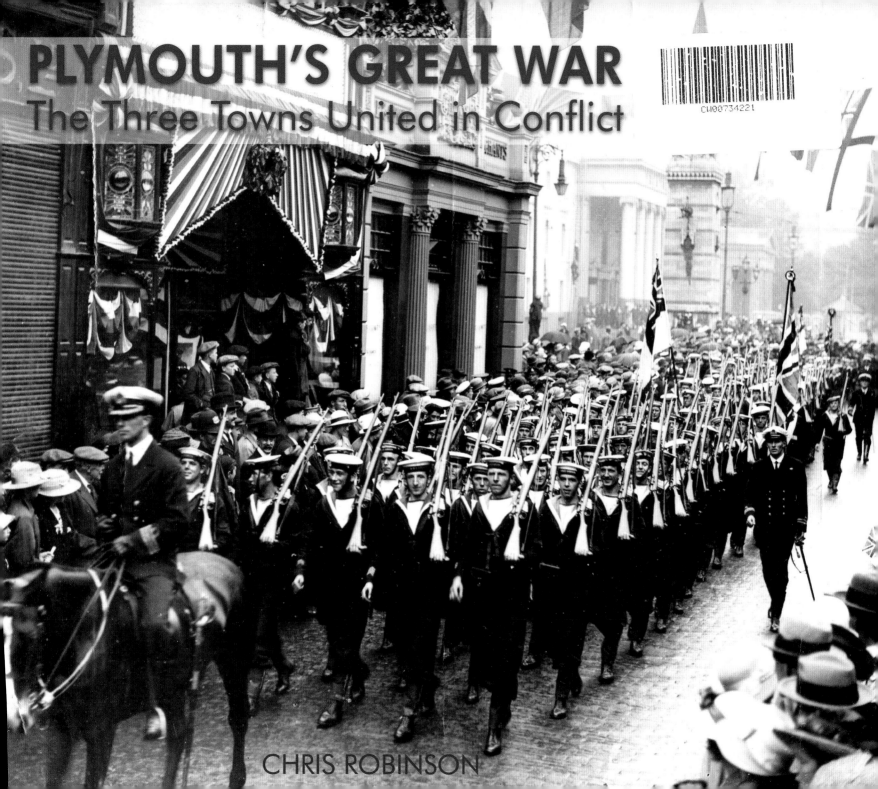

PLYMOUTH'S GREAT WAR
The Three Towns United in Conflict

CHRIS ROBINSON

British Library Cataloguing in Publication Data

Chris Robinson
Plymouth's Great War
The Three Towns United in Conflict

A catalogue record for this book is available from the British Library
ISBN 978-0-9569858-7-3

Written and illustrated by Chris Robinson
Layout Chris Robinson
© Chris Robinson 2014

First published 2014

Also available in this series:
Plymouth in the Twenties & Thirties
It Came To Our Door
Plymouth in the Forties & Fifties
Plymouth in the Fifties & Sixties

Published by
Pen & Ink Publishing
34 New Street, Barbican
Plymouth PL1 2NA
Tel: 01752 228120 /705337
www.chrisrobinson.co.uk

Printed and bound in Great Britain by
Latimer Trend & Company Ltd
Estover Close
Plymouth PL6 7PL

CONTENTS

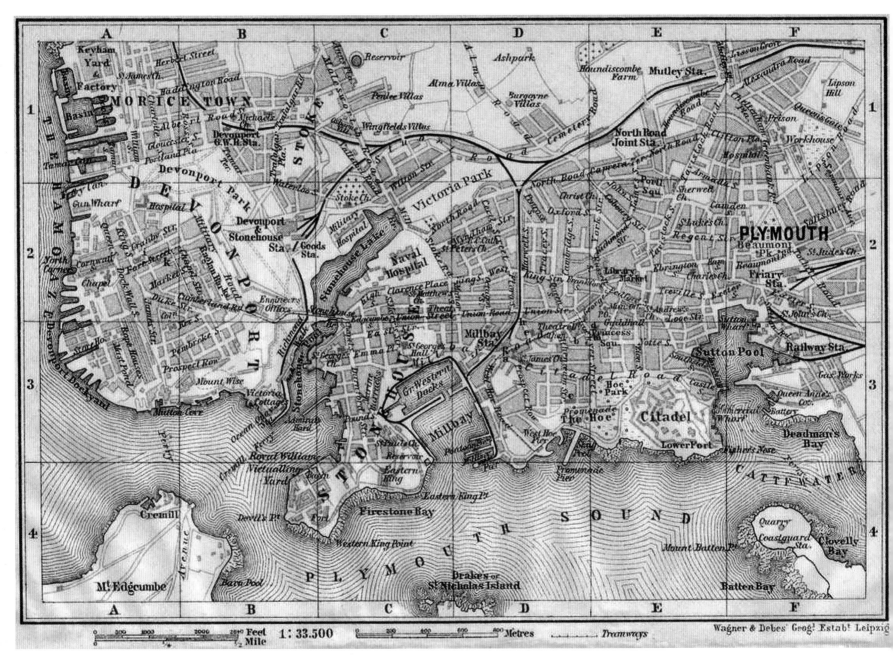

Mao of the Three Towns – Devonport, Stonehouse and Plymouth c.1910.

INTRODUCTION

Once upon a time there were Three Towns; Plymouth, (East) Stonehouse and Devonport, and they lived happily alongside each other for over 200 years.

Although their boundaries had long since become a little blurred, when the occasion demanded, they were fiercely separate and distinct. When the King, Edward VII, visited in 1902, a little more than a year after the death of his mother, Queen Victoria, and sometime before his coronation, it was a great, and nationally noteworthy, occasion. Each town claimed its right to greet the new monarch and his wife. Upon their arrival at North Road Station and greeting by the Mayor of Plymouth, the Royal Party was briskly paraded through the Three Towns. The Chairman of Stonehouse Urban District Council, regaled them with a second address in Union Street, and the Mayor of Devonport, another, at the Brickfields, before they were safely delivered into the Dockyard. The whole process had taken less than 45 minutes, but they had at least paid lip service to each of the Three Towns.

For most local residents, the Amalgamation of the Three Towns just over a decade later, made little difference to their lives – apart, of course, from those on, or employed by, the three individual councils. Thus at the end of 1914, Plymouth was not a hugely different place to the city of today: Tamerton Foliot, Plympton and Plymstock were still outside the boundaries and the population of the newly amalgamated Three Towns was around 210,000, making it at least three times bigger than its nearest rival in Devon and Cornwall – Exeter.

Clearly the devastation caused by the aerial bombardment of the Second World War was to have a profound effect on its appearance, and the drive to re-house displaced residents would lead to a major extension of its boundaries, but essentially, most of the early twentieth-century town, including Peverell, Mutley, Mannamead, Mount Gould, Prince Rock, Ford, Keyham and Prince Rock, stands little changed today.

However, it's hard now to imagine the levels of general deprivation: many homes had poor sanitation and large areas of the Three Towns were packed with densely crowded, poorly maintained slums. Only the affluent could afford the relatively recent innovation that was electricity. Communications were primitive, there was no radio or television and the telephone was only available to a comparative few.

Most people relied on their own two feet to get themselves around. The electrification of the tram system brought great improvements after 1901, but it didn't reach all parts. Train stations were dotted all around with stops at St Budeaux, Keyham, Devonport, Mutley, Lipson, Laira, Plympton, Plymstock, Oreston, Hooe and Turnchapel. There were no buses and very few cars on the road, and even those who could afford them couldn't drive them at much more than running pace – the limit set in Plymouth in 1909 was 10 mph.

The horse and cart was another option, but once war had been declared there were few horses to be seen on the streets of Plymouth as over the following four or five years, as almost all of them were required for war service (in the event over 480,000 of our horses were lost in the Great War).

Once wounded few if any were nursed back to health – unlike our servicemen: in the four and a half years of war, over a million British and Empire servicemen were killed and over twice that number wounded. Clearly, although Plymouth and other service towns had military and naval hospitals they were never going to be able to cope with the numbers of men coming back broken from France and Belgium.

At times too, the authorities struggled with the number of servicemen passing through the town. In the early stages of the war Plymouth was surrounded by tented training encampments as existing barrack accommodation at Raglan, Crownhill, Devonport, Stonehouse and the Citadel, was all at capacity and beyond. With its Army, Navy and Royal Marine bases operating in conjunction with Devonport Dockyard and the Royal William Victualling Yard, Plymouth had long been one of the most significant places in the country in times of war and the development, through the war, of a flying-boat base at Mount Batten added greatly to that reputation.

The massive naval presence in town of course meant that every ship lost at sea might have consequences for one or more families locally, and while such is not to say the news from the trenches might not always be devastating in its local impact, the losses at sea were great, and Plymouth felt them more keenly than most. Thousands of ships were sunk and sometimes hundreds of men were gone in minutes – not wounded but drowned, their bodies never to be recovered, their families forever to feel the pain.

Meanwhile one of Plymouth's key roles in what was originally dubbed 'the War to end all Wars' was to care for sick and wounded. Each major battle added to the ever-increasing list of casualties and one by one prompted the conversion of one or other of Plymouth's new board schools to a hospital facility.

After Mons in August 1914, the newly converted Salisbury Road received its first contingent of patients and five other schools were adapted. The Battles of the Marne and then Ypres added to the toll before the year was out, and, in the summer of 1915, Hyde Park School and Ford Workhouse were refashioned to accommodate ANZAC troops injured in the Dardenelles and Gallipoli.

The launch of the prolonged Somme Offensive saw 38,230 men injured on the first day alone and it wasn't long before Camel's Head School had been added to the list of medical outposts. By the end of the war dozens of hospitals had been set up around Devon and many more in the rest of England. Plymouth itself could, at its peak, accommodate thousands of men, but there was no national health service and provision of bed-space was courtesy of the Military Authorities, the Red Cross and Voluntary Aid Detachments (privately funded operations).

Plymouth's millionaire MP, Waldorf Astor and his wife Nancy, personally provided over £60,000 to the cause (the equivalent of many millions today) in the first year or two of the war alone, and were instrumental in improving the lives of many women and children locally.

The Astors were also influential in winning a contract to produce 5,000 shirts a week (later the figure doubled) for the Royal Army Clothing Department, work that gave vital employment to otherwise redundant seamstresses and women whose husbands were away. By April 1915 over 1,000 women were working on the scheme and over 200,000 shirts had been produced.

It is perhaps not surprising that the public perception of the role of women was to change so much during the war, certainly their local contribution to the war effort in terms of doing 'men's work' most notably the manufacture of munitions, was to have a great effect on our ultimate success in France. Nor was it a surprise that the pre-war campaign for female suffrage was to bear fruit after the war … or indeed that Nancy Astor was to become the first ever woman to take her seat in Parliament.

Society was changed forever by the war, the old upstairs/downstairs, servant, cook and mistress regime all but ended and the role of women was redefined as one of comparative, if not exact, equality with men.

The story of Plymouth leading up to and during the Great War is truly a fascinating one and one that hitherto has had scant attention from historians. It has been an education in itself to put it together and I hope it will educate, entertain and enlighten all those who read it.

Chris Robinson *October 2014*

Early in 1914 the boys of Plymouth College staged a grand gymnastic display, involving the whole school, on the school field. Over 200 lads took part and the final act saw 25 of them spread out to create the date 1914. Little could any of them have imagined just what the next four years would hold for them.

As it transpired over 500 past pupils were to take an active part in the war, many of them among those boys in the display and many of them members of the school's OTC (Officer Training Corps). Generally this pushed them to the front, quite literally when they signed up and tragically over 100 of those uniformed young men would never return. The percentage of loss – one in five – was consistent with Public Schools around the country and was almost twice that for the rest of the population.

Nowhere, perhaps, is this better illustrated than in the picture above, the 1914 school hockey team. Fresh faced young men, with hearts full of hope and who had no idea what lay ahead of them.

All went on to join the services after leaving school, but only seven would survive the Great War, as four of them, Henry Jago (standing, third from left), his brother, Edward (seated far right), Samuel Williams (standing far right) and Alan Hambly (front row right) would all make the ultimate sacrifice.

Henry Jago, who won the Military Cross and was mentioned in despatches by Field Marshal Haig, was killed in action on 24 April 1918 aged 23, his brother, Edward, who like Henry was also in the Devonshire Regiment, had earlier died of wounds on 1 July 1916, aged 20. Meanwhile Samuel Williams, who joined the Sherwood Foresters, was just 19 when he was killed in action on 16 October 1916, and Alan Hambly, another member of the Devons, was also 20 when he died of wounds, in France, on 22 May 1917.

7 March 1902: The King, wearing the uniform of an Admiral surmounted by a cloak, and the Queen, arrive at North Road Station.

THE EDWARDIAN EXPERIENCE

When it was announced that the 59-year-old King Edward VII was to make his first visit to the area since ascending to the throne in March 1902 it was sudden and somewhat unexpected. The Three Towns were thrown into turmoil – what form should the celebrations take, who should be invited and who should pay for it all. In the event the township of Stonehouse, the borough of Plymouth and The General Tolls Company funded the decorations from North Road Station to Stonehouse Bridge and Devonport came to its own arrangements.

'The whole three miles of streets were decorated in a most lavish and effective manner, for Plymouth had vied with Devonport, and Stonehouse with both, to make the occasion one of artistic interest, as well as of loyal celebrity' (Walling).

It was almost the first public duty the Royal couple had undertaken *'since the lapse of the year of mourning for the late Queen Victoria'.* The principal objects of the visit were to lay the foundation stone of the Dartmouth Naval College, and to launch the battleship *Queen* which had been laid down in Devonport Dockyard the previous year. Despite the apparent lack of planning time a fine programme was completed, indeed it was described by one local newspaper editor – Robert Walling – as *'the most elaborate and picturesque ceremonial ever carried out in Devon'.*

The station clock was reading 5.23 when the new Great Western Railway engine *Baden-Powell* (which had been rechristened *Britannia*) steamed into North Road Station two minutes ahead of schedule. *'The sight that greeted their Majesties on their arrival and during their progress through the Three Towns from Plymouth to Devonport was one which drew from them afterwards gracious econiums, a sight of which the like had never been seen by anybody in the history of the place.'*

The King, Queen and Princess Victoria leave North Road Station.

The decorations in and around the precincts of the station were laid on by Great Western Railways and were truly elaborate:
'There was a handsomely upholstered pavilion just outside the exit opening, with galleries for the privileged visitors, and on the opposite side of the road were huge stands erected over the railway sidings, accommodating the borough administrative bodies and their guests. Nearly all the Mayors and Mayoresses of Devon and Cornwall were there at the invitation of the Mayor of Plymouth, Mr JA Bellamy. Further west, on the same side of the road was a great stand on which stood 7,000 of the school children of Plymouth.'

Top: *The decorations in Bedford Street.* Above: *The King salutes the Army and Navy.*

Cobourg Street was one long row of grand stands, all crowded, every inch of space available on the gardens and house-fronts being occupied by sightseers.

Venetian poles were erected at intervals along the roadway on each side, and the lines between them were hung with strings of flags, with floral devices at intervals.

Pound Street contained a stand specially set apart for the Corporation employees. Here a man created a great deal of amusement by climbing a telephone pole with the aid of a piece of rope, and fastening himself near the top, where he obtained gratis an uninterrupted view of the cavalcade.

Enthusiastic cheering accompanied the whole of the progress through Old Town Street to Spooner's Corner, where a huge stand had been erected on the St Andrew's Cross garden.

From this point, with the old church and the Guildhall Buildings for background, and the scene in Bedford Street with its elaborate decorations, for a vista in one direction, the spectacle was as fine as at any part of the route.

The whole centre of Plymouth had been transformed by the aid of flags and flowers and coloured papers, and the blaze of colour and variety of decorations culminated at the widest part of the street, outside the Devon and Cornwall Bank, with a huge crown of ribbons, flowers and gilded paper suspended over the middle of the road. The Royal carriage passed immediately under it, and the King and Queen were observed to note with special interest the decorations in this neighbourhood.'

Fortunately the weather was perfect, with bright sunshine and balmy air – 'more like June than March' – as the procession made its way along George Street, turning right at Derry's Clock into Bank of England Place and into Union Street where the Royal Carriage pulled at its first stopping place, the boundary between Plymouth and Stonehouse.

There, at the junction of Phoenix Street, Manor Street and Union Street, and 'overlooked by the huge, handsome pile of the New Palace Theatre' (then the most impressive new building in the Three Towns), Mr Samuel Panter, a 61-year-old retired baker and Chairman of the East Stonehouse District Council, was waiting with colleagues and officials for the King. At ten minutes to six the Royal carriage arrived. The Royal party had been in Plymouth just 27 minutes.

Mr Panter was presented to the King by Lord Mount Edgcumbe, as was 42-year-old local solicitor, Richard Robinson Rodd, Clerk to Stonehouse Council.

An address was made by Mr Panter to the King and the King, in return, handed a brief reply to Mr Panter.

'The crowd began to cheer in a deafening fashion before the conversation was finished. This startled the horses, and the King, laughing, waved his hand and said "Stop a bit!" But the ceremony was soon over.'

By six o'clock, having crossed through Halfpenny Gate 'without a toll being collected', the Royal carriage arrived in Devonport.

'The surroundings of the scene were, of course, finer than at either of the other two receptions. It took place in a vast open space, backed by the battlements of Mount Wise and the green slopes of the Brickfields, extending away to the confines of Raglan Barracks.

The road leading to the north from the bridge, and passing by the L & SW station, was the one selected for the progress into the town proper. "Welcome to Devonport!" proclaimed a great blue and gold banner stretched across the end of the roadway, and in token of the importance of this first entrance of the King into the great Dockyard town the road has been re-named "King's Road", so that Devonport has one permanent reminder of the visit.'

Delivering his speech on behalf of the people of Devonport, the Mayor there, Edgar Leest, a young architect still in his twenties, was keen to point out to the King, in the second of a two-sentence address that: 'One of the first acts of your Majesty's Royal mother at the commencement of her illustrious reign was to confer the great privilege of municipal self-government upon the inhabitants of this town, who now crave permission to express their intense appreciation of the continued Royal favour so graciously signified by the presence of their beloved King and Queen in their borough today, and they pray God that the richest blessings of the Almighty may be bountifully bestowed upon your Majesty and your Royal house, and that your Majesty may long be spared to guide the destinies of a devoted nation, and to establish in the annals of the world the record of a glorious reign, justly renowned for the peace and prosperity of your Empire, and the happiness and contentment of your people.'

The address was enclosed in a beautiful silver-gilt casket on a pedestal of polished oak.

Top: *Presentation of the Address at Devonport.* Above left: *The Devonport Casket. 'The panels were filled by local views executed in enamel; the cover was crowned by a figure of Britannia; and a figure of a soldier and a sailor were on brackets at either end.'* Above right: *Edgar Leest, who became Mayor of Devonport on the sudden resignation of his predecessor.*

Top: King presenting medals at RN Barracks. Above: Departure of their Majesties.

In his reply the King said: *'I pray heartily that your municipality may continue to grow in efficiency and prosperity.'*

After a number of further presentations the procession moved on again.

'Dusk was now deepening, and the electric arc lamps which had been specially hung at short intervals over the centre of the thoroughfare were switched on, and spread a silvery light upon the scene, while to the west against the sky could be seen the outline traced in incandescent lamps of the classical form of Devonport's great Column.'

There was another large gathering by the Devonport Technical Schools and the entrance to Devonport Park. The whole route from Ha'penny Gate to the Dockyard was lined with sailors – bluejackets – and police, Fore Street, was thronged, as was Marlborough Street which had a huge floral crown suspended above the end of the road. Shortly after 6pm, and only a little more over three-quarters of an hour of setting foot in the Three Towns, the Royal carriage disappeared behind the Dockyard gates, leaving thousands of people to promenade along the *'gaily decorated route, now ablaze with illuminations.'*

The King and Queen were taken down between lines of lads from the training ships to the Royal yacht, *Victoria and Albert*, which was waiting for them at No 2 Jetty. Once on board the King hosted a dinner party for the Lords of the Admiralty, Lord Mount Edgcumbe, and other notables. All around them the warships in the Hamoaze were brightly lit while on Plymouth Hoe there was *'a display of fireworks on a scale of magnificence which had never been attempted in the West before'*.

The following day, Saturday 8 March, saw the Royal couple officiate at two events in the Dockyard – the launch of HMS *Queen* by Queen Alexandra and laying of the keel of *King Edward VII* by the King himself. Medals were also presented by the King, one of them to Basil Guy, who was awarded the Victoria Cross for his actions aboard HMS *Barfleur* as a midshipman two years earlier during the attack on Tientsin. His Majesty also conferred a knighthood upon Admiral Sturgess Jackson.

The Royal couple were also to have visited the Royal Naval Engineering College at Keyham, but an outbreak of measles meant that the plan was abandoned.

In the evening the King threw another dinner party on board the Royal yacht and there was a second spectacular firework display, this time on the Brickfields.

Sunday saw the Royals celebrate their wedding anniversary – their wedding in 1863 had been marked locally with the erection of Derry's Clock as a wedding gift. Thirty-nine years later they spent a relatively quiet day at Mount Edgcumbe after attending a church service in the Dockyard. In the evening they hosted yet another dinner party on *Victoria and Albert*.

On Monday morning they took their leave of the yacht just after

11am and were escorted, via the tender *Sir Richard Grenville*, to Great Western Docks at Millbay and thence to Millbay Station, where they boarded the Royal train at 11.40. By 4.25pm they were in London, after an impressive, non-stop journey of four and three-quarter hours.

'Their visit,' concluded Walling, '*was a memorable one, and its glory and interest will linger long in the West Country.*'

Curiously enough, the Three Towns did not have long to wait for their next Royal visitation for on Tuesday 14 July 1903 the Prince and Princess of Wales arrived in the Westcountry and once again Walling was on hand to record the event.

The 38-year-old Prince was no stranger to the Westcountry, but it was the first time his wife, Princess Mary (May) – and since mid-1901 the Duchess of Cornwall – had been this far west.

Certainly it did not take them long to get here: the Royal couple's journey from London to Plymouth attracted no small measure of publicity as being '*the fastest long-distance run ever accomplished.*'

The Great Western engine, *Cornishman*, pulled the Royal train out of Paddington at 10.40 am and steamed into North Road Station at 2.34 pm, 36 minutes ahead of schedule. The GWR officials were delighted to have recorded a time of 234 minutes and 45 seconds to cover a distance of 246 miles.

The train, however, didn't stop here then, as the Royals continued on into Cornwall, and it wasn't until late on the following Monday afternoon that the Royal train, this time pulled up from Grampound by the *Bonaventura*, arrived in Plymouth.

On this occasion the station stop was Millbay – which had undergone a '*magnificent transformation*' in the previous ten years.'

The usual dignitaries, and the band of the Royal Marines, awaited their arrival, as well as a Mr Thomas Tunstall, who was introduced to the Prince by the Mayor of Plymouth, Henry Hurrell. Thomas Tunstall, 79, was a retired engine driver who had driven the first ever train into Cornwall and had conveyed Prince Albert (the Prince of Wales's grandfather) to Saltash when Brunel's magnificent bridge over the Tamar was formally opened.

Once again the weather was extremely favourable and after the proceedings at the station had been concluded the procession headed through Millbay Road, past the Theatre Royal, into George Street and Bedford Street and then on to the Guildhall Square.

Top: *Passing through Bedford Street.* Above: *Reception at the Guildhall.*

Here some 4,000 schoolchildren were massed with a guard of honour in front of them. For the second time in fifteen minutes the Royal party was treated to an abbreviated version of the National Anthem as they met the members of the Corporation, who were gathered in a double line by the porch, the then entrance to the Guildhall.

Again addresses were presented and the Princess '*pressed an electric button which unveiled a tablet to the volunteers*' of the South African War. Within 22 minutes of their arrival in the Square, however, the Royals were on the move again.

Monday 20 July 1903, the Prince and Princess of Wales are received briefly by Dr William Corbett (Chairman of Stonehouse Urban District Council) in the early evening sun.

'At Stonehouse,' noted Walling, 'the precedent of 1902 was closely followed. At the dividing line between Plymouth and the township, close to the Palace Theatre, the representatives of Stonehouse awaited the arrival of the Prince and his consort. There was a guard of honour of Royal Marines, with the band of the division, and this part of the street was finely decorated.

Within an enclosure the privileged persons were gathered, and when the royal carriage drew up, the Chairman of the Urban District Council, Dr Corbett, presented HRH with an address of welcome. Mrs Corbett handed a bouquet to the Princess. Dr Corbett was presented to the Prince by the Lord Mount Edgcumbe. The royal reply to the address expressed the pleasure which it gave the visitors to pass through the township on their way to Devonport.

The ceremonial scene here, too, was very brief, and the procession passed on amid scenes of sincere greeting, through streets lined by Marines, to the Halfpenny Gate.'

The residents of Stonehouse did, however, get a second chance to see the Prince later in the week when he drove to the Royal Marine Barracks to inspect the Plymouth Division of the Corps – the Prince was the Colonel-in-Chief of the Corps and there was a huge inscription welcoming him stretched across the entrance archway.

'The battalion was assembled on the parade in review order, under Lieut-Col. Frederick Horniblow, and the fine band, under Mr Winterbottom, was in attendance. The Prince, who was accompanied by Sir Edward Seymour and Sir William Butler, inspected the lines, and the ceremonies concluded with a march past, a very fine sight indeed, the whole of the troops going by in columns of companies to the tune of "A life on the ocean wave" and returning in quarter column to the strains of "God bless the Prince of Wales".'

Meanwhile, to return to the original procession through the Three Towns, 'as the line of carriages swept round the corner from Edgcumbe Street, the glimpse that met the eye of the Royal party impressed them deeply,' recorded Walling.

Stonehouse Bridge was decked out in rainbow colours and 'thousands of flags waved in the breeze, stretched along and across the roadway, and thousands of people shouted and waved their hats and handkerchiefs in welcome, while beyond on the hill were the grand stands where the official and populace of the borough of Devonport waited to perform their part in the day's programme.'

Top: *Arrival at Stonehouse Barracks – Royal Marines line Durnford Street.*
Above: *March past of the Royal Marine Light Infantry at Stonehouse.*

'The Prince's carriage drew up in front of the dais at the Devonport boundary. Beyond it were the stands accommodating the guests whom the Corporation had invited to witness the ceremony. Above, on the slopes of the Brickfields, dense crowds had taken up places of vantage.'

Foremost among the Devonport notables was the then Mayor JC (James) Tozer, the eminent local draper, who was at the ceremony with his wife Henrietta and daughter, Dorothy. Mrs Tozer presented the Princess with a beautiful bouquet of flowers at the end of the formal proceedings at which point the 'venerable local magistrate' Dr Joseph May, was presented to the Prince.

Dr May had received a very enthusiastic greeting from the crowd and undoubtedly almost every local would have known him. Born on 19 February 1808, the ageing official had been in his mid-teens when Plymouth Dock was restyled Devonport, by Royal Decree, in 1824. Dr May had also been a member of the Town Council since the date of the incorporation of the Borough of Devonport in 1837. It was a truly remarkable record and the Prince chatted with him for a few moments before passing on (as fate would have it, Dr May himself passed on the following year, on 10 April 1904, all but ten years short of the entire duration of the period that Devonport existed as an independent borough).

The Royal procession subsequently moved through Fore Street, 'where the decorations were of an almost fairy-like description,' and then on into the Dockyard, and thence to Mount Edgcumbe where the Prince and Princess were staying as guests of the Earl.

The following day the Princess went up to visit 'Lord Mount Edgcumbe's romantic castle at Cothele, while the Prince went shooting with a party in Mount Edgcumbe Park.'

On Wednesday the Royal couple 'took a motor car trip on Dartmoor' calling in at Crownhill on the way. There local schoolchildren, assembled on a makeshift platform, sang the national anthem and Mrs Arthur Carlton, of Widey Court, presented the Princess with another bouquet.

Thursday, the penultimate day of their visit saw the Princess launch the *King Edward VII*, that her father-in-law had laid the keel of the previous year, and they successfully called into the Royal Naval Engineering College at Keyham, the venue that the King and Queen had had to forego visiting on their tour.

'One of the prettiest sights to be seen in the Three Towns, on the occasion of the visit of the Prince and Princess, was the brilliantly illuminated Electric Car of the Devonport and District Tramway Company. The Car, as it glided over the rails at night, was a gorgeous blaze of electric light of every conceivable tint, and was like a perfect picture from Fairyland, and was witnessed by thousands' (Walling, Doidge's Almanac 1904).

Above: *The Prince calls into RNEC Keyham.* Opposite: *Fore Street is brightly decorated.*

Top left: *20 February 1907, Prince and Princess of Wales at the opening of the Keyham Extension.* Top right: *Isaac Pearse, Chairman of the Stonehouse Urban District Council, reads the Proclamation of King George V at Stonehouse Town Hall.* Bottom left: *The Proclamation is read at Plymouth Guildhall.* Bottom right: *Alderman Littleton, Mayor of Devonport performs the same function, 9 May 1910, at Devonport Town Hall.*

Somewhat unusually it wasn't that long, in comparative terms, before the Prince and Princess of Wales were back in the Three Towns; this time to open the extension of the Keyham Steamyard, in February 1907.

A much shorter visit, there appears to have been no suggestion of there being a grand, albeit swift, stop-start procession through the Three Towns, nevertheless there seems to have been an expectation that the three key figures in each town should have been invited to a celebratory lunch aboard the Admiralty yacht. At least that appears to have been what the Mayor of Devonport, William Moon thought. Apparently he felt that as the main official in the town that the new dock extension reached out from, he should have been there, given that the Mayor of Plymouth, Sir Charles Radford, the wealthy head of Popham's drapery store, was invited.

It was not the first time that Moon, a 57-year-old baker, grocer and Wesleyan preacher, felt that the Commander-in-Chief, Sir Lewis Beaumont had snubbed him.

Consequently, Mr Moon and his wife Eliza boycotted the Royal visit 'and his townsmen pointedly kept off the streets for the Royal processions' (Gill 1979).

Clearly there had long been rivalries between the Three Towns and each of them, particularly Plymouth and Devonport, were fiercely defensive of their independence. To the outsider, the boundaries between them looked decidedly arbitrary in places and there were many stories of how the police in Plymouth would push drunks across to the other side of the road in Phoenix Street or Manor Street, and vice-versa. It must have seemed strange to many outsiders, and even a great many locals. But the divisions persisted, each Town went about its own business and, when after just nine years on the throne, King Edward died, each authority had its own ceremony to announce the succession of the Prince of Wales as King George V.

So how separate really were the Three Towns at the beginning of the twentieth century and how sensible was it for them to continue to pursue independent existences?

20 May 1910, the scene at St Andrew's Cross, on the day of the funeral of King Edward VII.

Fishermen cleaning nets on the Barbican's East Pier, c.1905.

PLYMOUTH & STONEHOUSE

Plymouth was undoubtedly the oldest of the Three Towns. Here was a collection of Tudor and Jacobean buildings without parallel in the Three Towns, indeed without parallel in the Westcountry as a whole. However in the last few decades of the nineteenth century, large-scale redevelopment projects had seen the loss of many fine, but neglected buildings.

Half of Looe Street had been removed to make way for the town's first Municipal housing scheme, much of Notte Street, Basket Street and Old Town Street had also seen quaint, ancient, wooden-framed pubs and properties replaced by bigger, more substantial brick-built buildings. The arrival of the tram was the impetus for a number of 'improvements' – as certain streets were widened and new perimeter buildings were erected several stories higher than the structures they were replacing.

But for a few lone voices protesting at the rate at which the town's heritage was being eroded, there was little opposition.

In 1861 local architect James Hine had published one of the first books locally to feature photographs of Plymouth's rapidly disappearing old buildings. A few years later John McDonald produced a book of sketches of *Nooks and Corners of Old Plymouth*, while Eldred and Wright did a similar job, with commentary, in 1901. Sybil Jerram followed suit in 1913 and around the same time, another notable local architect, Arthur Southcombe Parker, began a very thorough, four-year *Antiquarian Survey of Old Plymouth*. In it Southcombe Parker detailed those buildings in and around the town that he deemed particularly valuable and worthy of preservation.

Sadly not all of his advice was heeded, but it marked the beginning of a new attitude towards Old Plymouth, or the wider Barbican area.

New Street.

High Street.

Commercial Wharf looking towards West Pier..

Plymouth Hoe, a popular venue for promenaders and for the staging of major events, notably Coronation Day in 1911, when Smeaton's Tower was lit by Electric Lights and there were fireworks and a massive bonfire.

It wasn't really until the early nineteenth century that Plymouth extended much beyond its Jacobean boundaries and until part-way through Victoria's reign, the Hoe remained a rural hinterland largely populated by sheep and cows.

The construction of houses at West Hoe and on the northern fringe of what became the Promenade of the Hoe (literally 'high ridge'), gradually changed all that and, after the construction of the Plymouth Pier in the 1880s, the area became increasingly given over to genteel leisure activities. Victoria Park was created over the infilled upper reaches of Stonehouse Creek to provide playing-fields for the livelier young men of the town and monuments and memorials sprang up here and there around a more formally laid out park on the Hoe.

With the dawn of the twentieth century came a series of improvements to the Hoe bathing facilities. The temporary facilities for ladies were demolished and replaced by two-storey brick built bathing houses, while in 1902 plans were developed for the Tinside site.

The cliff face at Tinside was unsafe and after some necessary work had been carried out, the Local Government Board approved proposals and a loan to wall up the entrance to the Reform Cave and to provide proper changing facilities and a pool at a cost of just under £3,000.

Not everyone was happy though, as one press report noted: *'Whatever romanticists may think of the taming of Tinside, the Town Council has the blessing of all those who go down to the sea in bathing costumes, and such as are members of the Ratepayers' Association are torn by conflicting emotions.'*

Left: *The Hoe and Pier.* Above: *The new bathing facilities at Tinside opened by Mayor James Godding in 1913, for bathers and 'those who love to watch the many twinkling smiles of Father Ocean'.*

23

Mutley Plain, looking south, c.1909, the electric tram has replaced the horse tram, but no sign of a motor car or van.

Between 1690 and 1820 Plymouth grew very slowly, and the story in Stonehouse, prior to the construction of the Royal Naval Hospital in the 1760s and the Royal Marine Barracks in the 1780s and the Military Hospital in the 1790s, was very much the same. Meanwhile, Devonport, or Plymouth Dock as it was known throughout most of that period, was born and grew at a hitherto unprecedented rate, such that by 1820 it was the biggest township of the three, indeed it was quite the largest town in the county.

Once the Napoleonic Wars had ended however, so did that spectacular growth, and while it continued to expand during the nineteenth century, it did not compare with its more venerable neighbour, Plymouth.

Following the development of New Town (around the western end of Cobourg Street) in the 1820s, new housing was built up over one green field after another and, in a major move in 1896, Plymouth's boundary was extended to embrace one of the fastest growing areas – Mutley.

Mutley Plain had been largely levelled in the wake of the late-eighteenth-century Turnpike Acts. Ever the driest and most direct route into the town from the landward side, Mutley came into its own following the arrival of the railway – it was serviced by its own railway from 1871 and by the Plymouth Corporation Horse Tram system via North Hill and Houndiscombe Road, from 1895.

Six years later, the electrification of the system, in 1901, saw the route extended through the rapidly growing district of Peverell – an area that was to prove to be extremely fruitful too for the Co-op.

Top right: *Methodist Church in Cobourg Street.* Middle: *Mutley Plain looking north.*
Bottom right: *Peverell c.1904.* Above: *Top of Peverell Park Road c.1911.*

The vast improvement in the public transport network opened up all manner of opportunities, not least of which was the fact that housing estates could now be built further afield without greatly inconveniencing potential residents.

It also meant that certain attractions did not need to be within comfortable walking distance of these new estates. Of course it helped if they could be sited along the route taken by the Corporation trams, which is precisely where Plymouth's new Free Library and Museum was erected between 1907-10.

One of over 2,500 libraries in Great Britain and America funded by the Scottish-born American manufacturer and philanthropist Andrew Carnegie – as well as a great many other good deeds, he provided over £10 million for the initiative, a simply staggering amount of

money at that time – the new buildings represented a great leap forward in local education provision for all ages. Thornely and Rooke's classically designed complex cost around £13,000 to build – some of it met by public subscription – and the buildings replaced a relatively short-lived museum facility in Beaumont House.

Suddenly this area became a true cultural quarter as just a few years earlier, in 1892, the Victoria Science, Art and Technical School had opened on the other side of Tavistock Road. While Devonport was subsequently blessed with their own Municipal Science, Art and Technical Schools (which opened in 1898), neither they, nor their neighbours in Stonehouse had anything that could compete with Plymouth's new Museum, Art Gallery and Public Library.

Top left: *Looking up North Hill.* Middle: *The new Library, Museum and Art Gallery.* Bottom: *The Victoria Science, Art and Technical School.* Above: *Inside the Museum.*

Looking down the recently widened Ebrington Street from just below the newly built Drake Circus.

In other respects too, Devonport, and especially Stonehouse were steadily being eclipsed.

Old Town Street was a perfect example of this: whereas Devonport's major thoroughfare, Fore Street, dated from the eighteenth century when carriages were becoming commonplace, Old Town Street had its origins long before that, it was much narrower, with even more narrow side streets, it was also lined with ageing edifices, many of them dating back to a time long before Devonport was even conceived. Consequently, there was increasing pressure to widen and redevelop the entire street.

Quaint, centuries-old, two or three-storey hostelries like the 'Old Four Castles', the 'White Hart' and the 'Rose and Crown' all came down in the 1890s, as well as their equally venerable neighbours and in their place dozens of much taller, modern buildings sprang up. Drake Circus appeared at the realigned end of an opened-out Ebrington Street opposite the corner on which a huge new five-storey building appeared.

Other new developments were equally tall and, suddenly, Old Town Street was full of businesses clamouring to be at the bustling heart of Plymouth's now easily accessible town centre.

Looking up Old Town Street to Drake Circus and the junction with Ebrington Street and Tavistock Road.

Looking down Old Town Street towards Whimple Street.

Among those businesses keen to establish a major presence in the street was that started in Whimple Street by Joseph Spooner in the 1840s.

Initially specialising in *'Millinery, Drapery, Shawls, Furs and Fancy Goods'*, the business was expanded soon afterwards and by the early 1860s an additional outlet had opened in Bedford Street. By the 1890s Whimple Street had been abandoned and the company was now operating out of numerous premises, many of them interlinked, in Bedford Street, Market Avenue and Old Town Street.

That interlinking was almost to prove their downfall, as on the night of 14 June 1902, fire almost destroyed the whole of the Bedford Street and Old Town Street operations. It was a Saturday evening, most of the 800 or so staff had gone home, but, remarkably it was estimated that there will still around 180 people in the buildings when one of the assistants was thought to have knocked into a gas pendant in one of the windows of No.4 Old Town Street, thereby setting fire to some flammable material.

Huge numbers turned out to watch the horrific spectacle as the massed Fire Brigades of the Three Towns played some 21 hoses on the conflagration. There were over a 100 firemen from Plymouth alone at the scene as well as around three-quarters of the Plymouth Police Force. Almost all business in the town ground to a halt. All tram traffic through Old Town Street ceased and it was several days before the service could be resumed. Happily Chubb's Hotel next door to Spooner's was saved, albeit somewhat soaked and charred. By 2.30am Sunday morning, the fire had died down sufficiently for the Devonport and Stonehouse men to return home. Those businesses and the few residents in town that were fortunate enough to have electricity were left without, temporarily, and the collapse of a great pole belonging to the National Telephone Company, left hundreds of users without a connection until normal service could be resumed. The management of Spooner's was quick to recover from the tragedy and it was not long before the stores were once again fully operational.

In 1910 there was another fire in their Old Town Street premises, but again, far from spelling the end for the business it occasioned yet another new beginning and Spooner's came to boast one of the most state-of-the-art shopping experiences in the area.

Top left: The corner in peaceful mood. Middle: Spooner's fire 1902. Bottom: As the flames subside Corporation workmen endeavour to put the tram cables back in place.

Old Town Street looking north with a new Spooner's building.

Just as the top of Old Town Street had been refashioned in the 1890s so too was the bottom. Where previously the substantial graveyard of St Andrew's had stood opposite the properties on the eastern side of the street, as it stretched down to Whimple Street, so now a smaller garden at ground level occupied part of the space.

Prior to 1895 the level of the burial ground had been more than eight feet above ground level, providing a major visual barrier from almost every angle. Now the whole area was opened up and a large section of the site had been appropriated to allow trams access to Basket Street.

Significantly, Bedford Street had little intrusion from the trams, leaving pedestrians fairly free to negotiate the odd horse and cart, until the motor car came to be more of a presence on the roads.

Like Old Town Street, Bedford Street was also significantly redeveloped towards the end of the nineteenth century and dawn of the twentieth. The landmark building at the end of this busy banking street, the Globe Hotel, was demolished in 1899 and replaced by the towering, neo-gothic offices of the Prudential Assurance Company: its brick façade being very much a typical feature of this era of Plymouth town centre redevelopment, although the plum-red colour was a little different.

Top left: St Andrew's Cross stands in splendid isolation on the site of the old burial ground. Right: The new tram route around the top of the park. Above: Bedford Street looking east; John Yeo's on left between Lloyds Bank and Popham, Radford & Co. with Perkin Brothers, on the other side of the road.

Bedford Street, looking towards the new Prudential building.

George Street was another prime shopping thoroughfare and like Bedford Street it was tram-free, although it could be easily accessed at either end. The main tram terminal point for many routes was outside the Theatre Royal and Royal Hotel. Hackney carriages also congregated here as traffic converged from Millbay Road, Union Street, Lockyer Street and George Street.

This was a true focal point of the town and many a rendezvous was arranged around the 'four-faced deceiver' Derry's Clock. There was certainly no real equivalent in Stonehouse or, indeed, in Devonport.

Two popular venues – Genoni's Café and Cousin's Hotel – sat side by side opposite the Theatre Royal, just along from the 'Swan of Avon', 'Victoria Hotel', the 'Falstaff Inn', and the Café Royal (another Genoni enterprise).

Sandwiched between them were the offices of the Western Morning News, while back on the other side of the road, on the western side of the Theatre Royal, was one of the prime social centres for the educated and earnest Plymothian – the Athenaeum, housing the Plymouth Institute and Devon and Cornwall Natural History Society.

Derry's Clock looking down George Street.

34

The western end of George Street, featuring two of architect John Foulston's first projects in Plymouth, the Theatre Royal and Royal Hotel (1813) and the Athenaeum (1819).

Far left: *Looking down past the Royal Hotel at the bottom of Lockyer Street, with the Lockyer Tavern to the right and, beyond the clock tower and Bank of England Place, Union Street.* Left: *Looking down Union Street from Bank of England Place.* Top: *Foulston's Theatre Royal and the Athenaeum.*

Furthermore, the main centres of popular culture were literally just around the corner, in Union Street.

Laid out almost 100 years earlier at Foulston's behest, to allow easy access to the Theatre Royal from both Stonehouse and Devonport, Union Street was, from the beginning, a street of two halves: one in Plymouth, the other in Stonehouse. Initially the Plymouth section was populated by substantial properties accommodating the well-to-do – doctors, professors, solicitors – while the Stonehouse end saw an instant explosion of commercial activity as much-needed shops sprang up to service a population that had expanded significantly in the wake of the construction of the Naval and Military Hospitals and the Royal Marine Barracks.

In the 1820s and 1830s the massive programme of work, occasioned by the building of the Royal William Victualling Yard, further increased demand, as did the development, in the 1840s, of Millbay Docks and the arrival of the railway in 1849.

However these changes also altered the complexion of the area and saw a gradual exodus of the middle classes from the Plymouth half of the strip.

Thereafter, Union Street gradually became the main focus for fun. When the local authorities refused to grant Henry Reed the lease of the Theatre Royal (which he had run successfully with his father-in-law, John Newcombe, who had worked for years to make it a going concern), Reed decided to build and open his own theatre.

It was 1889, and in just 16 weeks, in the run up to Christmas he managed to convert a furniture factory less than a hundred yards to the west of the Plymouth–Stonehouse boundary into a theatre with the biggest stage west of Bristol and a seating capacity of 1,300, similar to that of the Theatre Royal.

True to the *'It'll be alright on the night'* tradition (the council had only granted a licence to the theatre the night before), Reed opened his new attraction on Boxing Day 1889 with a production of Cinderella.

Union Street from just under the railway arch looking back towards Bank of England Place in the far distance, with Farley's Hotel on the right in the foreground.

Henry Reed's Grand Theatre and Grand Theatre Hotel (the former 'Forester's Inn') on the far left, looking down into the eastern end of Union Street and the Stonehouse boundary.

The new building, which Reed styled The Grand Theatre, was an instant success and the crowds flocked to Union Street.

Small wonder therefore, when, less than a decade later, a small group of entrepreneurs (made up of an erstwhile touring group of 'Court Minstrels' – Horace, Louis and EJ Livermore, together with London millionaire Henry Pocock) were casting around for a site on which to build Plymouth's first purpose-built theatre dedicated to the Music Hall, they chose a site in Union Street, right on the corner of the Plymouth–Stonehouse boundary.

The site was already partly occupied by a 'Pandemonium' known as Fancy Fair, but the new development would actually stretch across four sites, 89, 90, 91 and 92 Union Street, as the New Palace Theatre and an adjacent hotel, erected at a cost of £185,000, was destined to become the most expensive development ever seen in the Westcountry.

Music Hall was entering its golden age, helped enormously by the exciting new medium – the gramophone. In August 1898, just two weeks before the New Palace opened, the first ever commercially recorded disc by a male vocalist, was released in this country – Ted Handy's comic song *They've All Gone in For 'Em*.

The new medium meant artists and performers could be heard by a wider audience than anyone had hitherto dreamt of and, of course, the generation that grew up listening to these discs were naturally curious to see what those people making them looked like.

Florrie Forde, the young Australian woman who started making records in 1903 and who was one of the first to record *It's A Long Way To Tipperary* in 1912 (on the Columbia record label), came to the Palace with Casey's Court Company in 1907–8 – she was paid the princely sum of £40 a week – that at a time when most people were on around £2 a week or less.

She would also record the popular wartime songs, *Pack Up Your Troubles in Your Old Kit Bag* and *Take Me Back to Dear Old Blighty*.

Florrie Forde.

The new New Palace Theatre in the early evening sun on the Plymouth–Stonehouse boundary.

Marie Lloyd, whose repertoire included *The Old Cock Linnet, When You Wink the Other Eye* and *She Sits Among the Cabbages and Peas,* was another favourite at the Palace, as was Ella Shields, whose husband wrote what became a massive hit for her – *Burlington Bertie.* In 1909 Harry Tate, who enjoyed great success with his routine written around the automobile craze, the *Motoring Sketch,* entertained the Palace audiences and the following year William Henry Crump, better know as Harry Champion, delighted his fans with renditions of his cockney anthems, *Boiled Beef and Carrots* and *I'm Henery the Eighth I Am.* In 1911 he released another massively successful recording – *Any Old Iron.*

With the advent of war, Union Street was *'once again packed with soldiers and sailors, pubs were nightly filled and rough-houses commonplace and the Palace weekly programmes saw a gradually diminishing number of acts by male performers who were soon to join the services'* (Playbill 1980 – Harvey Crane).

'The Palace with its red plush seats and gilded cupids stood on equal footing with the Theatre Royal in those days.' For the most part however, the nights at the Palace were more of a music hall nature than regular theatre. Indeed, one of the best places for regular theatre was the Rep, in Princess Square. Opened by George King, a noted actor in his own right, in 1915, it was one of the first repertory theatres in the country.

Meanwhile, back at the Palace, in Union Street, patrons would *'arrive at the ornate doors, to be welcomed by the resident manager with a smile and greeting, to walk through that cosy, mysterious, delicately illuminated corridor to the stalls, to hear the band in the pits and to receive a nod from the conductor – until that magic moment when the No.1 lit up on the sign at the stage side, and the heavy plum-coloured curtain silently swept upwards to reveal the opening act, generally a juggler or acrobat'* (Crane).

It was also in 1915 that the first 'revue' appeared at the Palace. It was branded *Sign Please* a title that reflected the push to recruit the nation's young manhood for military service. It was swiftly followed by another show, *Fall In.* The Palace had been ably run by Tommy Hoyle since 1912, and, when victory looked likely, he produced a a show called *All Clear.* Tommy also ran the 'Golden Lion' in Old Town Street.

They all played the Palace. Left to right: Lilly Langtry (a 'specialty act' famous for a string of early affairs with, amongst others, the Prince of Wales later Edward VII, the Earl of Shrewsbury, and Prince Louis of Battenberg), comedienne Nellie Wallace and Marie Lloyd. Opposite page: The New Palace Theatre and inset, Ella Shields.

Happily for its well-respected proprietor, business boomed. As it did for another new medium that arrived in the street around the same time – moving images – the silent cinema as it would become.

Just across the road from the Palace was another, slightly older Victorian building, St James's Hall. Capable of housing around 2,500 patrons, it was here, in 1897, that people flocked to see the new 'living pictures'.

Initially viewed on hand-cranked machines and lit by limelight, it wasn't long before Union Street had its first proper 'Picture Palace,' built by Horace Andrew on the site of the old Turkish baths in Union Street, on part of Flora Place. By the time Andrew opened his venue in 1911 there were already five other places in Plymouth and Stonehouse showing 'living pictures' – all but one of them (the *Theatre Elite* in Ebrington Street) in Union Street.

As well as theatres and picture houses, Union Street had more than its fair share of public houses. In 1914 there were around two dozen facing on to the street itself and dozens more if you ventured a short distance into the many side streets. There were also a handful in Edgcumbe Street, as the very end of the thoroughfare, leading to Stonehouse Bridge, was known.

For many a serviceman, for many a year, the challenge was to negotiate his way from one end of the strip to the other having a drink in every one along the way. The usual starting point for these men whose wages were always paid in cash, was the western end.

Small wonder that the street was deemed to be a prime place to create a new temple of temperance in the shape of the YMCA in 1917 – there were also a couple of other temperance institutions there – but they were not only hopelessly outnumbered by the number of pubs, but also by the number of breweries in the area!

In such an alcohol-fuelled setting it was, inevitably, a popular working environment for the ladies of the night: *'When Stonehouse was only a sanitary district, certain contagious disease laws did not apply there as in the towns proper. So all the prostitutes flocked to Stonehouse'* (Gill, *Plymouth A New History*).

The point at which Union Street, Stonehouse, met with Union Street, Plymouth runs at right-angles to the street either side of the New Palace Theatre. Inset: the new YMCA in 1917.

The west end of Edgcumbe Street, Stonehouse, leading on to Stonehouse (Halfpenny) Bridge. This section was later absorbed into Union Street.

Generallly, Stonehouse was quite reliant on the Services; its indigenous population had been in gradual decline since the completion of the Royal William Victualling Yard and in 1911 was a little under 14,000, the lowest it had been for 50 years. Occupying just under 200 acres, in population terms it was more than a tenth of the size of Plymouth and less than a fifth of the size of Devonport. The last of the Three Towns to have its own, dedicated Town Hall (it was built in St Mary Street, looking straight down Emma Place in 1849/50), Stonehouse was granted its own Board of Commissioners in 1851 and, following the Local Government Act of 1872, a Local Board. In 1894, that Local Board, resisted an application by Plymouth Corporation (under Section 54 of the Local Government Act, 1888) for the inclusion of the Local Board District of East Stonehouse within the boundaries of the Borough of Plymouth and that same year the Urban District Council was substituted for the Local Board.

It was not the first time a merger or incorporation with Plymouth had been mooted, nor would it be the last. In the meantime, Stonehouse controlled its own finances and had its own committees for: Works and Lighting; Sanitation and Water; Higher Education, and so on. Curiously enough, in Newport Street, it also had an electricity power station – the Devonport Corporation Power Station.

Top: *Stonehouse Town Hall.* Bottom: *Emma Place leading to Stonehouse Town Hall.*

Devonport Corporation Power Station, located in Newport Street, Stonehouse.

The Halfpenny Bridge, Devonport

THE PLYMOUTH BREWERIES LIMITED

Urban District Council
of East Stonehouse.

Year Book,
1912-1913.

CONTAINING
LISTS OF COUNCIL COMMITTEES,
STANDING ORDERS,
JUSTICES OF THE PEACE,
AND
GENERAL INFORMATION FOR THE
USE OF THE COUNCIL.

BRIMACOMBE & TOLCHARD, Printers.
The Valletort Press, Union Place, Stonehouse.

Note the wording on the image 'the Halfpenny Bridge, Devonport' – perhaps better known as Stonehouse Bridge as it straddles Stonehouse Creek. Inset right: Title page from the East Stonehouse Urban District Council Year Book for 1912-13.

DEVONPORT

In order to better service the town, on the grounds that the dominant local provider, Plymouth Corporation Tramways, showed little inclination to electrify the Devonport lines, the Devonport & District Tramways Company was formed in 1898 and given powers to create five miles of track within the borough.

Bearing the magnet-and-wheel crest of the British Electric Traction Company (who were behind the operation), the Devonport company used electricity produced by the Devonport Corporation Power Station alongside the Creek, in Newport Street, Stonehouse. The twenty-odd American-built trams, which went straight into service in 1901 were painted chocolate brown and cream and the drivers and conductors were instructed not to make *'disparaging remarks about the management of routes, or about the Officers of the company'*, nor were they to *'enter into unnecessary conversation with the passengers'*, or *'to make signs, motions or signals of any kind to men in charge of other cars'*.

The service began on 26 June 1901 and of the five principal routes, two ran from Fore Street (to Tor Lane via Stoke and Stuart Road via Wilton Street); two from Morice Square (to Tor Lane via St Levan Road and St Budeaux via Keyham) and one from Stuart Road (which ran to South Keyham via Tamar Terrace), with the last two later (after 1903) being extended to Saltash Passage.

For the most part, the overhead cables providing the power were fixed to metal brackets attached to lamp standards, which stretched out improbably over the roadway, although in some places, notably on Stonehouse Bridge, and along Albert Road, 'T'-type fittings were used.

Over the next few years Plymouth Corporation approached the Devonport & District Company about operating through-services along their lines, but the Devonport body weren't interested – however, amalgamation altered everything, as ownership of the tracks passed to the newly expanded Plymouth Corporation, who promptly made a generous buy-out offer to the D&D Company.

Opposite page and above: *Fore Street*. Top: *Devonport Hill and Stonehouse Bridge*.

ESTABLISHED 1911

Devonport, Morice Town and District

The World's
Best Pictures.

*Amusing. Instructive.
Dramatic. Refined.*

Picture Palace

William Street, **DEVONPORT.**

The House
for
**Exclusives and
Serials.**

Open every Evening, 6 to 10-30 p.m.

Matinees—Wednesday and Saturday.

William Street, the main route into Devonport from the Dockyard Gate in Albert Road. Left: Advertisement for the Picture Palace in William Street.

The new tram routes, venturing out into the rapidly growing parts of Keyham, Camel's Head, Stoke and Millbridge, were good news both for the residents and the workers in these areas. As the Dockyard expanded in the run up to the war and through wartime, so the regular tram service came to play an ever-increasing role in everyday life. With little competition from motorised transport and an absence of any omnibuses (until the 1920s), this was truly the golden era of the tram in the Three Towns.

Such is not to say that everything always ran smoothly. On 27 November 1914 a tram carrying a number of 'dockyardees' home from their night-shift duties was beset with brake failure and the vehicle ran out of control down the hill from Tamar Terrace to Paradise Place. Capsizing near the bottom it eventually came to a halt after hitting part of the wall around King's Road Railway Station. Three people died, one of them instantly. It was the second time that there had been a fatality on that stretch; on the previous occasion nine people had been injured, but only one man (51-year-old Isaac Searle) had died in the accident.

Electricity failure could also be a hazard – on at least one occasion a high tide at Stonehouse caused seaweed to enter the intakes of the cooling water for the Corporation generator and for several hours the trams were all brought to a standstill, forcing all passengers to walk home. Meanwhile, during the war, to comply with the semi-blackout conditions canopy headlights were removed from all those trams deemed to be visible from the sea and the top half of the saloon windows were painted blue.

Top: *Albert Road (Navy Row)*. Bottom: *Passage Hill*. Inset left: *November 1914 tram crash.*

The tram route up from Passage Hill curves around into Morice Square, past the Royal Albert Hospital and the entrance to Marlborough Street (inset).

All three of the routes into 'old' Devonport were serviced by trams – New Passage Hill, Devonport Hill and Fore Street, the latter was the main terminal point and it formed the nearest equivalent that Plymouth had to a rendezvous point like Derry's Clock. The route in from Pennycomequick stopped a little short of Chapel Street, while the route in from Plymouth and Stonehouse came via St Aubyn Street and exited via Chapel Street, leaving the western end of Fore Street, like almost all of Marlborough Street tram-free, as the route up New Passage Hill bent around into Morice Square.

Fore Street and Marlborough Street were also the principal shopping thoroughfares with Fore Street the busiest by any measure and while there was no Royal visit during King George V's coronation year you could almost be forgiven for thinking there was as the standard of decoration here and elsewhere was every bit as elaborate as it had been for the visit of his father nine years earlier.

Fore Street was particularly resplendent and, in Devonport Park, a massive bonfire, the equal of anything planned for the Hoe, was prepared. The main entrance to the Park was also given a truly Regal makeover.

June 1911, Coronation Fever in Devonport Park. Above left: Entrance enhanced. *Middle:* The unlit bonfire. *Top right:* Hog roast with James Day in the Park. *Bottom:* Fore Street is decorated.

While not quite matching the spectacular vistas available to visitors on the Hoe, Devonport Park nevertheless commanded extensive views in many directions and was hugely popular throughout the Edwardian era and beyond.

Its entrance was right on the busy tram route in and out of Fore Street and for the people of Devonport this was the place to promenade in your Sunday best, to feed the birds and to listen to the band.

In the aftermath of the South African War a Boer War pom-pom gun, captured as a trophy by the crew of HMS *Doris*, was mounted and presented, at the crew's expense, to their base-port town, Devonport. Vice-Admiral Sir Robert Harris and Admiral Sir Edward Seymour, who was then Commander-in-Chief at Devonport, officiated at the unveiling which was staged on Saturday 27 February 1904.

The South African War was largely a military affair, so the men of HMS *Doris* were particularly proud of their contribution, when the Vice Admiral Harris put together a naval brigade from *Doris* and dispatched them 800 miles inland with a contingent of 200 Royal Marines, to help the men of the Oxford and Bucks Light Infantry at Paardeberg.

Above: *Feeding the birds in Devonport Park.* Right: *A sailor steps out with his wife and daughter..* Opposite page: *Passing the entrance to Devonport Park, trams on the busy run into Fore Street.* Inset left: *The Doris Gun.* Right: *General view of the park.*

The well-populated Mutton Cove basks in the sunlight. Opposite page, top: The landing-pontoon at North Corner. Middle: Another view of Mutton Cove. Bottom: The Torpoint Ferry.

Initially maintained as open ground as part of the defences of the strategically important military and naval base that was Devonport, Devonport Park and the Brickfields were ultimately land-locked and there was no direct access from the sea or Stonehouse Creek. Indeed just like general access into the the town was restricted to three roads (each one formerly controlled by a drawbridge), so public access to the waterfront was restricted to three main areas: Torpoint Ferry/ Pottery Quay; North Corner, and Mutton Cove.

In 1905 the Torpoint Ferry was still a single-ferry operation. A proposal was put forward that year for a double-ferry service but the Admiralty, and indeed Devonport Corporation, weren't keen as it would have meant the ferry company expanding their waterfront area. An experiment was tried with two ferries operating from one installation, but the strain on the equipment was too great and efforts were abandoned.

However, not only was the Torpoint operation a single-ferry affair, it also stopped every evening at 9pm, leaving anyone desirous of making the crossing at the mercy of the watermen. In the 1890s, Reynold, the Torpoint tug operator, began an evening service with two small steamers, but escalating landing dues prompted him to withdraw in 1901.

Once again the waterman held sway, but then, the Torpoint Ferry Company started their own evening service, running two vessels – *Volta* and *Lady Beatrice* (nominally honouring Lady Beatrice Carew Pole) – on a triangular route between Pottery Quay, North Corner and Torpoint. In 1905 the route became a daily one too.

The Tamar was a busy waterway with all manner of craft. In 1910, following a collision between the Torpoint Ferry and a Naval Destroyer – mainly blamed on the fact that it was difficult to tell which way it was going – it became mandatory for both the Torpoint Ferry and that at Saltash, to hoist a red flag by day and a red light at night, to indicate their direction of travel.

Another bustling centre of waterborne activity was Mutton Cove. Here again there were a number of watermen available for river crossings, it was also a popular steamer stop and with water-travel never being entirely predictable, it was not surprising to find that there were a few public houses at each of these venues – Pottery Quay, North Corner and Mutton Cove – to help waiting travellers pass the time.

Saltash, Royal Albert Bridge.

Not surprisingly there were wayside inns on either side of the Saltash Ferry crossing too and ferry traffic was boosted by the new tram route which went as far as Saltash Passage on the Plymouth side.

One place where there was a marked decrease in passengers was at what was virtually the southernmost tip of Devonport – Ocean Quay at the end of Richmond Walk.

Opened in 1878 as a London & South Western Railway station – from 1886 it began catering for travellers arriving in Plymouth Sound in transatlantic liners – Ocean Quay enjoyed healthy competition with Millbay Station for a number of years. Until, that was, the friendly rivalry ended in tragedy, as in 1906 the L&SWR train was derailed after going through Salisbury Station too fast: 28 people were killed.

Four years later passenger traffic through Ocean Quay ceased and the facility became a goods station only.

Top: *Ocean Quay Terminal from Stonehouse and below: from Admiral's Hard. Opposite page: Keyham Station and Brunel's Royal Albert Railway Bridge.*

North Road Station c.1910. Opposite page: A train steams out of Mutley Station and two views of the recently refashioned Millbay Station.

TRAINS, TRAMS AND OTHER TRANSPORTERS

Predating the tram by a decade or two, the train continued to play an important role in the mass movement of people around the Three Towns and beyond. There were a whole host of small stations along main routes: notably St Budeaux, Ford, Keyham, Dockyard Halt, Mutley, Lipson, Laira, Plympton, Plymstock, Oreston and Turnchapel. Mutley Station, which opened on 1 August 1871, six years ahead of the station at North Road (Brunel had originally wanted the main station for the Three Towns to be at Eldad), was particularly busy with ticket sales averaging over 1,000 a day in 1913 – which, over the year amounted to 360,000, over 100,000 more than at North Road which was a joint station operated by GWR and L&SWR.

Great Western's Millbay Station, significantly upgraded around the turn of the century, was still the principal Plymouth Station, although the opening of Friary Station, off Exeter Street, in the summer of 1891 brought fresh competition from the London & South Western Railway, who had opened their Devonport & Stonehouse Railway Station (later known as King's Road) on the eastern edge of Devonport and just above the northern bank of Stonehouse Creek in 1877, the year before Ocean Quay and the same year as North Road.

The route into Plymstock had followed the development of Friary in the 1890s, while Plympton was on the main route into the Three Towns and was where the Iron Horse had first made its appearance back in April 1848.

Essentially this all meant that come 1914 there were still people around who could remember life before the train and the tram (notwithstanding Thomas Tyrwhitt's horse-drawn railway of 1823 that ran from Princetown to Crabtree and later to Coxside Creek).

Inside the tram shed at Milehouse.

In overall terms the era of the horse tram was relatively brief but undoubtedly significant, indeed the Plymouth, Stonehouse & Devonport Tramways Company, which formed soon after Parliament had passed the Tramway Act of 1870, has been hailed as 'the grandfather of all legitimate tramway companies' (Charles Klapper, *The Golden Age of Tramways* 1974).

The company opened its first, and, as it transpired, only route in March 1872 – the company was bought out within a year by the Provincial Tramways Company, which was also running trams in Cardiff and Portsmouth.

Traversing a distance just shy of two miles, it ran from Derry's Clock to Cumberland Gardens via Union Street and was soon extended (in 1874) to take in Fore Street, Devonport.

But for a short-lived experiment with steam trams in the 1880s, horse trams held sway around the Three Towns until the very end of the nineteenth century when authority was granted to Plymouth Corporation Tramways Department to electrify parts of the system.

Prince Rock became the first area to be thus serviced, as a new electricity generating station was created on the edge of the Cattewater and a tram shed was built in Elliot Road.

The first invisibly powered run was on 22 September 1899 and within a couple of years, electrification had spread right across the system. The northern route – to Compton – opened on 4 April 1901 and the tram depot there was enlarged.

Meanwhile, the Devonport & District Company, registered under the same piece of legislation in 1898, started work on laying out five miles of track in their patch and by the end of June 1901 had started providing electrified services in the borough that hitherto had long been *'disenchanted with being the Cinderella of the Three Towns in the matter of modern transport'* (Langley & Small, *The Trams of Plymouth* 1990).

Come 1914 the whole situation changed, following the Amalgamation of the Three Towns. Plymouth Corporation bought out the Devonport concern, lock stock and barrel, taking over its trams and its depots. Curiously however, because they were operating under the terms of a 21-year lease, the Stonehouse Company carried on until 1922, although they were forced to stop, briefly, on 11 November 1918, when, following the declaration of peace, the crowds in Union Street became so great that the trams were called back for fear of damage.

Top left: *A tram at Lane End, Compton (Hender's Corner, looking up Tavistock – Mannamead Road).* Top right: *Inside the tram workshop.*
Bottom right: *Outside the Milehouse tram shed.* Bottom left: *Driver and conductors of the St Budeaux tram pose for the camera.*

Left: *The Co-op's first steam lorry supplied by Robey & Co of Lincoln.*
Above: *Steam lorry belonging to a Devonport removal firm.*

While trams were exclusively for pedestrians, trains at least could carry both passengers and freight, as could ships. However, with road surfaces improving around the country and motorised transport a realistic alternative since the creation of the first petrol-driven vehicles in 1888, the commercial world increasingly looked to transporting goods by road and by other than horse-drawn vehicles.

In 1908 the Plymouth Co-operative Society road tested its first horseless carriage – a steam wagon. Purporting to be capable of carrying a five-ton load, the wagon was severely tested in its first month and when attempting to transport five tons of building materials to the Society's farm at Wiverton, the machine was strained and required costly repairs. Thereafter its capacity was capped at four tons – much to the frustration of the Co-op.

Six years later, with the advent of war and a great many of the Society's horses being requisitioned for military service, a decision was taken to set up a Transport Department. Pinwell's Yard off Vauxhall Street, and a site at Sutton Wharf, were both acquired in 1915 to garage a new fleet of motor vehicles, while another large site at Peverell (off Recreation Road) was bought with a view to utilising it for one department or another – one of which was intended to be Transport Maintenance. Change was on its way, but it was a bumpy and unpredictable ride until the use of the pneumatic tyre became more common in the 1920s.

Above: Ash & Sons, Cork, Wine & Spirit Merchants, of James Street, Devonport, promoting Guinness. Top right: An Anglo-American Oil Company vehicle carrying advertising hoardings in Plymstock. Bottom right: More Co-op lorries c.1915.

Italian-born local fish merchant, William Teglio, with his wife Jane, son Max and daughter Norah, c.1912; Max was then at Kelly College, he was killed in action in France in 1917.

SOCIAL LIFE, SPORT AND SCHOOL

Motor cars made little impact in the Three Towns before the Great War, indeed they were regarded with a degree of awe.

Dr Francis Pearse, who described himself as a 'happy bachelor' was apparently the first to own a motor car in the area. He bought his German-made Benz in 1900 (when it was about four-years-old and he was 28).

A locally born dentist with a practice on North Hill (he lived and worked at No.10 Queen Anne Terrace), Dr Pearse was a familiar sight around town.

Generally, however, cars were a rare sight before the war and even more scarce during the war as Defence of Realm restrictions limited the amount of petrol anyone could use. Lord Astor was fined £10 in April 1918 for 'causing petrol to be unlawfully used'.

His chauffeur evidently told police that Lord Astor was using the car on Government business and he too was fined – £2.0.0d.

Meanwhile, another early motor in Plymouth was Francis Hawke's Ford Model T Laundaulette. Francis obtained his first driving-licence in 1912 (it was signed by the Chief Constable) and ran a garage and taxi business in Greenbank. He also had one of the first petrol pumps in Plymouth -– it was installed in the front garden of his house in Greenbank Terrace.

The car was often used for weddings, for the bride, with the guests following on horse and cart.

CO 53, Dr Pearse in his 1896 Benz.

CO 1642, Francis Hawke's Model T Ford, in 1918, sold that year for £155.

Plymouth Pier, opened in 1884 and home to one of the area's more enduring skating-rinks, although many complained that the pillars (see inset photo) got in the way.

Cars were no means the only wheeled options available for family entertainment, there was another, much smaller item that, fitted with revolving pieces, proved immensely popular in the Edwardian era – the roller-skate.

Roller-skating had been popular since the 1870s and in relatively quick succession eight or nine venues opened up around the Three Towns to cater for the craze. One by one, with the notable exception of the Pavilion Pier on the Hoe, the various skating emporia closed, but then almost out of nowhere the craze grabbed the nation in a spectacular way in 1909. Vast new rinks were opened in Ebrington Street and in the old soap works at Millbay.

The Ebrington Street rink was the first of the new wave, and its massive hall measured over 450 feet (150 yards) in length. Styled the new 'American Roller-Skating Rink', it opened on Friday 17 September 1909 and it was followed barely two months later, by the opening of the Millbay Rinkeries on Thursday 11 November.

Vast spaces capable of accommodating up to 500 skaters at a time, they were popular meeting-places and were equipped with coffee-bars and refreshment centres as well as offering exercise opportunities.

'The idea that Rinking is a passing fad must be banished once and for all, and one has only to pay a visit to any of the Rinks to be convinced of the grip which this exhilarating and pleasant pastime has on the public,' proclaimed one guide published in Plymouth in 1910. *'It is a matter for wonder, however, what the crowds of Skaters that are now seen on the various Rinks throughout the Country did with themselves prior to the advent of Rinking.'*

There were speed trials, races (backwards, egg-and-spoon, balloon, three-legged, wheelbarrow, sack, and so on), displays of 'Fancy Skating', Fancy Dress Carnivals, team sports, notably hockey and surprisingly perhaps, football, and dancing:

'Dancing on Skates has become very popular with both sexes, and nothing is more delightful than waltzing on Rollers, or the more favourite two-step, which is a decided improvement upon, and a welcome relief from, the ordinary round and round variety.'

Military Bands provided the musical backdrop and the venues typically offered three, two or three hour sessions a day – morning, afternoon and evening – truly fun for all the family.

Top right: The American Roller Rink in Ebrington Street. Bottom, from left: Opening advertisement for Millbay.; Millbay Rinkeries Manager John Brock with his daughters in 1910; an anonymous skater; Millbay Rinkeries entrance, Millbay Road.

Graffitti on Smeaton's Tower.

William Chubb with the bomb.

Perhaps the skating at the Pier fared better than some of the other venues because the Hoe was a natural magnet for so many people. Undoubtedly it was what prompted some militant suffragettes to plant a bomb in the entrance to the Hoe's most iconic feature, Smeaton's Tower, in April 1913.

Bearing the crude legend *'Votes for Women! Death in Ten Minutes'* the home-made device was discovered by a passer-by, William Chubb. Measuring six inches long and containing half a pound of powder, the cylindrical canister had a fuse soaked in parafin oil. The wick had apparently been lit, but must have blown out in the wind.

It was thought that the damage to the tower could have been quite serious had the bomb gone off as was apparently intended.

There was also an earlier graffiti attack on the outside of the tower. In a message intended for the Home Secretary, Winston Churchill, who was evidently due to sail into the Sound on board Enchantress, a suffragette statement was daubed in large letters: *'To Churchill – No security until you give women votes, no matter how big the Navy'*. It would appear, however, that no-one felt too threatened by this apparent threat to local security and that same year the opening of the new bathing facilities at Tinside started a major programme of improvements to the Hoe foreshore.

Long-popular with the local swimming fraternity, there were a number of clubs already associated with the area – the Seven O'Clock Regulars, the Shackey Pool Stragglers and the Tinside Champions.

Recent improvements had already seen an upgrading of the ladies' changing and swimming arrangements, and the new building work around Tinside (where apparently in the past changing had been in a tin hut as opposed to a wooden shack around the other side – hence the names), was primarily intended for the men.

In the event, Tinside was opened up to both sexes and all ages, a facility for everyone in fact.

The new Hoe swimming facilities.

The ladies' bathing pool, west of Tinside.

Christening the new Tinside bathing arrangements.

Another family-friendly, and indeed generally family-run affair was the travelling fairground. Whiteleggs, Hancocks, and Anderton & Rowlands were all regular visitors to the Three Towns. West Hoe and Richmond Walk were among the prime pitches and it was at the latter that tragedy struck the Hancock operation in the early hours of a cold night in December 1912.

The culprits were a large group of suffragettes who had been waiting to greet their leader, Emmeline Pankhurst. Unfortunately, Miss Pankhurst had been arrested before landing in Plymouth (from America) and the 5,000 ladies waiting to meet her went on a march and ended up setting fire to Fox, Elliot & Company's timber yard at Richmond Walk. Sparks from the conflagration flew over to the Hancock's Great Worlds Fair which had set up at Richmond Walk for the winter season.

'The fire took hold and all but reduced the palatial gilded Roundabouts and Switchbacks to charred debris. The boards proudly lettered with

the words "Patronised by Royalty" lay blackened and in ruins.

'The fairground business Sophie ran with brothers, William and Charles, had grown to be the most successful in the West, and Sophie battled with her fellow showmen to salvage what they could, suffering burns to her hands as a result' (Steven Smith & Keith Scrivens, *Hancocks of the West* 2006).

Hailed as one of the most celebrated of West Country business women Sophie was 'a tough, shrewd and successful woman,' and was 'in no need of emancipation. Nor was she a women to cross; it was said that her vocabulary of swear words was larger and better than any man's and that she could go on for half an hour without repeating herself.'

Tragically the Hancocks were not insured for such a loss and it was devastating for the business.

Top: 'Hancock's Fair at West Hoe, Plymouth with Swingboats, Motorcar Switchback and Helter Skelter.'
Bottom: *The switchback to the right is burnt out as are the gallopers to the left. Inset left: Sophie Hancock and her family.*
Right: *With the men away fighting in France the girls look after the Shooting Galleries open at Richmond Walk during the war.*

In marked contrast to the glitz, glamour and noisy excitement of the fairground, one way of passing the time that had been popular since the days of Drake, was bowls. Remarkably, however, there had been no record of a bowls club, or even green, on the Hoe since Sir Francis reputedly finished his game and went to face the Spanish Armada back in 1588.

Admittedly it did not help that, until 1845 there had been an Act on the statute books (dating from Henry VIII's time) forbidding anyone to play bowls unless they were *wealthy and well-to-do*.

What is more the English Bowling Association was only formed in 1903 so it wasn't entirely surprising. Post 1903 clubs sprang up very quickly around the country and in January1907 a letter was written to the local press bemoaning the fact that: *'the town of all England, indeed of all Britain, which should possess a bowling green, has none.'*

A Plymouth club was promptly formed – the Plymouth (Sir Francis Drake) Bowling Club – and, while they waited for a suitable green to be created on the Hoe, the newly formed club held its games on ground to the side of Plymouth College at Ford Park.

The following year, on Wednesday 6 May 1908, the Mayor of Plymouth, Sir Charles Radford, head of the successful local retail store, Popham and Rodford, bowled the first official woods at the opening of the Hoe Bowling Green.

Among the leading lights of the club in the early years, experiencing success at Club, County, National and International level from 1911 onwards, was the man who had been appointed Plymouth Argyle's player manager in 1905 – Robert Jack.

Top right: 6 May 1908 Mayor Radford opens the new bowling green on the Hoe. Middle: The Mayor bowls the first wood. Bottom: The new site viewed from Lockyer Street. Inset: The club is formed and plays its first games at Plymouth College.

Robert Jack had come to Argyle in 1903, from Burslem Port Vale and was one of, it not the first, professional footballer on the team's books – Plymouth Argyle were formed as a professional club that year, arising out of the ashes of Argyle Athletic.

A Scot, Jack had started out playing for his native Alloa in 1893, as a 15-year-old, and had signed for Bolton Wanderers in 1895 where he became their leading goalscorer and earned the nickname of the 'Flying Scot'. In 1901 he moved to Preston North End for a season before moving to Burslem.

His spell at Argyle looked as if it too might be brief as at the end of his first season as player-manager, and now 30, he moved to Southend United.

Argyle, meanwhile, were struggling. Plymouth had become a hotbed of rugby as both Devonport Albion and Plymouth Rugby Club were fielding teams as good as any other in the country.

Attendances at Home Park were dwindling and doubts were cast about the viability of running a first-class team in the town. A Committee of Management was formed and for three years ran the club, but it fared badly and Argyle found themselves facing a grave crisis, one that was only averted thanks to a new board being put together.

Clarence Spooner and his younger brother, Stanley (who ran Spooner's huge drapery business) both *'devoted, time, money and energy to save Argyle from extinction'* (Sid Tonkin, *All About Argyle 1903-1963*). One of their first moves was to invite Bob Jack back to Home Park - he accepted and their faith in him was well rewarded.

Bob Jack went on to spend the next 28 years at Home Park during which time Argyle were twice League champions, runners-up eight times, and only ever ended up in the lower half of whatever league they were in four times. More than once he turned down an offer to join a top club and he brought many famous footballers to Home Park to wear the Argyle colours. *'He was one of those managerial giants of whom it has been said, knew the football game inside out'* (Tonkin).

Top: *Plymouth Argyle 1903–4 Standing l-r: Walter Anderson, Herbert Winterhalder, Charlie Clark, John Fitchett, Jack Robinson (goalkeeper), Andy Clark, Johnny Banks, John Picken, Bob Jack. Seated: Tom Cleghorn, Bob Dalrymple, Billy Leech, Archie Goodall (Captain), John Peddie (another Scottish striker who later played with Picken at Manchester United), Harry Digweed, Frank Brettell (Manager). Bottom: Plymouth Argyle line up for the 1911-12 season. Inset: Bob Jack puts in a call.*

Jack's return to Home Park witnessed a period of consolidation: Argyle were in the Southern League, an attempt had been made in 1909 to get the Football League to form a Third Division, but a *'misguided minority'* foiled the bid.

Meanwhile, teams like Tottenham Hotspur, West Ham, Fulham and Cardiff managed to get themselves elected to the Second Division and the only chances Argyle got to play top-flight sides was in the FA Cup.

In 1913 the season Argyle won the Southern League, they knocked Preston North End out of the competition and were rewarded with a home tie against Manchester United, with the celebrated Billy Meredith. Over 20,000 were there to see Plymouth bow out 2–0.

The following season after first-round success against Lincoln, Argyle travelled to Roker Park, where they played a Sunderland team that included Charles Buchan, Charlie Thompson and other internationals. Over 37,000 watched as Sunderland scraped a 2–1 victory.

The advent of war before the 1914/15 season even started was to prove problematic for the services-based area. Argyle, like many other teams, lost players to the Army and most clubs had difficulty keeping a regular side together. Nevertheless, the season limped on *'and there was a sense of relief when the Football Association wisely decided to suspend League Football for the duration of hostilities'* (Tonkin).

Many players joined the 'Footballers Battalion' and among those never to return was the popular Billy Baker who played over 200 games for Argyle (1909–15) and who was killed in Serre, during the Somme campaign, in 1916.

The intervention of war meant that no regular football was played at Home Park until the start of the 1919–20 season.

Top: *A trick cyclist is removed from the Home Park pitch by seven burley policemen, possibly at the Cup clash with Spurs in 1910.* Above: *Devon derby 1910 style, Argyle v Exeter.* Far Left: *Billy Baker who played over 200 games for Argyle.* Left: *A football special tram pulls into Milehouse depot.*

AUSTRALIA & PLYMOUTH.

The war, of course, was to impact on all sporting activity locally, however of all sports perhaps the one best placed to maintain some sort of presence throughout, was rugby.

At the dawn of the twentieth century, when Argyle were just turning professional, rugby, although essentially an amateur game, was both popular and successful locally. Both Devonport Albion (at the Rectory) and Plymouth Rugby Club (at South Devon Place), drew big crowds and dominated the sporting headlines.

In 1901 when the first moving pictures were taken of a rugby match, the game in question was between Leicester and Plymouth. In 1909 when the visiting Australian rugby team were here on tour, they played Welsh clubs, English county teams and just one English club side – Plymouth – at South Devon Place. Albion were at home to Bristol that day – 16 January – and Argyle were at home to Swindon, nevertheless 9,000 watched the 'Wallabies' play, and beat, Plymouth.

In 1911, Devon, largely composed of Plymouth and Devonport Albion players, won the County Championship. The following season they again made the final, against Northumberland. The game was played at the Rectory, in front of a 14,000 crowd. Apart from one man, Snell of Seaton, the Devon team was made up of Plymouth and Devonport Albion players. Devon won 29–0, Edwards, Harvey, Hayman, Baker, Jago and Butcher all ended up on the scoresheet.

A number of the local stars represented their country too, most notably James Peters. Born to a West Indian father in Manchester in 1879, Peters joined Knowle Rugby Club, near Bristol, in 1900 and some members resigned. Two years later he moved to Plymouth, working in Devonport Dockyard as a carpenter. A teetotaller, he played for Plymouth and in 1903 he played for the County side.

In 1906 the 'outstanding half-back' helped Devon win the County Championship – that same year the South African touring team initially refused to take the field against Devon because of Peters. A campaign was mounted for Peters to play for England and on 17 March 1907 he became the first black man to play for England, in a match against Scotland. He won five England caps – it would have been more had it not been for racial pressure. Devon, with Peters, won the County Championship again in 1907 and Peters, an elusive runner who 'got away like a boxer' when he was tackled, played on with Plymouth until 1912 (despite losing three fingers in a Dockyard accident in 1910).

Top: *Plymouth 1907 with James Peters front right.* Middle: *Plymouth and the 'Wallabies' 1909.* Bottom: *One of the wartime sides, RN Depot, Devonport, Champions of the UK 1917–18.*

Top left: *The ground at South Devon Place.* Top right: *Saturday 17 September 1910 Plymouth College v Butlin's team (the school took up rugby after 26 years of football, in 1903).* Bottom left: *Stanley Budd (Bristol) holding the ball for Stanley Edwards (Plymouth, Devon and England) in game for RN Depot 1917–18.* Bottom right: *Albion v United Services at Keyham c.1919.* Inset: *James Peters of Plymouth Rugby Club, the first black man to play for England.*

Boxing was another popular spectator sport in the Three Towns, and appreciation of the 'noble art' increased dramatically upon the opening of the Cosmopolitan Gymnasium in 1907.

Originally operating out of a *'ramshackle barn of a building in Mill Street, sandwiched between a brass foundry and sugar refinery'* the Cosmo was also known as Hancock's Winter Gardens. Here, under a corrugated roof, could be found a funfair and all the paraphernalia associated with the fairground and circus life. Between 1907 and 1924 – barring two short stoppages – here was staged what became *'the longest running weekly boxing show in the history of British boxing. In its time it even eclipsed the National Sporting Club in the regularity of its shows'* (Ron Hellyer).

It was at the Cosmo that the legendary black Heavyweight Champion of the World, Jack Johnson, made his only competitive appearance in the British boxing ring – he beat Ben Taylor in eight rounds.

It was in June 1908: *'The Casmo was jam-packed to its tattered doors and rafters; many had to be turned away. Over 5,000 spectators crammed into the old barn which, at that time, only had chairs thrown haphazardly round the ring, in the middle of the building'* (Fighters of the Old Cosmo - Clive Mumford 1975).

In 1910, the then English Champion, 'Iron' Hague, came to the Cosmo and was knocked out by Plymouth's sailor-boxer PO Curran in the 15th round, sending the crowd home delirious.

Almost every other champion of the day fought at the Cosmo at one time or another. The club was set up by Silas Alger and two other local sportsmen in 1907. They used to hold their planning meetings in the 'Talbot' pub in Union Street and before long they were joined by the landlord Harry Jenkins. Harry soon became the principal figure in the running of the Cosmo, which, with the addition of stands and seating, became a significant venue on the circuit.

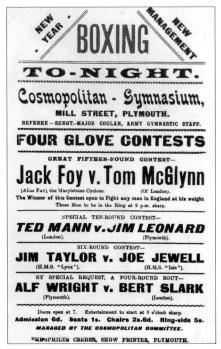

Above inset: Harry Jenkins, of the Talbot and the Cosmo. Above left: Jack Johnson, heavyweight Champion of the world, who fought his only British bouts in Plymouth. Right: One of Theophilus Creber's Cosmo posters.

When war was declared, Jenkins, like other promoters up and down the country, closed his venue. However, it was notable that the Cosmo had always attracted a large number of service personnel and almost immediately he was besieged by military and naval personnel across the Three Towns, to re-open, and so, in October 1914, he wrote an open letter to the press.

He had closed down to encourage men to serve their country, that was now happening, but, he said, *'the crisis continues and seeing that there are so many troops in training in this fortress, it has occurred to me that the time for re-opening has arrived – for three reasons.*

1. That I have had several applications from the new troops, some who are professional boxers.

2. Boxing is part of their physical training and any exhibitions will further serve to keep them fit and serviceable.

3. That those not already versed in the noble art of self defence may come and learn.

'The winter season,' he announced, would be staged, *'for the benefit of the local war fund.'*

Interestingly enough, two years later, the Cosmo was raided by the police and military authorities, who took the particulars of 200 young men who appeared to have no exemption certificates. Otherwise it was business as usual.

There were, of course, many sports that could continue throughout the war, the difficulty lay, not in finding people wanting to compete, but in trying to organise regular team sports with fixtures all across the country. Conversely the fewer participants needed, like boxing, the easier it was to stage sporting events.

Plymouth Argyle had evolved out of Argyle Athletic, an all-round sporting club that promoted football, cricket, running, swimming, cycling, boating and even, for a spell prior to being admitted to the Southern League, whippet racing. Cycling events and running races were almost exclusively for boys and men, however, and each passing year witnessed an increase in the number of entrants.

With many of the prominent businesses in the Three Towns employing large numbers of people, it was common for the business owners to sponsor sporting events just for their own staff and families.

The Co-op, celebrating their 50 year jubilee, staged several children's sports days in August 1910. One at the Rectory attracted 1,100 children, a week later a similar event at Home Park drew an attendance of 2,600 children, and by the time the third and final event was held, at South Devon Place a fortnight later, over 4,600 children appeared to join in the fun.

Clarence Spooner, as well as helping to bank-roll Argyle in 1899, with his brother, had also earlier organised the Avenue Recreation Club for all employees of Spooner & Co.

Businesses then were mainly locally owned and not part of some vast chain or retail group and employees were encouraged to feel part of one big family.

Top right: *'Olympic Games Home Park, start of the 5,000 metres race'* (Doidges 1913). Middle: *Girls' Co-op Jubilee race in Central Park 1910*. Bottom: *Plymouth College Sports Day 6 April 1906*. Above: *Gilbert Butcher, 16, wins a 440 yds race at Home Park, 1904.*

Left: St Budeaux couple Frederick and Florence Johns with some of Frederick's cycling trophies. Top: Ford Park, Plymouth College - July 1905 Bellamy batting without gloves. Above: Keyham Cricket Club, 1911. Opposite page top: Plymouth College school pool, 1911. Bottom: 6 April 1906, Macklin tackles the high jump at the School Sports Day.

Schools were the main source of sport for most young people, but not all offered the wide range available at Plymouth College. They were particularly well blessed, not only in having playing-fields on their doorstep, unlike so many of the new schools that appeared around the turn of the century, like Hyde Park and its architectural twin Salisbury Road, but, also thanks to the magnanimous gesture of its assistant master, Joseph Thompson, they had their own swimming-pool.

In 1902 Thompson defrayed the cost of the pool as well as paying to have the fives courts relaid, projects which, combined, cost over £1,000, an enormous sum when you consider that most teachers were then earning less than £100 per year.

At the end of 1900 a report on education in Plymouth's fifteen board schools revealed that there were a total of 323 teachers (58 more than in 1897) in service, but only half of them had teaching certificates. A quarter of these Board School teachers were paid over £100 per annum, but most, 46% received between £50 and £100, while 30% earned less than £50.

Fortunately for Plymouth College, Thompson was a man of independent means and although he was a passionate advocate of adequate salaries and improvements in rates of pay for teachers, he himself didn't need to earn anything from his work.

Swimming subsequently flourished at the school, as did any number of other sports, including cricket, hockey, football, fives and from 1903 onwards, rugby football.

That same year School Boards disappeared and respective corporations became the Local Education Authorities and a new system of primary and secondary schools was fashioned out of the old system.

By that time, Devonport had already built nine new board schools, in the wake of the 1870 Education Act, and Plymouth had erected twice that number – all of them great limestone piles with barely a blade of grass between them. There were new schools in Stonehouse, too. However, it's worth remembering that education was not free until 1891 and that the provision of education had improved remarkably within a relatively short period. After all, one of the statistics revealed in the census required by the 1870 Education Act, was that there were then some 2,000 children in Plymouth who were receiving no education at all.

Top: *Farriers at work in the autumn of 1914 as Plymouth College's playing-fields are taken over for military preparations.* Above left: *The field is deployed for exercising horses.*
Right: *The Cricket Pavilion alongside the makeshift cookhouse.* Opposite page: *Salisbury Road School (top) and Hyde Park School, both of which were used as wartime hospitals.*

With the advent of war and the requisitioning of at least ten local schools 'for billeting and other purposes' it meant that some 5,000 local children had been displaced by the middle of August 1914. Most, however, were found alternative premises, nevertheless the school leaving age was just 12 and although it was possible to stay beyond that time, many chose to leave.

For those who stayed, locally the dockyard and the armed services were among the main options for the boys, only a very few went on to further education. The new technical college in Plymouth and Devonport offered some post-school opportunities and evening classes for the more mature student who wished to improve their knowledge, or in some instances gain qualifications that would help improve their ability to teach. But there were few University places, indeed there were few universities and, apart from Oxford and Cambridge and a handful of Scottish Universities, they were nineteenth century institutions (London, Lampeter, Durham, Wales and Belfast) and the others – Birmingham (1900), Liverpool (1903), Leeds (1904), Manchester (1904), Sheffield (1905) and Bristol (1909) – were even more recent.

However, during wartime, with so many men away from home, there was no shortage of employment opportunities, but not everyone was keen to see children working.

Isaac Foot, at a meeting of the Plymouth Education Committee in February 1916, proposed that: 'no child under the age of 14 should be employed or engaged in street trading'. However, he was unsuccessful and eventually the alterations to the recommendation of the sub-committee, who placed the limit at 11 years, was adopted. Another addition, that no boy should be employed as a lather-boy, or any other similar occupation in any barber's or hairdresser's shop, proposed by the Vicar of St Andrew's Arthur Perowne, was added as was another clause suggested by Mr Foot to the effect that no child should be engaged as a billiard-marker.

Not all parents welcomed the move: 'No doubt those in authority who make these bye-laws have their bread buttered both sides, but do they ever think of the poor folks who have to earn bread before it can be eaten? When one has children at the age of 11 or 12 one looks to them to earn, if only a few pence to help buy food, clothes or footwear.

Only a mother knows what a godsend their little help is, also it keeps

Salisbury Road Schools, Plymouth.

22570   Photo Tourists Association.   Turnham Green W.

other children from finding mischief. Perhaps the only reason for the street trading bye-laws is because some parents spend their children's money on drink. Therefore all have to suffer for a few, just as some critics class all soldiers' and sailors' wives, but there are good and bad in all classes of life. I think it is very hard for those who have fathers, husbands, sons and brothers fighting for their King and Country and freedom, and those left behind to look after the welfare of the towns and countries to impose such bye-laws such as to stop children from earning until 14 years of age. What do they care about the poor widows with large families?'

The missive was signed – *PRIVATE WIFE AND A MOTHER*

Clearly every set of circumstances was different, another letter to the local press, this time from a *'Friend of Children'* addressed the issue of children and cinemas:

As cinemas are in the present much in the limelight, I would be glad to know at what age children may enter unattended. This evening at 6.30 passing along Union Street I noticed two little ones standing in the bitter wind outside a public house. As I stood there looking at the poor mites (boy four and a girl eight) a woman came out and gave them money telling them to go to the pictures. She then, looking completely relieved, entered the "pub" again having got rid of her encumbrances in a manner pleasant to all. By the look of her she was likely to remain "soaking" for an indefinite time – till she was "put out" no doubt.'

These were difficult times all round and the three boys who were given six strokes of the birch rod for putting metal bottle-stoppers on tram-lines so that they flattened out and resembled a penny, which they could then use in a slot machine for chocolate or cigarettes (no less than 90 were found in a machine near the Pier) may have felt hard done by, but there was a noticeable increase in juvenile crime during the war. At a meeting of the Clerical and Lay Conference of the Deanery at Plymouth in March 1916 the Rev Charles Teape spoke of the increase in juvenile crime in the town during the year, a fact which he attributed in large measure to the exciting pictures exhibited at cinemas. Magistrates were recognising all over the country that the increase in juvenile crime was largely due to the determination on the part of children to get into picture shows. The Chairman, Rev Perowne, was glad that some of the worst films, which had passed the so-called censor in London, would not be shown in Plymouth. Meanwhile, Rev JP Barker contended that one of the reasons for the increase was the short hours which children were now putting in at school.

Top: *Girls at play on the roof of the Higher Elementary School, Stoke, which was requisitioned as a Military Hospital.* Middle: *St Ursula's School, Beacon Park.* Bottom: *Inside a classroom at St Ursula's.*

J Hayne Pillar, a active member of the Plymouth Co-operative Society instructs a class of young boys on the effects of alcohol consumption on the heart.

Top left: 21 January 1907 Salisbury Road Baptist Church is officially opened. Top right: The completed church. Right: the interior of the premises. Below: The pass issued to the Reverend Herbert Hill in November 1914 after the Church was requisitioned by the Military Authorities for use as a Hospital. Opposite page top: 22 May 1909, the foundation stone is laid at the corner of Hyde Park Road and Peverell Terrace for the new parish church of St Gabriel. Bottom: Dignitaries process along Hyde Park Road towards a Provincial Grand Lodge meeting of Freemasons at Plymouth College.

No. 50 Ward.............. Territorial Hospital,

Salisbury Road

Plymouth, Nov 26th 1914.

Admit Rev H Hill to Visit No. _____

Salisbury Road Baptist Chapel Regt., between the hours of 2

p.m. and 4 p.m. on Wednesdays and Sundays. any day

TO BE GIVEN UP AT THE ENTRANCE GATE AND RETURNED ON LEAVING.

This pass must be renewed every month. is permanent

Registrar, 4th Southern General Hospital.

CHURCH, CHAPEL, AND COMMERCE

The number of clergy in the Three Towns had grown spectacularly during the nineteenth century, reflecting the growth in population generally, with every denomination anxious to provide a church or chapel for their prospective congregation as the housing estates were developed.

Plymouth, Peverell, Mount Gould and Lipson were areas of rapid expansion at the dawn of the twentieth century and churches sprang up accordingly. St Gabriel's (1910), was the main Church of England destination in Peverell, a few years after Peverell Park Methodist had opened, while the Catholic Church of St Edward the Confessor appeared in 1911 and a facility for the local Baptists not long afterwards.

In Mount Gould, St Simon's appeared in 1907, a new parish carved from St Jude's. Completed in the same year was Salisbury Road Baptist church, both of them appearing two years after the new Wesleyan church in Mount Gould and the Bible Christian base in Embankment Road.

Meanwhile St Augustine's was finished in Lipson Vale, in 1904, and ten years later phase one of St Mary the Virgin at Laira was ready for worshippers. A new Weslyan building was opened at Laira in 1906 and, in 1915, a Congregationalist chapel.

Other notable C of E additions were St Barnabus (1904) in Wilton Street and St Mary's (1911) in Cattedown, with new Wesleyan establishments at Compton (1900), Camel's Head and Pennycross (both 1907), Primitive Methodist foundations in Cobourg Street (1908) and Keyham (1910), where there was also a new Catholic building – the Church of the Holy Redeemer (1902).

Faith clearly loomed large in daily life: *'I have faith in our destinies'*, proclaimed the King, in his speech on the eve of war.

'I shall be strengthened in the discharge of the great responsibilities which rest upon me, in the confident belief that in this time of trial my Empire will stand united, calm, resolute, trusting in God.'

Curiously enough, the King's cousin, Kaiser Wilhelm, also entreated his people to trust in God: *'May God's blessing be with you.'*

Perhaps it was no surprise that after the war, and the loss of so many millions of men on both sides, many started to question that faith.

9 September 1901, opening of new grocery store in Station Road, Keyham.

One institution in which more and more people were investing faith in the late-nineteenth and early-twentieth centuries was the Plymouth Co-operative Society.

Established locally, only in 1860, no other organisation dovetailed more harmoniously with the expansion of the Three Towns. Formed initially to ensure that the working man wasn't being seen off either in terms of how much he was paying for food and clothing, or in terms of the quality of those items, the Co-op with its system of re-investing profits and rewarding loyal customers with a dividend taken out of any surplus generated, was an instant success in Plymouth (although it struggled due to poor management in the early days in Devonport). Just as churches were being built at an unprecedented rate across the Three Towns to cater for the spiritual needs of the populace so the Co-op opened shop after shop to serve the consumer needs of those same people.

From humble beginnings in Catte Street on the fringe af Sutton Harbour – a first floor shop run by part-time volunteers – selling unadulterated *'flour, oatmeal, lard, dried fruits, tea and sugar; the main ingredients from which a meal could be made at the time'* (John Webb – the Society's first secretary), the Society very quickly started to grow and to diversify.

Before they had celebrated their first anniversary they had moved to bigger premises, and then bigger still within two years. By the end of their first decade they were dealing in coal, footwear and clothing.

Then they took on a dairy, then a bakery, then a farm.

In 1892 they opened their impressive Central Premises on the corner of Frankfort Street and Courtenay Street in town. It was quite simply the biggest retail development the Three Towns had ever seen.

All the while their chain of smaller stores continued to spread. On 9 September 1901 their 23rd grocery store opened, as well as their 16th butchery in Station Road, Keyham.

Every time a new housing development appeared, the Co-op was on hand to service it with a new shop or two and because they had ready funds they were able to expand in a way individual traders could hardly hope to aspire to. In 1902 they even started building their own houses, although that experiment was relatively short-lived.

Unlike their move into mobile shops, which came in March 1903 with the introduction of their first horse-drawn greengrocery van.

1903, an early Co-op grocery van in St Michael Avenue, Keyham.

1903, the new Co-operative store at the junction of Weston Park Road, Peverell Park Road and Hyde Park Road. Opposite page top and bottom: The new Co-op bakery in 1906. Middle: The new Co-op restaurant, opened April 1909 – three course lunches were 1/6d (7p).

Designed to meet the needs of their members who lived in areas where there was no handy Co-op store, or just to provide a regular service for different neighbourhoods, these too were an instant success and before the year was out a further twelve vans had entered service and four more had been ordered.

Of course, it wasn't long after that that it occurred to the Society that they may as well start manufacturing their own carts and carriages, which they did at Coxside.

By this time the economies of scale were beginning to make a whole host of other opportunities possible and so it was that they set about building a massive new warehouse on North Quay and a bakery and a stables at Peverell.

It was an almost unbelievable success story and one that local independent traders were deeply jealous – and resentful – of. Indeed in February 1905 the so-called Traders' Publishing Association Ltd in conjunction with the Argus Printing Company, produced a newspaper called *The Tradesman and Shopkeeper*.

Circulated within the Plymouth area, the paper alleged that the Plymouth Mutual and Industrial Co-operative Society was in the throes of bankruptcy and that the building of the Bakery at Peverell had stopped and the new Warehouse at North Quay was going to be sold off. It also suggested that the 1904 balance sheet was faulty and members were withdrawing their capital.

All of the allegations were without foundation, but were nonetheless damaging. The Society took a stand and sued for libel in the High Court of Justice in London in April 1906.

Three times Mayor of Plymouth, local solicitor John Thomas Bond, took up their case. The Society's books were examined thoroughly and revealed that their actual assets over liabilities were standing at over £100,000; the judge was prompted to remark that he wished he was half as bankrupt as the Society.

The Co-op was duly awarded £4,000 damages against the Traders' Publishing Association and £1,000 against Argus Printing.

In the meantime, numbers continued to rise and the business continued to expand. In 1900 membership had stood around 25,000, by 1913 it had risen to 40,000.

The declaration of war in 1914, however, brought fresh challenges and a reawakening of middle-class prejudice against the Co-operative Movement generally.

War-relief committees were set up in towns and villages across the country and Co-op members, whose societies had given generously to these bodies, were denied representation. Similarly, military service tribunals were packed with private traders, who seemingly took great delight in sending Co-op workers out to the Front while somehow exempting their own employees.

'One society lost 102 out of its workforce of 104, while surrounding shopkeepers were keeping their sons out of uniform. Some army officers sent in to oversee the process had naively explained that the Co-op was an unfair competitor in any case and should be closed down.' The situation wasn't helped by the fact that the Government had appointed Lord Devonport, *'a wholesale grocer and competitor of the Co-op'* (Birchall 1995), as wartime Food Controller.

In the Three Towns, by the end of 1915, some 209 Co-op workers were serving out of a total of 363 who were then eligible to be called up. Three months later that number had risen to around 300. In the new laundry, all the van drivers had been called up and 53 wash-house women had been moved to munitions work, leaving the department in a difficult position.

By the summer of 1916 the number of those called up had risen to 350 and by May 1917, with the criteria for call-up having changed, there were now 700 employees serving in the Armed Forces with the Society magnanimously making up the difference to families of the shortfall between what the services were paying and what the employees had been paid before they were called up.

All these measures took their toll on the Society's resources, but none compromised their integrity, and membership rose dramatically. By 1918 the roll had risen by almost 50% to 60,000 and the number of staff now employed across the Three Towns had risen from 1,521 to 2,400. Trade, meanwhile, had gone from just over three-quarters of a million to just over two million pounds.

They had lost horses to the war effort, but had invested in motor vehicles. They had bought a ship, only to have it requisitioned by the Admiralty. They had opened a jam factory when there had been serious concerns that the fruit from the Tamar Valley might be wasted because it could not be transported for sale elsewhere and towards the end of the war, following the refusal of the Local Authority to establish National Kitchens, they provided almost 60,000 meals in six months, mainly for children on the Barbican and in Stonehouse.

At that time the Co-operative Society was a loose collection of thousands of independent Co-operatives up and down the country, and locally there was no one in their league.

Spooner, Popham Radford, Perkin Brothers, Dilleigh, Dingle and Underwood & Co., were among the major retailers in Plymouth, with JB Love and JC Tozer in Devonport. Apart from banks (notably Barclays and Lloyds) and insurance companies (Prudential, Commercial Union, Norwich Union ...) national chains were relatively inconspicuous on the high streets. They could already be found before the war: H Samuel's had a jewellery shop in George Street, WH Smith's had a stationers in Mount Pleasant Terrace, Stead & Simpson had a shoe shop in Bedford Street and Hepworth's had clothing stores in Plymouth (Bedford Street and Union Street) and Fore Street (Devonport), but they were few and very far between. Almost all of the businesses across the Three Towns were locally owned and run, like the 60 or so tobacconists that could be found around the area before the war, and like the then newly established Lawson's ironmongery in Frankfort Street (1904), Wray & Co, jewellers, in Union Street (1908) and WH Joce, King Street, plumbers and gas fitters (1908).

The businesses tended to be very specific too, few general shops or department stores and a heavy reliance on boys on bicycles for lightweight deliveries.

Some businesses could be contacted by telephone, via a three- or four-digit number at most. The *Western Weekly Mercury* number was simply Devonport 7, while their editorial number was 163, and their commercial department was on 413. One of the Three Towns older established businesses, Balkwill & Co, Chemists (whose origins stretched back to William Cookworthy in the early eighteenth century) had the telephone number 31, while Swiss & Co, who published a regular Post Office directory and handled the advertising on the trams around the Three Towns – the medium giving *'the greatest publicity at the lowest cost'* – could be contacted on Devonport 43.

Interestingly enough, their 1908 *Post Office Directory* doesn't appear to list any of the Three Towns Co-operative stores in its trade directory pages. It's worth noting, incidentally, that while there were a huge number of Co-operative Societies around the country, locally the early attempt to set up a Society in Devonport and Keyham had failed and in Stonehouse no separate attempt was ever made, and so, to all intents and purposes the Plymouth Co-operative & Mutual Society had long since regarded the Three Towns as one.

Top: *Marks & Spencer, Fore Street, Devonport 1917 with Muriel Bennett in the centre.* Above: *William Henry Joce and son, King Street c.1911. Opposite page: Albert Pengelly, Union Street 1919, tobacconist or tobacnist (the mistake was made by a chatty signwriter who wasn't paying attention to his work – annoyed at first Pengelly relented when he realised people were coming in to point out the mistake, and often buying something. Thereafter he called all of his other outlets 'tobacnists').*

Fire in Duke Street, Devonport c.1910: 'Queen's Head Hotel' far left, next to Breen's with the Co-op on the other side of the street and the Market in the distance. One of the young girls watching proceedings is Dolly Lampen, whose father, Samuel, the Market weigh-man, kept the Market clock going. Right: Devonport Fire Brigade.

AMALGAMATION

As time rolled by the notion of Devonport, Stonehouse and Plymouth being three entirely separate self-governing entities became increasingly questionable.

The ever-improving public transport system was blurring the boundaries year by year, physically and commercially, and the idea that each town needed to have its own departments responsible for sanitation, policing, collecting and disposing of refuse, and supplying gas, water and electricity was becoming increasingly difficult to defend.

Time was when Stonehouse Creek had provided a clear-cut topographical divide between Devonport and its near neighbours, but the infilling of the upper section and the opening of Victoria Park at the dawn of the twentieth century made that much less obvious. Meanwhile, the division between Plymouth and Stonehouse was by then almost completely arbitrary.

Furthermore, the idea of merging the Three Towns was far from new – it was discussed by the then newly formed Plymouth Chamber of Commerce back in 1814 – and it had been revisited by various bodies in the years since. However, it wasn't until the threat of war became all too real that serious action was taken as 59-year-old Major-General Arthur Pole Penton (General Officer Commanding, Plymouth Defences) declared that, in the event of an emergency he didn't want messengers frantically cycling off to the Mayor of Plymouth, the Mayor of Devonport and the Chairman of the Stonehouse Council seeking consensus on something requiring an instant decision.

Parliament agreed and 'The Local Government Provisional Order Bill for the unifying of the Three Towns' was eventually passed despite a vigorous campaign by the Devonport authorities to stop it – the campaign was still raging after the war started.

Victoria Park, c.1904.

Essentially, however, the Devonport case was very weak in key areas. The indigenous Devonport businessmen (many of whom were Devonport councillors) may well have feared a gradual erosion of Devonport's influence over its own destiny, and they may well have been justified in those fears, but the majority of its inhabitants were not overly bothered.

Nevertheless that didn't stop the Devonport fathers from fighting the decision in Parliament, indeed they spent thousands of pounds contesting the issue.

However, on Wednesday 5 August 1914, in the same paper that the local population learned that Britain was now at war, they also read about the conclusion of the Amalgamation case that had been heard by a Select Committee of the House of Lords.

The first witness on that last day of the hearing was Dr William Corbett, leader of the Stonehouse Council. Doubtless, much to Devonport's dismay, Corbett contested that Stonehouse welcomed the proposal, but added that they wanted to see the bridge tolls removed and would not be happy to just join with Plymouth.

'We are out for the amalgamation of the Three Towns because we think it is the proper thing and are willing to give up a good deal to attain that object,' he added. And when asked by the Duke of Wellington if he, Corbett, thought that Devonport had any interests opposed to Plymouth, he replied, *'None whatever – they are absolutely one.'*

Their interests according to Corbett may have been one, but not in the eyes of Devonport's prime protagonists. However the timely declaration of war supported the merger, particularly as it meant that Plymouth Sound was now 'boomed'. The measure had been taken to prevent enemy shipping entering the harbour but it also meant that it was now difficult for Devonport to discharge their refuse barges out at sea, which was the Town's main means of waste disposal. Plymouth, by comparison had a 'destructor' which would continue to work in wartime.

Plymouth's position was also infinitely superior in terms of water supply. Plymouth, argued Dr Hill, a Durham County health official and witness to the case, had 110 days water supply while Devonport was very much living *'from hand to mouth, as she had a storage of 14 days' supply only.'*

In the event, Royal Assent for Amalgamation was confirmed on 10 August 1914 and the formal execution of the proposal took effect on Sunday 1 November. The following day, a Monday, was declared a general holiday and saw the local electorate go to the polls to return a new Town Council for Greater Plymouth. Far from being a day of celebration the day was described as being *'as dull as the November day on which it fell,'* its significance being massively overshadowed by the War.

Opposite page: *Devonport Corporation Cleansing Department c.1902.* Above: *Last assembly of Devonport Borough Council.* Inset: *Burrator.*

THE WESTERN MORNING NEWS, WEDNESDAY, AUGUST 5, 1914.

Britain Declares War on Germany.

THE DIE IS CAST.

BRITAIN DECLARES WAR ON GERMANY.

THE KING'S FLEET.

HIS MAJESTY'S MESSAGE TO OFFICERS & MEN.

"THE OLD GLORIES."

GERMANY DECLARES WAR ON BELGIUM.

The die is cast. England last night declared war on Germany.

This followed what amounted in effect to an ultimatum from Great Britain to Germany on the subject of the preservation of the neutrality of Belgium. Mr. Asquith read in the House of Commons correspondence which had passed on the subject, and said that the Government could not regard the communications received from Germany up to that time as in any sense satisfactory. In the telegram which the Government have sent to Berlin a reply was required to be made by midnight. The reply was received before that hour, but it was unsatisfactory.

Germany last night also declared war on Belgium.

As was anticipated, Admiral Sir John Jellicoe

WAR DECLARED.

ULTIMATUM TO GERMANY ON BELGIUM.

REPLY UNSATISFACTORY.

The German answer to the British Ultimatum was received last night.

It was unsatisfactory, and at seven o'clock war was declared on Germany.

THE BRITISH ULTIMATUM

When the Speaker took the chair in the House of Commons yesterday afternoon there was again a crowded attendance.

Mr. Bonar Law asked the Prime Minister if he had any statement he could make to the House.

Mr. Asquith, who was received with general cheers, replied: In conformity with the statement of policy which was made by my right hon. friend the Foreign Secretary, a telegram was sent early this morning by him to our Ambassador in Berlin. It was to this effect:—

The King of the Belgians has made an appeal to his Majesty the King for diplomatic intervention on behalf of Belgium.

His Majesty's Government are also informed that the German Government has delivered to the Belgian Government a Note professing friendly neutrality for maintaining a free passage through Belgian territory, and promising to maintain the independence and integrity of the kingdom and its possessions at the conclusion of peace, but threatening, in case of refusal, to treat Belgium as an enemy. An answer was requested within twelve hours.

We also understand Belgium has categorically refused this as a flagrant violation of the law of nations.

His Majesty's Government are bound to protest against this violation of a Treaty to which Germany is a party in common with us, and must request an assurance that the demand made upon Belgium will not be proceeded with, and that her neutrality shall be respected by Germany.

(Cheers.) Yesterday we asked for an immediate reply. (Renewed cheers.) We received this morning from our Minister at Brussels the following telegram:—

The German Minister has this morning addressed a Note to the Belgian Minister for Foreign Affairs stating that, as the Belgian Government had declined the well-intentioned proposals submitted to them by the Imperial Government, the latter, deeply to their regret, is compelled to carry out, if necessary by force of arms, the measures considered indispensable in view of the French menace.

Simultaneously, or almost immediately afterwards, we received from the Belgian Legation here in London the following telegram from the Belgian Minister for Foreign Affairs:—

General Staff announce that territory has been violated, Gemmenich, near Aix-la-Chapelle.

Subsequent information tends to show the German force has penetrated still further into Belgian territory.

We also received this morning from the German Ambassador here a telegram sent to him by the

WAR ON BELGIUM.

DECLARATION BY GERMANY LAST NIGHT.

["London Standard" and "Western Morning News" Special.]

Brussels, Tuesday.

An official announcement has been issued that Germany has made a declaration of war against Belgium.

The second German Note to Belgium (says Reuter's Agency) is of a very threatening character. Notification was made by the German Minister at Brussels late on Monday night to the Belgian Government, stating that, following the Belgian answer to the German ultimatum, Germany declared that she is prepared to carry through with force of arms, if necessary, the measures she considers essential.

THE KING'S SPEECH.

Brussels, Tuesday.

The King delivered the following speech to the Deputies:—

Never since 1830 has a graver hour sounded for Belgium. The strength of our right and the need of Europe for our autonomous existence make us still hope that the dreaded events will not occur.

If it is necessary for us to resist an invasion of our soil, however, that duty will find us armed and ready to make the greatest sacrifices. Our young men have already come forward to defend the fatherland in danger. One duty alone is imposed on us, namely, the maintenance of a stubborn resistance, courage, and union.

Our bravery is proved by our faultless mobilization, and by the multitude of the voluntary engagements. This is the moment for action. I have called you together to-day in order to allow the Chamber to participate in the enthusiasm of the country. You will know how to adopt with urgency all the necessary measures.

Are you decided to maintain inviolate the sacred patrimony of our ancestors? No one will fail in his duty, and the army is capable of performing the task. The Government and I are fully confident. The Government is aware of its responsibilities, and will carry them out to the end, to guard the supreme welfare of the country. If a stranger should violate our territory he will find all Belgians gathered round their Sovereign, who will never betray his Constitutional oath.

I have faith in our destinies. A country which defends itself wins the respect of everyone and cannot perish. God be with us!

Speaking in the Chamber to-day, M. de Broqueville, the Premier, announced that the 14th and 15th classes of the Reserves had been called to the colours, and then read the German Note and the Belgian reply.—Reuter.

ENGLAND'S ACTION.

RECEIVED WITH FRANTIC DELIGHT IN ST. PETERSBURG.

St. Petersburg, Monday.

Thousands of people made demonstrations to-day before the British Embassy here. Sir George Buchanan, the Ambassador, appeared at the window and addressed the crowd amid frantic cheering.

He declared England's perfect sympathy with Russia. The Secretary of the Embassy, standing beside the Ambassador, then raised cheers for Russia.

An Imperial Ukase has been published announcing the introduction of a military censorship.—Reuter.

TO THE NAVY.

KING GEORGE'S MESSAGE TO OFFICERS & MEN.

"THE OLD GLORIES."

"SURE SHIELD IN HOUR OF TRIAL."

The following message has been addressed by the King to Admiral Sir John Jellicoe:—

"At this grave moment in our national history I send to you, and through you to the officers and men of the fleets of which you have assumed command, the assurance of my confidence that under your direction they will revive and renew the old glories of the Royal Navy, and prove once again the sure shield of Britain and of her empire in the hour of trial.

"GEORGE R.I."

The above message has been communicated to the senior naval officers on all stations outside of home waters.

FOOD PRICES.

PUBLIC EAGERNESS TO OBTAIN SUPPLIES.

As was anticipated, food prices in Plymouth continue to advance, though there is believed to be no immediate danger of scarcity, and therefore no need for householders to get in large supplies. A rush only has the effect of contributing to the rapid upward movement. Meat shows the most surprising rise. Since Saturday there has been an increase of from 2d. to 2½d. per lb in beef, and a big rise in lamb and mutton. Fish, bacon, sugar, and other commodities are also dearer.

Mr. John Ross, of Plymouth Market, states that the butchers considered it unnecessary to call a meeting of the local association, inasmuch as the public realised that the big increase of wholesale prices must mean a corresponding enhancement of retail prices. He, with others of the butchering trade, was, however, very much surprised at the extent of the rise in butchers' meat. They had not anticipated that it would be anything like as large, but were obliged to guard themselves.

It is satisfactory to know that the bakers are not at present contemplating a further addition to the price of bread, and this should go far to reassure the public. Since the crisis began, however, flour has risen from 12s. to 13s. a sack, and the public seem quite willing to pay the present increased price of bread. Millers do not care to make any real quotations, owing to the wild state of the market and the desirability of await-

ADMIRAL JELLICOE.

ASSUMES SUPREME COMMAND OF HOME FLEETS.

The Admiralty announce that, with the approval of his Majesty the King, Vice-Admiral Sir John R. Jellicoe, K.C.B., K.C.V.O., has assumed supreme command of the Home fleets, with the acting rank of admiral, and Rear-Admiral Charles E. Madden, C.V.O., has been appointed to be his Chief of the Staff. Both appointments date from yesterday.

SIR JOHN R. JELLICOE.

Vice-Admiral Sir John Rushworth Jellicoe, who becomes Commander-in-Chief of the Home fleets, was born on December 5th, 1859, and attained the rank of vice-admiral on September 18th, 1911. He entered the navy in July, 1872, and was promoted lieutenant in August, 1880, with three first class certificates. He was lieutenant of the Agincourt during the Egyptian war, 1882, for which he received the medal and bronze star, and in the following year was the winner of the £80 prize at the Royal Naval College, Greenwich. Shortly after he was appointed a junior staff officer of the Excellent, gunnery school at Portsmouth, then under the command of Capt. (now Lord) Fisher. In 1886, when gunnery lieutenant of the Monarch, he received the Board of Trade silver medal for a gallant endeavour to save a shipwrecked crew near Gibraltar. In the late eighties and early nineties he served for some time at the Admiralty as assistant to the director of naval ordnance (Capt. Fisher), and in June, 1891, was promoted commander. His next ship was the Victoria, flagship of Sir Geo. Tryon, Commander-in-Chief in the Mediterranean, and he was in her when she was sunk in collision in June, 1893.

In January, 1897, he was promoted to captain, and in December of the same year was appointed to the Centurion, flagship of Sir Edward Seymour, Commander-in-Chief on the China station. In this capacity he acted as chief staff officer to the expedition which attempted to relieve the Pekin Legations in June and July, 1900, being severely wounded. He was highly commended in the admiral's despatches, and received the C.B. in the November following. In 1902 he was appointed captain-superintendent of contract-built ships, and the year after naval assistant to the Controller of the Navy (Sir William May). In August, 1903, he succeeded Rear-Admiral Bridgeman in command of the Drake, in the Cruiser squadron, but returned to the Admiralty in February, 1905, as director of naval ordnance, which appointment he held during a most important period of gunnery development, including the completion of the first all-big-gun ship the Dreadnought. His share in the design of that vessel was recognised at her launch in 1906, when King Edward conferred the K.C.V.O. upon him.

Attaining flag rank in February, 1907, he was appointed in the following August rear-admiral in the Atlantic fleet. He relinquished this post a year later, and within two months succeeded Sir H. B. Jackson as Third Sea Lord and Controller of the Navy. He remained at the Admiralty this time for a little over two years, and in December, 1910, was appointed to the command of the Atlantic fleet, with the acting rank of vice-admiral. He received the K.C.B. in the Coronation honours in June, 1911. He was appointed a Second Sea Lord on December 9th, 1912.

REAR-ADMIRAL MADDEN.

Rear-Admiral Chas. E. Madden has just relinquished the command of the Second Cruiser squadron in order to succeed Rear-Admiral A. G. H. W. Moore as Third Sea Lord. He was born in September, 1862. He served in the Egyptian war of 1882, and received the medal. Attaining the rank of captain in June, 1901, he commanded the Orion, depôt-ship for destroyers at Malta, from April to November, 1902, when he became flag-captain to Rear-Admiral Fawkes, commanding the Cruiser squadron, in the Good Hope. He received the fourth class of the Royal Victorian Order from King Edward in August, 1903, and in November, 1904, was attached to the Admiralty for special duties. In February, 1905, he was appointed naval assistant to the Controller of the Navy (Captain, now Vice-Admiral, Sir Henry Jackson), and the following June was married to the daughter of Sir Charles Cayzer, Bart., M.P. In December, 1905, he succeeded Capt. (now Rear-Admiral) Bacon as naval assistant to the First Sea Lord (Sir John Fisher), and as such received the C.V.O. on the occasion of King Edward's visit to Portsmouth on August 3rd, 1907. Nine days later he was appointed to command the Dreadnought, as flag-captain and chief of the staff to Sir Francis Bridgeman, Commander-in-Chief of the Home fleet. He

NAVAL ADDITIONS.

ADMIRALTY ACQUIRE FOUR NEW SHIPS.

TWO DREADNOUGHTS.

TO BE NAMED "AGINCOURT" AND "ERIN."

The Admiralty announces that the Government have taken over the two battleships, one completed and the other shortly due for completion, which had been ordered in this country by the Turkish Government, and the two destroyer-leaders ordered by the Government of Chile.

The two battleships will receive the names Agincourt and Erin, and the destroyer-leaders will be called Faulkner and Broke, after two famous naval officers.

THE TWO BATTLESHIPS.

SULTAN OSMAN I.

One of the Turkish battleships referred to is the Sultan Osman I., which has just been completed by Sir W. G. Armstrong, Whitworth, and Co. (Ltd.), and left Devonport about three weeks ago after being docked at the North Yard. As was reported at the time, she was the largest vessel ever docked at Devonport. She has a length of 642 feet overall, and a beam of 89 feet, there was no dock on the Tyne which could hold her comfortably; hence the decision to send her to Devonport. Between perpendiculars the Sultan Osman I. measures 623 feet, and draws 27 feet at mean load displacement and 29 feet at maximum draught. Laid down originally to the order of the Brazilian Navy on September 14th, 1911, as the Rio de Janeiro, she was at one time the largest warvessel under construction in the world. With her displacement of 27,500 tons she shares at present with the Japanese battle-cruiser Kongo, delivered by Messrs. Vickers last year, the distinction of being the greatest warship yet completed either here or abroad. However, there are now several warships approaching completion which equal or exceed the new battleship in displacement, such as the Queen Elizabeth, of 27,500, the Tiger, of 28,000, the American Pennsylvania, of 31,400, and the Japanese Fuso, of 30,600 tons. As a matter of fact, for a time after her first keel-plate was laid she was intended to surpass even these monster ships.

A DARING PROPOSAL.

Her designer had in his eye a vessel of 31,600 tons, with a total length of 690 feet, and her armament was to have consisted of twelve 14-inch weapons, instead of the 12-inch now fitted. Other designs of even greater magnitude, involving the installation in the one case of eight 16-inch and in the other of ten 15-inch guns, were originally projected. A change in the Presidency of the Brazilian States resulted, after some progress in construction had been made, in the substitution of the present 27,500-ton design for the enormously costly ship originally planned. In 1913 the Brazilian Government came to the conclusion that the Rio de Janeiro was unsuited to their requirements, and arranged with the builders for the cancellation of the contract. In her stead an order has been placed with Messrs. Armstrong for a battleship of about 30,000 tons, which will be armed with 15-inch guns, more in accord with modern tendencies. The Rio de Janeiro was not long in the market before the Ottoman Government raised sufficient money to buy her. Launched on January 22nd, 1913, the Sultan Osman I. was eighteen months on the stocks. The Turkish Government are stated to have paid £50,000 more than the original contract price, so that she has cost the Turkish Government £2,725,000 in all.

LARGE NUMBER OF TURRETS.

With regard to her design, the new Dreadnought is remarkable for the large number of turrets which she carries. The seven turrets, which are disposed on four different levels, each carry two 50-calibre 12-inch guns.

Wednesday 5 August 1914, Western Morning News, page 5.

WAR

'The die is cast. England last night declared war on Germany.'
So ran the opening line of one of the main news stories on page 5 of the *Western Morning News* on the morning of Wednesday 5 August, 1914. Elsewhere, in a *'Summary of To-Day's News'* we read: *'Great Britain declared war on Germany at seven o'clock last night.*

How King George, by a personal appeal to the Czar, did his utmost to avert a general European conflict is revealed in an official communication issued in London last night.

A Russian force on the Prussian frontier is reported to have been repulsed by the German garrison. Fighting on French territory continues. It is stated that the Belgian frontier has also been crossed.'
Sifting information from other columns in the almost exclusively text-driven pages readers were told that:

'The all-embracing ambition of the German Emperor [who incidentally, like Czar Nicholas of Russia, was a cousin of King George] *... is undoubtedly the moving spring for the whole war.*

England is entering the war with clean hands and a clear conscience, and can face the verdict of history in the war with nothing to retract or blush for.'
Meanwhile another correspondent noted that:

'Historians will find the official report of yesterday's momentous proceedings in the House of Commons very like the play of Hamlet with the Prince of Denmark left out. No indication could be gathered from the Speaker's record in Votes and Proceedings that Sir E Grey made a momentous speech upon the European crisis, or that the House of Commons did anything unusual except pass the "Postponement of Payments Bill" though all its stages rapidly. No motion was before the House when Sir E Grey spoke, and, of course, no division was taken. There was, therefore nothing to be written on the records. I find that many people have been puzzled that the House did not divide upon the question of peace or war.

"I cannot see that the House of Commons authorised the Government to declare war," said one critic today. He would have had little doubt on the subject if he had been present at yesterday's epoch making sitting, and listened to the tense, fierce cheers of the overwhelming majority of the House as Sir E Grey described the measures he had taken.

The Government knew from these signs that they had Parliament, and through them the great majority of the nation at their back, and they would not insult the intelligence of the House by asking members to vote on the question whether England should vindicate her honour or disgrace herself.'

Not all politicians were in favour of the move, however, and two of only four photographs to appear in the paper – all of them on the front page – were of 66-year-old John Burns, President of the Board of Trade, and 76-year-old Viscount Morley of Blackburn, Lord President of the Council, both of whom had tendered their resignations.

However the paper claimed that the high-profile Liberal departures would encourage the Opposition of *'that restless element in our population, including Socialists, who are too unpatriotic to sink their prejudices in the interests of the nation'*.

Furthermore, there was talk of some Liberals prophesying that the war will mean *'the smash up of the Liberal party and the eclipse of all their hopes'*.

John Burns   Viscount Morley of Blackburn.

Admiral Jellicoe   *Lord Kitchener.*

The other two front-page photographs were of Lord Kitchener, his Majesty's Agent and Consul General in Egypt, *'who it is rumoured, will take over the office of Secretary for War, at present held by the Premier'* and Admiral Lord Jellicoe *'who was yesterday appointed in supreme command of he Home Fleet'*.

There was, incidentally, absolute confidence in the Home Fleet, as the King himself had put it when addressing his remarks to the officers and men of the Senior Service, in a speech widely quoted in the paper: *'under your direction they will revive and renew the old glories of the Royal Navy, and prove once again the sure shield of Britain and of her empire in the hour of trial.'*

A panel of experts, headed by the Asquith-appointed Frederick Huth Jackson, a noted financier, had already proposed that the British Government should *'assume the risk of insuring British ships against war risks all over the world – and thereby set free the commerce of the Empire at this critical time.*

The Board of Trade, working in conjunction with the insurance groups, will take a share in the liability for safety of the vessels, but will themselves accept all risk for the safety of the cargo.'

In other words, the Navy will either save shipping from capture, or the Government will foot the bill for the loss.

'Vessels sailing from New York to Buenos Ayres, or from any portion of the Far East, or, indeed, any part of the world, will be offered the same facilities as those coming direct to England with foodstuffs and raw materials.

"We want them to keep the seas," said the Chancellor of the Exchequer, whereas the existing insurance policies force them to fly to port and stay there. In this way the Government hope to keep going the whole mechanism of our sea-borne trade. They have sufficient confidence in the strength of the Navy to feel sure that the financial losses which they may incur will not be of an overwhelming character.

'All these measures,' concluded the paper's feature writer, *'bring home to the public the complexities and ramifications of modern warfare, but they will serve to mitigate the suffering of noncombatants, and smooth the path to the speedy resumption of business when peace once more reigns in Europe.'*

The expectation was clear: the Navy would sort any problems that arose at sea and anyway the war was not likely to be a long one. As was noted elsewhere in the paper that day: *'If war had to break out in Europe it could not have occurred at a more convenient moment for us. The Home fleets were practically at war strength when the first rumble of coming trouble was heard.'*

What is more: *'home supplies are exceptionally large, there being four months wheat supply available, and English fruit is plentiful and ready for marketing.'*

No amount of such reassurances, however, could prevent an element of panic: *'A very unworthy course of action has been pursued during the last day or two by a large number of people who ought to know better and who ought to set an example to their fellow citizens of unselfishness rather than the reverse. There has been a run on gold, and a run on the provision dealers, some people buying large quantities of dry foods and tinned foods, as though they were provisioning their homes for a siege.'*

One supplier was quoted as saying, *'We have people who usually order from 7lb to 14lb of a certain commodity asking for a hundredweight'.* While another report stated that *'sugar had almost doubled in price and the cost of coal had increased by 20%'.*

Somewhat worryingly, there was also a notice in the paper to inform the public that 'owing to the War and subsequent stress of business Colliers Stores, Dilleigh & Co, Lipton Ltd., and Underwood & Co., are withdrawing price lists and, aren't sending out reps but are taking orders via post and telephone.'

However the largest advertisement in the paper was for Pratt's Motor Spirit – White Rose and Royal Daylight Lamp Oils, and the proprietors were proudly boasting that they have made 'NO advance in the wholesale prices of any of our products and see no necessity for an advance under the present conditions'.

Oil lamps were still very important to the average household; in 1914 only 1,753 consumers locally were connected to mains electricity and by the end of the war there were still less than 10% connected nationally.

The times were changing, however, as was expressed in a review of Graham Wallas's The Great Society, newly published by MacMillan at 7/6d and reviewed in the Western Morning News that day, 5 August 1914: 'Mr Wallas uses the term 'Great Society' to signify that transformation or extension of the social scale which has resulted from the many mechanical inventions of the last century. Railways, telegraphs, &c., have altered our relationships. In more primitive days men were related to one another as individuals, they lived in small, almost self-dependent, village communities. Now the usual everyday relationships are those of huge impersonal concerns, vast organisations, no longer those of single individuals.

As an example of this interdependence – as contrasted with the days when a man stood or fell by his own endeavours – we may quote this sentence: The widow who takes in washing fails or succeeds according to her skill in choosing starch or soda or a wringing-machine under the influence of half-a-dozen competing world-schemes of advertisement.'

Everyone was now fair game for the advertisers, who were spending more and more money trying to increase their share of the market – and newspapers were the main vehicle for such large scale advertising. There was still a place for the small ad though: 'Wanted immediately good FOOTMAN-VALET,' 'Wanted Good Plain Cook,' 'Cook General or House-Parlour Maid,' 'Governess for girl 11, boy 7,' and 'Woman, 23 years of age, good worker, honest, and sober, but subject to periodical epileptic fits, which only last a few days monthly, requires a place (through mistress getting married).'

There were also a number of horse, pony, carriage and cart

advertisements: 'Cheap Landau, light, single horse, with brake and lamps; £6 to clear.'

Despite the advances of the modern world this was still, for the time being, the age of the horse, although to accommodate the new motorised methods of transport the roads were improving as a story, courtesy of the AA and MU revealed: 'Tar spraying is in progress between Crownhill and Roborough. Half-width of road is being done. Road repairs are being carried out five and half miles north of Plymouth. Full width of road is being done, and two steam rollers are at work.'

With the outbreak of war however, transport owners were soon likely to find their vehicles requisitioned: 'All transport required by the Army Service Corps which is demanded through Messrs Turpin and Sons must be provided at once by other transport owners, or it will be taken' (WMN 5 August 1914).

Of course with Devon and Cornwall being dominated by farming communities it was interesting to note on page four that: 'Farmers' representatives in Parliament are taking steps to impress upon the Army authorities the necessity of avoiding measures which will interfere with the gathering of crops. For instance, farm horses now used in harvesting cereal crops in England and Wales, should, it is suggested, be exempt from impressments for Army requirements.'

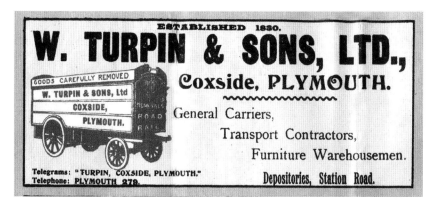

'I understand,' the reporter, added 'that the Government will work on these lines, being anxious, as Mr Lloyd George has said, to facilitate the ordinary business of the nation to the utmost degree.'

Among the other stories reported in the same edition of the paper it was reported that the wife of the sitting MP for Plymouth, Mrs Waldorf Astor, while addressing the Salvation Army Home League at Congress Hall at the Octagon, said that she had always been an advocate of better homes and houses for the working-classes:

'Years ago I thought it would be better to spend money on housing rather than on the Navy, but my husband says it is better for the poor to have bad houses than to have none at all, which would be the state of affairs if the they had no navy capable of defending them.'

As well as the situation on land and sea, the paper was keen to point out the potential aerial threat that modern warfare now presented:

'The best sky fleet is that of Germany. The German machines are uniformly good, while German pilots hold nearly all the important records. The number of machines which German aeroplane firms are capable of building at normal rates is approximately 2,000 per annum. Of the French military aeroplanes it is questionable whether more than 250 are of much war utility.'

Russia's aeroplane building capacity is small; it is doubtful if it exceeds two hundred per annum' and … 'contrary to general belief, Austria has no airships whatever, although she has a Zeppelin under order.'

Meanwhile, elsewhere in the paper it was reported from Brussels that yesterday 'the French Minister informed the Belgian Minister of Foreign Affairs at 2.30 this morning that three dirigibles were flying towards Brussels having invaded Belgian territory.'

Aerial warfare was very much a new phenomenon and represented an, as yet, unknown threat. Closer to home, however, there were already issues for concern, perhaps the most disappointing of which was the threat posed by pickpockets – a situation exacerbated by the dense crowds congregating around the windows of the newspaper offices anxious for breaking news ahead of publication. In Exeter the previous day Police had to issue warning notices because they had received 'no fewer than seven complaints of stolen purses' from such a crowd.

Meanwhile another unnamed correspondent reported: 'We are informed that three men of suspicious character were discovered late on Saturday night endeavouring to break through the wire entanglements which have been erected along the coast at Renney on the outer and eastern side Plymouth Sound.

Information is indefinite … but it is stated that they were fired upon by the sentries, and captured.

Intelligence is refused by the military authorities, but it is understood that the three individuals are not Englishmen, and that they have refused to speak.'

These were tense times. A new proclamation decreed that 'all enclosed War-office and Admiralty properties' of which there were many in and around the Three Towns, 'are now prohibited areas under the Official Secrets Act, and that any person approaching such a place must halt the instant he is challenged by a sentry, as otherwise he will run the risk of being mistaken for a hostile emissary and be fired at.'

The terms of the King's Petition, issued on the declaration of war, again reported in the Western Morning News that Wednesday and signed off by Major-General Penton, in charge of the Garrison Town, read: 'I hereby, in pursuance of powers given me by the Army Act, give notice that Regular troops, Special Reserve troops, and Territorial Force troops forming part of the garrison of the fortress, will be billeted as necessary upon the inhabitants of the Three Towns during the continuance of the present emergency.'

It was also reported that '…for the purposes of facilitating the movement of troops, the Government has assumed control of the railways.'

After weeks of speculation suddenly the situation was very real. Dotted around the other pages there was news of many events – regattas, tennis matches and other sporting occasions being cancelled, with many servicemen pulling out of competitions and their competitors getting 'walk-overs' into the next round of whatever competition it was.

A good deal of page eight was taken up with news of servicemen being called up, rounded up, camps being struck, men being billeted temporarily and then moved on. By and large, however, the troops went off singing and cheerful, and although 'some employers are left very shorthanded, there are no grumblers'.

In other arenas life still went on as usual: The Theatre Royal Plymouth was host to Robert Courtneidge's No.1 Company in Oh, Oh, Dolphins; The 'Nobodies' were at the Pier Pavilion on Plymouth Hoe; the Grand Theatre in Stonehouse was staging A Woman's Revenge; and at the Devonport Hippodrome, you could see the 'famous revue – Fancy Meeting You.'

Leaving for the front: A typical scene in a rural setting – a family says farewell at Lipson House.

Before the week was out, however, a number of further restrictions had come into force under the terms of the Defence of the Realm Act – DORA. They included not allowing people to: melt down gold or silver; fly kites; light bonfires; buy binoculars; write letters abroad using invisible ink; ring church bells; trespass on railway lines or bridges; give bread to horses or chickens; buy brandy or whisky in railway refreshment rooms; spread rumours about military matters, or talk about naval or military matters in public places.

In Plymouth, where this was likely to be particularly difficult, especially in situations where alcohol might be thought to loosen tongues, the Fortress Commander, Penton, closed all the pubs for six weeks. He also introduced restrictions on the sale of alcohol a year before the rest of the country and, in October, he decreed that women were not allowed to purchase drinks after 6pm. And then, a month later, he determined that all pubs should close at 9pm and remain closed until 9am the following day, with the additional proviso that servicemen were not allowed inside pubs until midday and that, furthermore, civilians were not allowed to buys drinks for servicemen and servicemen were not allowed to buy drinks in bottles for consumption off the premises.

The following year some of the measures introduced by Penton, like the restricted hours and the 'no treating', were adopted nationally.

'It is,' proffered Penton in his official communiqué, in August 1914, 'an act of mistaken kindness to offer anything which may help unfit members of HM Forces.'

Furthermore, 'any publican who serves either a Sailor or Soldier with an amount of liquor which is likely to render him unfit to perform his duty will be most severely dealt with by the Fortress Commander under the powers conferred upon him. All ranks of Society are earnestly desired to observe this notice.'

It is far from clear how effective the measures were, as one letter to the local press from Vox Populi, of Stonehouse put it, 'I do not think the order could have been very stringent as some houses are still serving females irrespective of that Order, while other houses are abiding by that rule which is another very unfair way of doing business.'

The self-styled 'voice of the people' had started their missive in the belief that it was 'General Penton's wish that only certain women were to be debarred, not respectable women whose relatives are now at the Front fighting'.

Adding a dismissive comment about 'all those piffle merchants who haven't the common sense to know that when women go out for the evening they don't carry a horse trough, or a milk jug'.

It was indeed an odd ruling, particularly as there were quite a number of pubs in Devonport that were run by female licensees, among them the 'Avondale', the 'Duke Street Inn', the 'Barnstaple', the 'Lord Beresford' and the 'Lord Hood'.

There was clearly some sort of problem, however, as a later newspaper report alluded to an 'increase of drunkenness among women, about which many magistrates are complaining'.

The report noted that 'many of the offenders are wives of soldiers on active service, and when a woman of this class came before Magistrates yesterday it was stated that the woman had suffered from delirium tremens'.

The report continued: 'She was drawing half the wage her husband had earned in civil employment, besides the War Office allowance of 1s7d [about 8p] a day.'

Lord Sanderson, a former foreign office civil servant, promoted the idea of war clubs for women. The 74-year-old bachelor spoke of his own spirit of restlessness that drove him to his own club. Working women, he believed, must have the same desire to meet and talk things over, but if they had no club, then the pub was the only alternative.

Speaking in Plymouth just before Christmas 1914, he said it was a marvel that there was not more drinking among these women.

'But the clubs must not be too homely, the nearer they get to the public house, without drink, the better.'

A little later, Lady Egerton, the wife of the Commander-in-Chief of the Plymouth Station, sponsored and opened a club for wives and mothers of servicemen at 64 Emma Place, Stonehouse.

It was to be the first of three and anyone wishing to join it was welcome to go along, mindful that they could transfer to the one in Plymouth or Devonport as and when they opened.

The entrance fee was set at 2d, with a weekly subscription of another 2d, with tea available at a penny per head. The club was to be open between 2.30 and 9pm each day.

'All applications for membership are to be made to the Parish Secretary who will have membership cards, which are always to be shown at the door.'

Another almost fanatical follower of the Temperance movement was Mrs Waldorf Astor (as she was invariably referred to). Addressing the King Street Wesleyan Brotherhood on the drink question, Mrs Astor contended that the best way to keep men from drink was to put something in their hearts.

'More harm,' she said, *'has been caused to our soldiers by drink than has been done to our soldiers in France by the Germans and it was imperative that some steps should be taken to put a stop thereto.'*

While her statistics may have been questionable her motives, and indeed those of her husband, certainly weren't. Waldorf Astor sent at least two cheques for £30,000 to the Red Cross during the first year of the war, a phenomenal sum considering a typical Naval Commander would have been paid £365 a year and the Admiral of the Fleet himself, just a little more than £2,000 per annum. They also provided a number of recreation halls for servicemen locally, the first of which was opened at Crownhilll on 10 November 1914. Tragically it was burnt down a year or so later and in April 1916 Major Astor and his wife provided a brand new replacement.

The main provider of such recreational facilities however was the YMCA. In the opening months of the war they established 18 temporary tented resources and in 1917 the organisation opened an impressive new set of more permanent premises in Union Street.

Top: *Winifred Brown outside the 'Princess Royal' in Cornwall Street, Devonport.*
Bottom: *The new YMCA building in Union Street, opened 26 October 1917.*

Work had begun on the new centre on the last day of February 1917 and the completed property was opened eight months later, on 26 October, by the seventh child – and third son – of Queen Victoria and Prince Albert, HRH Field Marshal Prince Arthur, Duke of Connaught and Streathearn.

The 67-year-old Duke had joined the Army over 50 years earlier and had spent the early part of the war in Canada where he had served as the first Governor General of Royal descent. Prince Arthur had lost his wife earlier that year and was thus a widower like 74-year-old Dr Charles Hingston, who was then the President of the Plymouth YMCA. A Justice of the Peace and an eminent physician, Hingston presided over a merry band of more than 150 voluntary lady workers and two dozen night patrol workers – men – most of whom were beyond the age of military service and who *'have met thousands of men during the night hours at railway stations'* … and who presumably suggested the YMCA as a place to rest and relax, rather than look for an hotel or a guest house, or whatever, at some strange hour of the night or day. The YMCA was, after all *'open day and night to all the Allied Forces'* and according to the booklet put together soon after the end of the war, saw *'a continual stream passing in and out when the men are off duty'*.

The facts and figures certainly spoke for themselves: in the two years since the Union Street operation opened it was said, in 1919, that *'a million customers have been served by our lady workers; 61,000 men have occupied beds; 407 concerts, lectures, and social gatherings have been held in our Hall – every one of them an unqualified success; 128,952 letters have been written and posted and 22,800 games of Billiards have been played.'*

The social functions were all organised by a Committee of Servicemen and as the *Camera Impressions* indicated: *'It will be seen that "Jack" and "Tommy", mingle quite happily'*.

Meanwhile, reading through the list of names of those who donated £20 or more to the endowment of the 22 cubicles that formed a part of the bedroom accommodation we see plenty of familiar local worthies, among them: Sir Henry Lopes; Brigadier General the Lord St Levan; the late Earl of Mount Edgcumbe; Sir John Jackson; the late John Yeo; Henry Hurrell; Messrs Wakeham Bros.; Miss Bayly of Seven Trees and the Voluntary Workers at Goodbody's Sailors' and Soldiers' Recreation Room.

Top: *The Refreshment Room.* Middle: *The Billiard Room.*
Bottom: *The Recreation Room.* Opposite page: *Emergency beds in the full YMCA.*

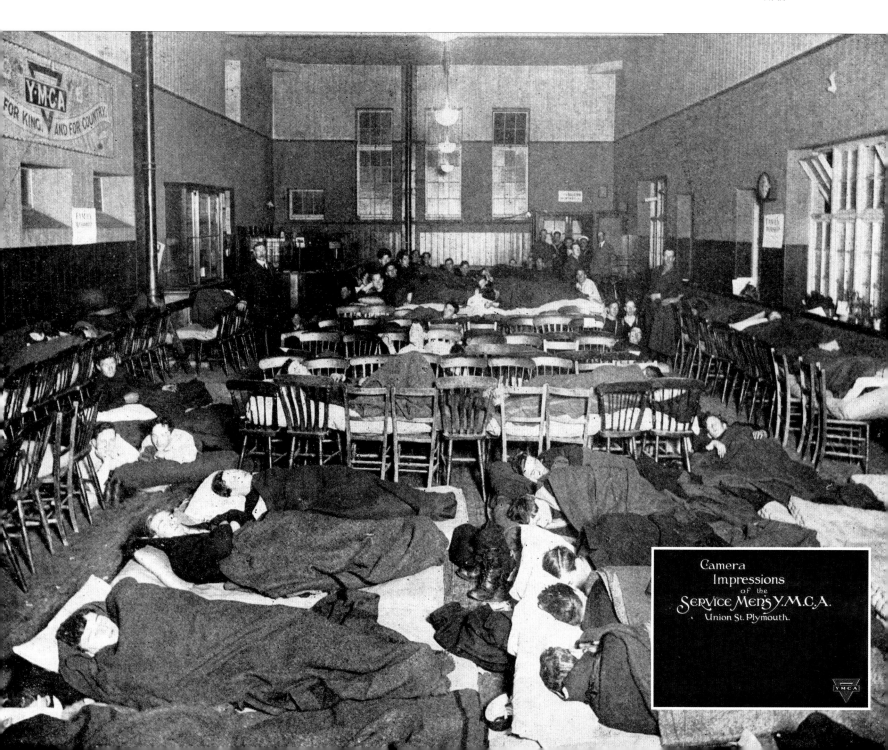

Camera
Impressions
of the
Service Men's Y.M.C.A.
Union St. Plymouth.

Top left: *Agnes Weston and Sophia Wintz.* Top right: *Royal Sailors' Rest, Fore Street looking west.* Above: *Fore Street, looking east.*

Another great friend of the serviceman, particularly all sailors, and of the alcohol-free entertainment emporium was Aggie Weston, who, since 1876 had been offering *'Coffee, Comfort, and Company'* all for a penny. Having started in Devonport, she subsequently opened similar enterprises in Portsmouth, Portland and Sheerness. Before long the Devonport experiment was expanded: firstly by the purchase of a second, neighbouring building, and then, just over ten years later, by the purchase of the whole of the Fore Street/Edinburgh Road corner site. This, in turn lead to the opening, in the late 1880s (around the same time as the Royal Naval Barracks were first occupied), of what became, in 1892, thanks to a Royal Warrant from Queen Victoria, 'Agnes Weston's Royal Sailor's Rest.'

Much of her work was accomplished with her great friend Sophia Wintz, *'but for whom I could not chronicle one tithe of the work that has been done'* (Agnes Weston, *Under Fire* 1917).

And there can be no doubt that between them the two women achieved a tremendous amount, their tireless efforts appearing to know no bounds:

'The work of a lifetime seemed crowned,' wrote Miss Weston in *Under Fire*, 'when, on Sunday, May 7th, 1916, exactly 40 years from the date of its first opening, before a great gathering over 1,000 strong, sailors, soldiers, sailors' wives and mothers, old pensioners and other seafaring people were able to declare the new extensions open.'

The new addition was called the Royal Block, by special permission of His Majesty the King and like all their buildings the new premises were all *'legally and safely vested in Trustees, so that, in the event of the deaths of myself and Miss Wintz, the work would go on, on its own lines, and we have a splendid staff of workers for the different departments of the work, so that all is provided for the future, as well as the very uncertain future at present will permit.*

Miss Wintz and myself are Honorary Managing Trustees,' she continued in quite candid form, 'we receive no emolument whatever, but, on the contrary, give considerably to the funds from our private incomes. I merely mention this to show that nothing comes to us from these large businesses, we have not the proverbial "axe to grind". All profits are spent on the work itself.'

And certainly they were very large businesses, as Miss Weston herself observed, *'Our Royal Sailors' Rests seem to do more and more service every year: the three buildings at Portsmouth and Devonport, including* the little Home at Keyham, accommodated 471,798 Seamen, Marines and Soldiers, with beds during the last year – nearly half a million – an increase on the previous year of 92,621.'

Clearly there were times here, like in the YMCA, when the beds were all taken, hence: 'These sleepers do not include a large number who had to put up with a shakedown in the Reading Rooms or the Large Hall at crowded times.'

But however much money the business generated it was never going to be enough, especially in wartime, because it wasn't just the servicemen Aggie Weston supported, it was their wives and mothers too: 'We are in touch with every widow and bereaved mother and have been able to advise and help them in many ways.

They set grand examples of patience and courage, and in the thousands of letters that we have received, it has been grand to read how nobly they are bearing up under such crushing sorrow. The mothers often have need of help, as they are not pensioned, and if the boy sent the money himself, instead of allotting through the Admiralty, they would get no gratuity, so that my war chest will need constant replenishing.'

A Legacy Form was included at the end of the publication and, with a statement that almost seemed to suggest that she thought the end for her was in sight, she concluded: 'And so my story is ended, and I thank God that I have lived to work through these terrible days.'

The following year circulation of a monthly newsletter they had taken to sending to sailors (in the past Miss Weston had sent handwritten missives to men serving away from home) reached some 600,000 readers per issue.

Miss Weston, known to many blue jackets as 'Mother' Weston, also published a journal Ashore and Afloat, to further Christian beliefs, charitable behaviour and temperance, among sailors.

In June 1918, her efforts were publicly recognised when, at the age of 78, she was made a Dame Grand Cross of the Order of the British Empire. Sadly just four months later, and a few weeks before the end of the war, Miss Weston died, in Devonport. In an unprecedented move the decision was taken to accord Dame Weston a full ceremonial Royal Naval funeral, an honour never before conferred upon a woman.

The streets were lined as the funeral procession made their way to Weston Mill cemetery where Miss Weston was laid to rest.

October 1918: two views of the funeral procession for Dame Agnes Weston. Inset: Cover of Under Fire, booklet produced by Agnes Weston in 1917.

Landing Party of Boys returning from Cremyll to HMS Impregnable.

A LIFE ON THE OCEAN WAVES

Britain's twentieth-century heavy-metal Navy was a far cry from the wind-blown wooden warships of the past. No longer was it necessary for the 'sailor to run aloft and lay out on a yard arm to reef and furl,' ran one account of 'The Training of a Lad' in 1905, less than a decade before the start of the war. 'The picturesque sail drill with boys and instructors aloft is no longer one of the sights of the Hamoaze.'

In many other respects however, little had changed in the training regime. At that time around 3,000 boys a year were being recruited into the Senior Service, most now had to be at least thirteen-and-a-half-years-old and once he had been handed a ticket with his ship's number and issued with a hammock – he was in.

'His life on board ship may now be said to commence, and full of work it is without a doubt, with his class, twenty all told, who are all allotted to one instructor, and who mess together and are practically one happy family for the rest of their training service.

He turns out at 5am, lashes up his hammock, stows it away in the nettings (a space in the bulwarks on the upper deck), washes himself, (having a bath twice a week, for on board a man of war "cleanliness is next to Godliness,") has a cup of cocoa as a "stand by," and falls in for cleaning ship and scrubbing decks.

This brings him to 7 o'clock, when about three-quarters of an hour's gymnastics and boat pulling gives him a splendid appetite for his breakfast, which comes at quarter past eight. This consists of coffee, and bread with butter or pork on alternate days. Falling in half-an-hour after breakfast for inspection, church service is held under the chaplain, and the different classes are marched off for instruction.

Members of all religious denominations are accepted in the Navy – Churchmen, Roman Catholics, Dissenters and Jews. The King accepts any of his physically fit boys as sailors if they are of good character and have their parent's or their guardian's consent.

Not many Jews as a fact join, but they are accepted when they do come, if "fit" and with them as with Catholics or Dissenters, special arrangements are made for worship, and in the case of Hebrews for their feasts and diet.

The ordinary routine course of a second-class boy on board the Impregnable or Lion is seven months. During this time he attends school on board under properly qualified and certificated schoolmasters. A large and well-equipped schoolroom is fitted on each training ship, where every boy continues his shore scholastic training, and has every opportunity of adding to it. There is even an advanced class which goes as far as trigonometry. His other subjects consist of seamanship, gunnery, and gymnastics, an equal amount of each being taught.

Tea is served at about half-past three to four o'clock in the summer, after which the boys land for cricket, football, or a general romp about the recreation field on the Cremyll or Cornish side of the Hamoaze. In the winter they have tea on their return to the ship at about five to half-past. This consists of tea, bread and different kinds of jam. Supper at seven o'clock consists of tea, bread and butter, and on alternate evenings dripping is served out; the time from the hammocks being got out of the nettings and slung up to the beams ready for use (8pm), being devoted to doing odd jobs, writing letters, reading, &c. At 9pm all turn in.'

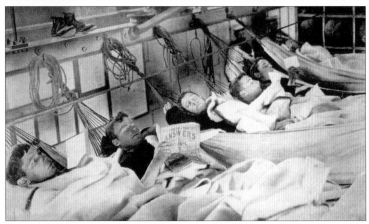

Top: *The 'manly art' recreation aboard HMS* Lion. *Middle: 'This is the way we wash our clothes,' Jack's Laundry. Bottom: A little light reading before 'lights out.'*

Once they had completed their seven months' training these boys (most were still under 15) were now able to call themselves first class boys, a rank which conferred certain privileges, not least of which was an increase in pocket money – he was now given a shilling a week (5p) to spend – small beer compared to what he might earn as a grown-up sailor. Indeed it was about a fifteenth of what regular sailors earned in a week. They were allowed to buy beer, two pints each per evening, and that was on top of their daily tot of rum, issued at 'six bells' or 11 am each day. It wasn't compulsory to take the tot incidentally and abstainers were allowed 1/6d (an extra 7p) per month in lieu.

Not that the young boys had that option of course, but it should be remembered that all board and lodgings, heating and lighting were included and on joining the Navy each boy was served out with a kit of clothing – free. Then, on being advanced to the status of first class boy an additional set of kit was issued, bringing the value of his free clothing to around £10 – '*a supply of clothing which will compare very favourably with that of any ordinary boy in civilian life, and is indeed better than that of the sons of most of the artisan class.*'

Sailors were generally in charge of their own uniforms, however, and that included washing and ironing ... and any running repairs: most sailor's ditty boxes (white wooden affairs measuring about a foot long and nine inches deep and storing all manner of personal effects – photographs, letters and knick-knacks) contained a needle and thread.

Another advantage of being a 'lad' in the Navy was that they were all taught to swim. Remarkably, at that time over 50% of the men in the Merchant Navy were unable to swim, as indeed were the vast majority of the population and drownings were commonplace – especially among young children messing about in creeks and rivers and at the seaside.

Young sailors also learned all manner of skills that might serve them well in civvy street, not least of which was the readiness to follow instructions and obey orders:

'*Indeed it may be safely said that all the lads may be happy as the proverbial sandboy, if they only behave themselves; for the careless and bad there are penalties, for the well behaved boy punishment has no terrors.*'

Top left: *Telegraphy students.* Top right: *Barrack room, grog time.* Bottom left: *The loading machine.*
Bottom right: *The Maxim Gun – 400 rounds per minute.*

Discipline was of the utmost importance, as indeed was the Navy itself, as our scribe, William Crockett – a 53-year-old photographer, who lived in a large house in Durnford Street with his wife and nine children – was at pains to point out:

'Of the vital importance of the Navy to the Empire it is hardly necessary to speak, yet it is a fact that the value of our first line of defence to the very life of our nation is scarcely realised. There are thousands of people in these islands who have never seen a ship or been within sight of the sea, and who do not grasp the fact that upon the supremacy of our Navy all of us depends.

Bread is cheap, yet but little of the corn from which it is made is grown in Britain; meat is within the purchasing power of even the very poor, yet the sheep and beeves roamed on pastures far removed from England. Our staple articles of food have been imported from countries far away from our land, and it is safe to state that without the vast supplies received from our colonies and abroad, our teeming population could not be fed. Yet year by year the producing area of these islands has decreased, and at the present day it is quite impossible to feed our population with the food grown only at home. It has become necessary for this reason to consider more carefully the vital importance of our Navy to our national existence. In war time the food of rich and poor will almost entirely depend upon the strong arm and watchful eye of the "boys in blue."

We shall always have to largely depend upon our Army and the auxiliary forces to defend our ports from hostile raids, but it is upon our sea power that we rely for the protection of our sea borne commerce, our food supply in time of war, and above all our protection from invasion.

If our Navy is from neglect suffered to fall from its present high standard of efficiency, or is from lack of funds allowed to grow weaker in power, and suffers crushing defeat from a hostile force, then the sun of Great Britain has for ever set as a great power among the nations, and no armies within these shores can prevent an enemy making his own terms, for he, by cutting off our food supplies can starve us into submission.'

Doubtless even William Crockett had little idea just how prophetic his words would turn out to be less than a decade later when war was declared.

The size of Britain's Navy and the size of its Empire, was without parallel at the beginning of the twentieth century, and it was Britain's blockade of the coastal areas of Germany's African colonies that had played a key part in the Boer War, and had a crippling impact on the German economy. The situation had also inclined Kaisar Wilhelm to increase the size of his navy and spur his very willing Grand Admiral, Alfred von Tirpitz, to unwittingly start an international naval arms race. The Germans aimed to construct a fleet that was around two-thirds the size of the British fleet, which was always going to be difficult in the light of Britain's 'Two Power Standard' where it had been effectively aiming, since around 1890, to have a navy that was at least as big as the next two biggest world navies put together (then French and Russian).

Whatever the logic, by 1914 the British Navy was boasting some 49 battleships and over 200,000 sailors, while the German fleet included 29 battleships and a shade under 80,000 men – which made it by then the second largest navy in the world. The Germans had also significantly stepped up their submarine production, a move that would prove devastating to the Allies.

However, it was a line of mines that led to the first British naval casualties of the war, less than 36 hours after hostilities had been declared. The mines had been laid by SMS *Königin Luise*, a former holiday ferry that the Germans had converted into a minelayer. On the very night war had been declared the *Königin Luise* had steamed into the North Sea to lay mines off the Thames Estuary.

The next day, 5 August 1914, HMS *Amphion* and ships of the 3rd Flotilla, were carrying out an arranged search when they were tipped off about a suspicious craft that appeared to be 'throwing things overboard.'

Four destroyers gave chase and the *Königin Luise* was sunk; the *Amphion* picking up 46 survivors from the German crew of 100. Ironically, however, while making her way back to Harwich early the following morning, *Amphion* hit one of the mines that the *Königin Luise* had laid the previous day. A fire broke out, the captain was rendered unconscious and there were a few fatalities. While attempting to restore order, and decant men into rescue boats, more mines were struck and within 15 minutes the *Amphion* had sunk.

Some 150 British sailors were lost, along with 18 of the German survivors.

The German Fleet in Plymouth Sound

Top: *German Fleet in Plymouth Sound, 1904*. Above: HMS Amphion *sunk on 6 August 1914.*
Inset: *Cover of Puck magazine, depicting the super powers playing war games.*
Opposite page: *Entrance to Devonport Royal Naval Barracks.*

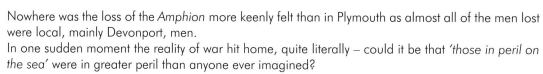

Nowhere was the loss of the *Amphion* more keenly felt than in Plymouth as almost all of the men lost were local, mainly Devonport, men.

In one sudden moment the reality of war hit home, quite literally – could it be that *'those in peril on the sea'* were in greater peril than anyone ever imagined?

The first great test came later in that first month of the war.

The Germans had not anticipated the speed with which Britain would be able to transport its Army on to mainland Europe and were not expecting a major challenge in the North Sea. The Admiralty for their part, mindful of the fact that modern warships needed fuel, not wind, to propel them realised that the historically effective ploy of blockading fleets in their home ports was going to be difficult, particularly with submarines entering the equation for the first time, and with mines an additional and ever-growing menace. It therefore became obvious that a more proactive approach was needed.

The Heligoland Bight, located near the mouth of the Elbe, and a key part of one of the busiest shipping lanes in the world – from Hamburg to the Straits of Dover and the English Channel – was of crucial importance to the German fleet. Hence the idea of ambushing patrolling German destroyers there was promoted.

A fleet of 31 destroyers and two cruisers, under the command of 39-year-old Commodore Reginald Tyrwhitt, with submarines under Commodore Roger Keyes, led the attack, with six further light cruisers and five battlecruisers in support – the latter under Vice-Admiral David Beatty.

In the event, three German light cruisers, one destroyer, and a couple of torpedo boats were sunk, with the loss of over 700 lives. Some 336 Germans were taken captive, while only 35 British sailors were killed, including at least one Devonport man, Able Seaman Frederick Coker.

The result was hailed as a great success back home, although it could so easily have been a disaster. However, the Germans had no idea how close that call had been and the Kaisar was clearly unsettled by the incident and decreed that the *'fleet should hold itself back and avoid actions which can lead to greater losses.'*

As Churchill later observed: *'They felt as we should have felt had German destroyers broken into the Solent and their battle cruisers penetrated as far as the Nab. The results of this action were far-reaching, henceforward, the weight of British Naval prestige lay heavy across all German sea enterprise ... The German Navy was indeed "muzzled". Except for furtive movements by individual submarines and minelayers, not a dog stirred from August till November'* (The World Crisis 1923-27).

Top: WJ Douglas, one of Amphion's *many local casualties.* Above: HMS Monmouth.

And when November came the action wasn't in the North Sea, it was in the South Pacific, at Coronel, off the coast of Chile, where Vice-Admiral Graf Maximillian von Spee's cruiser squadron met up with Rear-Admiral Sir Christopher Cradock's much smaller squadron, on 1 November 1914. Both HMS *Good Hope* and HMS *Monmouth* were lost with all hands. This cast another veil of gloom over the area as *Monmouth* was another locally manned vessel and hundreds of Plymouth families were bereaved.

Meanwhile, arriving in Valparaiso harbour, von Spee and his fleet were welcomed as heroes by the German population there. However, von Spee himself refused to join in the celebrations and when eventually presented with a bunch of flowers he reportedly commented: *'These will do nicely for my grave.'*

The astute commander was rightly fearful of the British response. He did not have to wait long.

A few days later two dreadnought cruisers from the Grand Fleet arrived in Devonport, they were to be victualled and made ready for a special mission in the South Atlantic. That mission was to intercept von Spee before he could do any damage to the crucial Atlantic trade routes into Britain. The Admiralty surmised that von Spee would hold rendezvous at the Falkland Islands and wanted the dreadnoughts, *Invincible* and *Inflexible*, to steam down there with all possible haste. On Monday 8 November the Admiral-Superintendent of the Yard informed the Admiralty that the earliest they could be made ready for departure was midnight on Friday 13th.

'Ships are to sail on Wednesday 11th,' came back the reply from the 39-year-old First Lord of the Admiralty, Winston Churchill, 'if necessary the dockyard men should be sent away in the ships to return as opportunity may offer.'

And sail they did on the 11th, with Vice-Admiral Doveton Sturdee in command of a growing squadron which, in addition to the dreadnoughts, came to include three armoured cruisers and two light cruisers. Four weeks later, on 7 December, Sturdee arrived in Stanley. The following day von Spee and his German squadron, unaware of the newly arrived British presence, attempted to raid the Stanley supply base, and in the ensuing confrontation von Spee's squadron was destroyed.

With Christmas now approaching and all hope of the war being over by then long since gone, the country was stunned and outraged on 16 December when the Imperial German Navy mounted an attack on North East coastal towns of Scarborough, Hartlepool and Whitby. Over 1,000 shells were fired into the seaside ports and 93 people were killed and a further 438 injured. There was instant indignation that the Germans could commit such an act, after all most of those casualties were civilian (86 killed, 424 injured), and the story generated interest around the world, notably in America, where it started to impact on the 'neutrals' there.

In Britain, more specifically there was anger at the fact that the Royal Navy's protective shield had been penetrated, particularly as their intelligence suggested that the Germans were planning something in the area. However, Admiral Franz Hipper was able to conduct his raid and get his fleet back home to safety with little more than surface damage to three of his cruisers.

The incident helped fuel growing concerns that the Germans might be planning an invasion and the 5th Battle Squadron was re-based at Sheerness to guard against that eventuality.

As well as provoking widespread indignation the incident also provoked a powerful recruitment campaign.

Vice-Admiral Sir Lewis Bayly was put in command of the operation and duly spent New Year's Eve 1914 undertaking gunnery exercises with his fleet off the Dorset coast. The weather was not thought to be conducive to submarine attacks and so when HMS *Formidable*, at the rear of the fleet was struck by a torpedo from *U-24* at 2.20am it came very much as a bolt out of the blue. Thoughts of trying to get the pre-Dreadnought-class battleship closer to the coast were quickly deemed to be in vain and the Captain gave the order to abandon ship. Less than 30 minutes later a second torpedo struck; rescue boats were launched and two of the fleet cruisers came alongside and somehow managed to pick up around 80 men in the early-morning gloom, in what were now very difficult conditions – there was a 30ft swell hindering the process.

A number of others were hauled to safety by a passing trawler, however 35 officers, including the Captain, Noel Loxley, who went down with his ship, and some 512 men were lost out of a total complement of 780.

'*This was staggering news for Plymouth,*' recalled RAJ Walling, '*and it spread a gloom over the country,*' (Story of Plymouth).

Most of the men were Chatham based, but there were a dozen or so Plymouth and Devonport men lost on that first day of 1915 and there were few grounds for optimism at the start of the New Year.

One heartwarming story did come out of the episode however. It concerned the 'Pilot Boat' pub in Lyme Regis where a number of the bodies drawn from a drifting life raft were laid out in the basement. The landlord's dog, a half-collie named Lassie, found her way in amongst the bodies and started licking the face of one of them. Not satisfied with that she then lay alongside the prone body of Able Seaman John Cowan for more than half an hour, nuzzling and warming him with her fur. Before long and to everyone's surprise the seaman eventually stirred and was subsequently taken to hospital where he made a full recovery. Cowan later returned to the pub to thank Lassie and before long the story had spread like a virus around the Senior Service.

A few weeks later, 24 January, there was a more substantial encounter between ships of the British Grand Fleet and the German High Seas Fleet. This time the action was near Dogger Bank, in the North Sea and the British under Beatty came off best. Although a battlecruiser and a destroyer were both incapacitated, and 15 men were killed, the Germans, under Franz Hipper again, lost their armoured cruiser, *Blücher*; had serious damage to another battlecruiser with 189 men captured and over 950 killed.

The battle was a morale booster for the country as a whole, but mistakes were made by the British Commanders, both with regard to targeting and signalling, mistakes that would come to cost them dear again, the following summer, at Jutland, in the North Sea just west of the northern extremities of Denmark.

The German plan, masterminded by Admiral Reinhardt von Scheer (who had recently replaced the less aggressive Admiral von Poul) had been to lure out and destroy a significant section of the Grand Fleet, as part of a wider strategy to relax, or even end, the British blockade of shipping in and out of Germany's limited stretch of coastline.

As a prelude to this, on 24 and 25 April 1916, the German navy attacked the coastal towns of Lowestoft and Yarmouth to trigger a British response.

Fortunately, the British learned from intercepting communications that a more major fleet manoeuvre was imminent and so on 30 May Admiral Sir John Jellicoe set out from Rosyth with the intention of meeting up with Admiral Sir David Beatty and his section of the Grand Fleet from Scapa Flow.

The following day Beatty came upon Admiral Hipper and his fleet of 40 ships a little sooner than the Germans were expecting and hostilities commenced across a distance of around 10 miles. Just after 4.00pm the British battlecruiser *Indefatigable* was taken out by enemy fire and 1,000 men were lost when a magazine on board exploded. Further losses followed – *Queen Mary* being hit and subsequently sinking in just 90 seconds.

The German's numerical disadvantage was redressed with the arrival of Admiral von Scheer's High Seas Fleet and shortly after 6.30pm another British ship, the *Invincible*, having been struck, belied her name and sank.

The fighting continued until nightfall at around 10.30pm by which time some 250 ships had moved into the battleground, 25 of which (14 British and 11 German) had slipped beneath the troubled waters. Jellicoe positioned himself in such a way as to try and cut the Germans off from their base, so that the fighting could be continued after sunrise, but von Scheer managed to make his escape.

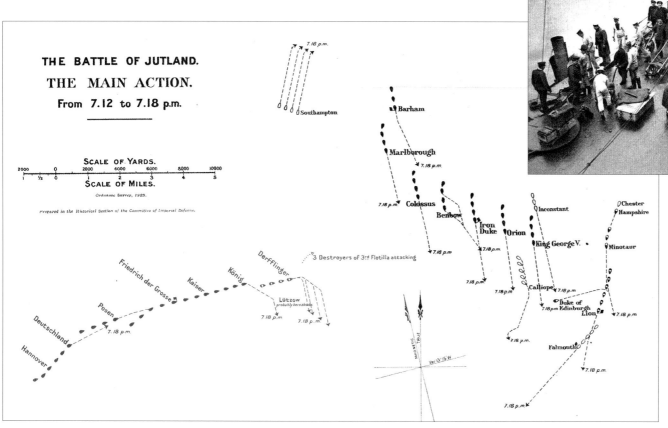

THE BATTLE OF JUTLAND.

THE MAIN ACTION.

From 7.12 to 7.18 p.m.

SCALE OF YARDS.

SCALE OF MILES.

Ordnance Survey, 1923.

Prepared in the Historical Section of the Committee of Imperial Defence.

Southampton

Barham

Marlborough

7.18 p.m.

Colossus

Benbow

Iron Duke

Orion

Inconstant

King George V.

Chester

Hampshire

Minotaur

Calliope

Duke of Edinburgh

Lion

Falmouth

3 Destroyers of 3rd Flotilla attacking

Derfflinger

Lützow probably herebouts

König

Kaiser

Friedrich der Grosse

Posen

Deutschland

Hannover

Above: *Shells being landed on HMS* Lion.

Left: *Countless accounts of the Battle of Jutland were subsequently generated, with critics divided over who to blame for what. Detailed maps were drawn up giving blow by blow representations of the action, one series running to over 20 plans covering less than ten hours, some looking at just 10-minute snapshots.*

Long after the war, experts were still debating the affair.

Indefatigable *was hit by shells from the German battlecruiser* von der Tann. *They caused massive explosions, the second of which blew pieces of the British battleship some 200 feet into the air. Only two crewmen survived – over 1,000 died.*

The Royal Navy had 151 combat ships at the Battle of Jutland, an officer on board one of them, HMS Obedient, of the 12th Destroyer Flotilla, later recorded this account of the loss of the Devonport-based Defence: 'From ahead, out of the mist there appeared the ill-fated 1st Cruiser Squadron led by the Defence. At first, the Defence did not seem to be damaged, but she was being heavily engaged, and salvoes were dropping all around her. When she was on our bow, three quick salvoes reached her, the first one "over", the next one "short" and the third all hit. The shells of the last salvo could clearly be seen to hit her just abaft the after turret, and after a second, a big red flame flashed up, but died away again at once. The ship heeled to the blow but quickly righted herself and steamed on again. Then almost immediately followed three more salvoes. Again the first was "over", the second one "short" and the third a hit, and again the shell of the hitting salvo could be clearly seen to strike, this time between the forecastle turret and the foremost funnel. At once, the ship was lost to sight in an enormous black cloud, which rose to a height of some hundred feet, and from which some dark object, possibly a boat or a funnel was hurled into space, twirling like some gigantic Catherine-wheel. The smoke quickly clearing, we could see no sign of a ship at all - Defence had gone.'
And with it over 650 locally based servicemen.
(www.devonheritage.org)

The British casualties were huge, over 6,000 men lost, 600 more wounded and 177 taken prisoner. Meanwhile, the Germans lost just 2,500 men and had 500 wounded. Both sides, nevertheless, regarded the battle as a victory – the Germans chiefly because they had sunk twice the tonnage of the ships they had lost. The British, however, still had a seaworthy fleet and the Germans, despite one or two minor forays were never again in a position to challenge the British Navy in the North Sea. Jutland proved to be the only full-scale clash of battleships in the Great War.

At the end of that year the German navy focussed its efforts on unrestricted submarine warfare, attacking Allied and neutral shipping heading in and out of Britain – a strategy that would ultimately bring the United States into the war and accelerate the end of hostilities.

Meanwhile, back home in the Southwest, Walling would later record of Jutland that: 'No single battle in history has inflicted such loss and suffering on Plymouth. The Lion, flagship of the Vice-Admiral, Sir David Beatty, was a Plymouth ship. The tale of damage she sustained, which put her out of the fight and caused the Admiral himself to transfer to a destroyer, was read with horror.'

In all five of the ships lost and four of those badly damaged were Devonport-manned.

'There were crowds outside the newspaper offices for hours awaiting casualty lists, and for weeks after the streets seemed full of black widow's weeds' (Gill - *Plymouth A New History*).

The losses locally were huge. Over 600 Devonport-based men were lost on both the *Indefatigable* and the *Defence* as well as around 40 Plymouth-based Royal Marines on each ship. A further 50 locally based lads were lost on the *Warrior*, on the *Invincible* and on the *Queen Mary*, with a similar number lost on the *Lion*, while there were more than a dozen local casualties on the *Tiger*.

All in all over 1,500 Devonport-based sailors were lost at Jutland, along with over 100 Plymouth-based Royal Marines: small wonder that the town was in mourning – there would have been barely a soul who did not lose a friend, relative or general acquaintance on that fateful day.

Although, mercifully, there was not another naval battle of this scale during the war, the loss of life at sea continued unabated, to such an extent that by November 1918 the number of casualties in Plymouth-manned ships exceeded 7,000.

Some time after the war the Western Daily Mercury editor Robert Walling published a list of the vessels manned from the Plymouth port division (excluding only minor craft) that were lost, and, with a few additional bits of information, it makes uncomfortable reading, as throughout the period barely a month went by when his paper was not reporting on some tragedy that would have touched on his readers

The impact of the German U-boat offensive which stepped up a gear after the Battle of Jutland is also very evident.

6 August 1914: HMS *Amphion* (light cruiser 3,440 tons) mined. 132 lost.

8 September 1914: RMS *Oceanic* (merchant cruiser) ran aground and wrecked off Shetlands, was carrying Royal Marines to help with stop and search.

20 September 1914: *Pegasus* (light cruiser 2,135 tons) sunk by gun fire from SMS *Koenigsberg* in Zanzibar harbour – 30 Devonport men, 3 Plymouth men lost 55 crew wounded.

1 November 1914: *Monmouth* (armoured cruiser 9,800 tons) sunk by von Spee's squadron at Coronel.

3 November 1914: *D5* (submarine) sunk by drifting mine. 21 men lost (14 Devonport) 5 survivors

27 December 1914: *Success* (destroyer) wrecked off Fifeness in heavy gales.

19 February 1915: *Goldfinch* (destroyer 747 tons) wrecked off one of the Orkney Isles.

18 March 1915: *Ocean* (battleship 12,950 tons) Dardanelles – torpedoed from shore (one Devonport fatality)

18 April 1915: *E15* (submarine) Dardanelles – stranded and blown up by crew.

13 May 1915: *Goliath* (battleship 12,950 tons) Dardanelles - torpedoed by Turkish destroyers 570 out of a complement of over 700 lost, mostly Devonport sailors, but quite a few Plymouth marines.

25 May 1915: *Triumph* (battleship 11,985 tons) Dardanelles – torpedoed. 75 lost about a third Devonport men.

27 May 1915: *Majestic* (battleship 14,900 tons) Dardanelles – torpedoed by U-21 off the Gallipoli peninsula. 49 lost, mostly Devonport but some Plymouth Marines.

10 June 1915: *No.12* aka HMS *Moth* (torpedo boat 263 tons) torpedoed by U-boat. Chatham manned.

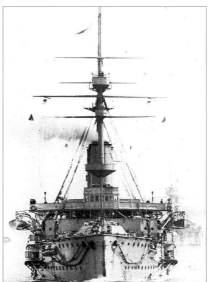

Top: *Crew members on HMS* Goliath. Bottom left: *Goliath.* Bottom right: *HMS* Majestic *sent out to join in the Dardanelles Campaign to clear the Turkish Straits and assist the Allied landings at Gallipoli, is struck by a torpedo from U-21.*

Black Prince: Another Jutland victim with 27 Devonport men lost. Bottom: There were Devonport men lost on 23 of the ships involved in the action at Jutland, most on board Defence, Indefatigable, Invincible, Warrior, Queen Mary and Lion.

20 July 1915: *Rhianon* (armed yacht 138 tons) mined and sunk in North Sea. Crew of 5 lost.

1 October 1915: *J6* (submarine 1,210 tons) built in Devonport and sunk by Q-ship *Cymric* off the Northumberland coast when she was mistaken for *U6* not *J6*. *Cymric* raised the White ensign and opened fire, scoring a number of direct hits. Only when survivors were seen in the water was the mistake realised. 15 men were lost out of crew of 45.

28 October 1915: *Argyll* (armoured cruiser 10,850 tons) wrecked Bell Rock – All hands saved.

5 November 1915: *Tara* (armed boarding steamer 1,862 tons) torpedoed and sunk by *U-35* in Eastern Mediterranean. 12 lost rest of crew (80 plus) taken POW.

27 December 1915: *TB46* (torpedo-boat 79 tons) foundered – sank in tow.

11 February 1916: *Arabis* (sloop 1,250 tons) torpedoed, by German destroyers in the North Sea. At least 44 Devonport men out of 54 lost, another 20 or so taken prisoner.

9 March 1916: *Fauvette* (armed boarding steamer 2,644 tons) mined and sunk in North Sea, 15 men lost 48 survivors.

24 March 1916: *E24* (submarine) mined and sunk in North Sea, at least 11 Devonport men out of 35 crew lost.

25 April 1916: *E22* (submarine) torpedoed by *UB-18* off Great Yarmouth. All 31 lost (at least 6 Devonport men)

27 April 1916: *Nasturtium* (sloop 1,250 tons) mined at the entrance to Valletta Harbour, Malta, 6 Devonport men lost and one other – HMS *Russell* hit and sunk in same area on the same day.

13 May 1916: *M30* (monitor 535 tons) Gulf of Smyrna – sunk by Ottoman shore based coastal artillery, 4 lost all Devonport men.

31 May 1916: *Indefatigable* (battlecruiser 18,750 tons) Jutland – sunk by gun fire. 1,000 lost – 2 survivors, rescued by the Germans

31 May 1916: *Defence* (armoured cruiser 14,600 tons) Jutland – blown up by German gunfire. 900 lost, mostly Devonport-based.

31 May 1916: *Nomad* (destroyer 1,025 tons) Jutland – sunk by gun fire. 8 lost - one Devonport man.

31 May 1916: *Invincible* (battlecruiser 17,250 tons) Jutland – blown up. 1,026 lost, at least 50 Devonport men.

31 May 1916: *Queen Mary* (battlecruiser) Jutland - blown up. 1266 lost, at least 50 Devonport men.

31 May 1916: *Lion* (battlecruiser, 26,270 tons) Jutland, damaged – 93 lost, around 50 Devonport men.

31 May 1916: *Tiger* (battlecruiser 28,500 tons) Jutland, damaged – 22 lost, including a dozen Devonport men.

1 June 1916: *Warrior* (armoured cruiser 13,550 tons) Jutland – disabled by gunfire. 67 lost, 51 Devonport men.

6 July 1916: *E26* (submarine) lost in North Sea unknown cause, at least 9 of the crew (of 31 lost) were Devonport men.

9 August 1916: *B10* (submarine) Tied up after taking part on the blockade of Pula (Croatia), was the first submarine to be sunk by aircraft bombs (from an Austrian Naval Air Service craft).

13 August 1916: *Lassoo* (destroyer 1,010 tons) torpedoed and sunk by *U-10* off the Maas Light Ship in the North Sea. At least half of the half a dozen of those lost were Devonport men.

14 August 1916: *Remembrance* (Q-ship 3,660 tons) torpedoed and sunk by *U-38* in the Mediterranean. 2 lost.

19 August 1916: *Nottingham* (light cruiser 5,440 tons) torpedoed and sunk by *U-52* in North Sea almost all of the 39 lost were Devonport men.

19 August 1916: *Falmouth* (light cruiser 5,250 tons) torpedoed and sunk by *U-63* in North Sea, 12 lost, 13 wounded.

22 August 1916: *E16* (submarine) mined and sunk off German coast. All 31 crew lost including at least 9 Devonport men.

1 December 1916: *E37* (submarine 662 tons) lost in North Sea. All crew (30) lost including at least 7 Devonport men.

3 December 1916: *Perugia* (Q-ship 4,348 tons – peacetime collier) torpedoed and sunk by *U-63* off southern coast of France. 8 men, all Devonport based, lost.

22 December 1916: *E30* (submarine 667 tons) mined off Suffolk. All crew (30) lost.

23 January 1917: *Simoon* (destroyer 1,072 tons) sunk by gunfire from German destroyer *S.50* in North Sea. 48 men lost including a couple of Devonport men.

25 January 1917: *Laurentic* (armed merchant cruiser) mined and sunk off Northern Ireland. 354 passengers and crew lost including over 40 Devonport and Plymouth-based men.

1 March 1917: *Pheasant* (destroyer 1,025 tons) mined and sunk off the Orkneys. All lost including over 70 Devonport men.

Top: HMS Nottingham - *postcard published by Abrahams & Sons of Devonport.*
Bottom: Laurentic: *the White Star liiner that had carried Canadian troops to Plymouth in October 1914.*

HMS Vanguard: The vital parts of the new ship - she was commissioned in 1910 and was moored at Scapa Flow when an accidental explosion saw her sink almost instantly killing over 800 men on board.

12 March 1917: *E49* (submarine 662 tons) mined off Shetland Islands by mine laid by German *UC-76* two days earlier. All crew (30) lost, including at least 6 Devonport men.

13 March 1917: *Warner* (Q-ship 1,273 tons) torpedoed, west of Ireland by U.38, casualties unknown, some survivors picked up by *D3* Submarine.

16 April 1917: *C16* (submarine 292 tons) Harwich - sunk after being rammed accidentally by HMS *Melampus* (it was the second time she had been sunk – previous occasion in 1909 – both times she was salvaged and re-commissioned. All 16 hands lost.

5 May 1917: *Lavender* (sloop 1,200 tons) torpedoed and sunk by *UC-75* off coast of Southern Ireland, St George's Channel. 22 lost, almost all Devonport men.

25 May 1917: *Hilary* (merchant cruiser) torpedoed and sunk by *U-88* on her way to refuel at Scapa Flow. 4 lost.

28 May 1917: *TB4* (torpedo boat) accidental explosion. 14 lost (12 Devonport men).

11 June 1917: *Zylpha* (Q-ship 2,917 tons) torpedoed by *U-82* in Atlantic and sank four days later.

14 June 1917: *Avenger* (merchant cruiser 15,000 tons) North Scotland – torpedoed by *U-69*.

9 July 1917: *Vanguard* (battleship 19,560 tons) Accidental explosion at Scapa Flow – the worst accidental loss in the history of the Royal Navy. Although not a Devonport manned ship there were over 40 Devonport men among the 804 casualties – there were only 2 survivors.

15 July 1917: *Redbreast* (fleet messenger 1,313 tons) torpedoed and sunk by *UC-38* in the Mediterranean – 42 lost including at least 8 Devonport men.

26 July 1917: *Ariadne* (cruiser used as minelayer 11,000 tons) torpedoed and sunk by *UC-65* in the English Channel – 34 lost mainly local.

7 August 1917: Bracondale (Q-ship 2,095 tons) torpedoed three times by *U-44* in North Atlantic. Casualties unknown. Did manage to inflict damage on U-boat which didn't dive again and which was rammed and sunk five days later off Norway by HMS *Oracle*.

9 August 1917: *Recruit* (destroyer 1,075 tons) mined and sunk in North Sea – over 50 casualties, mostly Devonport men.

10 August 1917: *Dunraven* (Q-ship 3,117 tons) torpedoed by *UC-71* and foundered, sinking as it was being towed back to Plymouth. Only one fatality.

13 August 1917: *Bergamot* (sloop 1,290 tons) torpedoed and sunk by *U-84* in the Atlantic. 14 lost.

16 August 1917: *Bradford City* (Q-ship – former collier, *Saros* 3,683 tons) torpedoed by *U-28*.

16 September 1917: *G9* (submarine 703 tons) opened fire on HMS *Pasley* by mistake and was subsequently rammed by the British ship. Only one of *G9*'s crew of 31 survived, Stoker William Drake.

18 September 1917: *Contest* (destroyer 957 tons) torpedoed and sunk by *U-106* in the SW Approaches to the English Channel – 35 lost, almost all Devonport men.

2 October 1917: *Drake* (armoured cruiser 14,100 tons) torpedoed by *U-79* – 18 lost about half Devonport men.

2 October 1917: *Brisk* (destroyer 790 tons) mined SW of Bull Point, County Antrim while going to assist HMS *Drake* – 31 lost, almost all Devonport men.

9 October 1917: *Champagne* (merchant cruiser 5,360 tons) torpedoed and sunk by *U-96* in Irish Sea – 47 lost.

17 October 1917: *C32* (submarine) Gulf of Riga – blown up by crew after running ashore.

21 October 1917: *Marmion* (destroyer 1,030 tons) accidentally rammed by HMS *Tirade* while escorting a convoy across the North Sea and sank in atrocious conditions – 76 lost, almost all of them Devonport men.

18 November 1917: *K1* (submarine 2,010 tons) sunk after collision with *K4* off the Danish coast to prevent her being captured. 56 crew rescued.

18 November 1917: *Candytuft* (sloop 1,290 tons) torpedoed and sunk by *U-39* in the Mediterranean - 9 lost, Devonport men.

16 December 1917: *Arbutus* (sloop 1,290 tons) torpedoed and sunk in St George's Channel by *UB-65* – 8 lost, all but one Devonport men.

23 December 1917: *Tornado* (destroyer 1,091 tons) mined in North Sea near Maas Light Vessel. Germans had laid minefield a few week earlier and newly launched *Tornado*, was due to help protect a convoy along with HMS *Torrent* and HMS *Surprise*, and others. Tragically all three were sunk and 252 men were lost, including 75 men from the *Tornado*, almost all of them Devonport men.

Top: *Sloop Anchusa*. Bottom: *Submarine D6*.

25 December 1917: *Penshurst* (Q7 Q-ship 1,191 tons) torpedoed and sunk by *U-110* in St George's Channel. 2 naval casualties.

12 January 1918: *Narborough* (destroyer 1,010 tons) wrecked on the Pentland Skerries off the Orkneys – lost, with her sister ship, *Opal*, in very poor visibility. One survivor from the two ships – 188 lost more than 20 of them Devonport men.

14 January 1918: *G8* (submarine 703 tons) lost in North Sea – reasons unknown. All crew (31) lost, mainly Portsmouth and Chatham but some Devonport men.

20 January 1918: *M28* (monitor 570 tons) sunk by gun fire from *Goeben* in the Battle of Imbros in the Aegean. 11 (all local men) of her crew of 69 lost.

20 January 1918: *Louvain* (armed boarding steamer, formerly SS *Dresden* 1,830 tons) torpedoed by *UC-22*. 227 lost, many of them Devonport men.

29 January 1918: *E14* (submarine) Dardanelles – gun fire from shore artillery.

31 January 1918: *E50* (submarine 662 tons damaged in collision with *UC-62* off the North Hinder Light 19 March 1917) mined off the South Dogger Light Vessel. At least 12 of 31 casualties local men.

15 March 1918: *D3* (submarine) English Channel – bombed by mistake by French airship. 29 lost incl. at least 6 Devonport men.

4 April 1918: *Bittern* (destroyer 360 tons) lost in collision off the Isle of Portland with SS *Kenilworth* (whose skipper was later found to be negligent). 63 lost, all Devonport men.

10 April 1918: *Magic* (destroyer) mined ENE of Fanad Head – 25 lost, almost all Devonport men.

1 May 1918: *Blackmorevale* (minesweeper 750 tons) mined and sunk in North Sea. 26 lost.

5 June 1918: *Snaefell* (armed boarding-steamer 1,368 tons) torpedoed and sunk by *U-105*. 8 lost.

28 June 1918: *D6* (submarine) torpedoed and sunk by *U-73* off the west coast of Ireland. 23 lost.

16 July 1918: *Anchusa* (sloop 1,290 tons) torpedoed and sunk by *U-54* of Northern Ireland. 78 (of crew of 93) lost, almost all of them Devonport men.

30 July 1918: *Stock Force* (Q-ship 732 tons) torpedoed and damaged off Start Point by *U-80* whom she counter attacked and damaged. *Stock Force* later sank in Bigbury Bay.

Another Abrahams' of Devonport postcard: Caption reads H.M. Monitor '27' in action in the Dvina River whilst co-operating with land forces against the Bolsheviks, afterwards blown up during the retreat from the Troitsa to prevent her falling into enemy hands. September 1919.

2 August 1918: *Vehement* (destroyer 1,272 tons) mined in Heligoland Bight. 48 lost, almost all Devonport men.

8 September 1918: *Nessus* (destroyer 1,022 tons) sunk in collision with HMS *Amphitrite* in the North Sea.

30 September 1918: *Seagull* (torpedo-gunboat 735 tons) lost in collision in the River Clyde.

20 October 1918: *Mechanician* (escort ship 9,044 tons) torpedoed and sunk by *UB-35*

1 November 1918: *G7* (submarine 703 tons) lost at sea – last British submarine to be lost in the War. All crew (31) lost, at least 6 Devonport men.

10 November 1918: *Ascot* (minesweeper 810 tons) torpedoed and sunk by *UB-67* off the Farne Islands in North Sea. 51 lost.

22 November 1918: *G11* (submarine 703 tons) ran aground near Howick, north of her base at Blyth. 2 men lost during evacuation.

5 December 1918: *Cassandra* (light cruiser 4,120 tons) Baltic – mined. Operating against the Bolsheviks 10 men lost 400 evacuated.

5 May 1919: *Cupar* (minesweeper 800 tons) mined and sunk off the Tyne.

4 June 1919: *L55* (submarine) involved in the anti-Bolshevik campaign postwar, *L55* probably sunk by hitting a British-laid mine. 42 lost including several Devonport men.

17 September 1919: *M27* (monitor 570 tons) North Russia – scuttled after running aground.

The list is not exhaustive and represents just a fraction of the Allied and neutral ships lost in the Great War. Estimates suggest that over 6,000 ships were sunk by German and Austro-Hungarian U-boats alone, over 100 of them were very large vessels of over 10,000 tons – this list mentions less than a dozen in that category.

It will also be noted that HMS *Ascot* was sunk on 10 November 1918, the day before Armistice was declared, giving the hapless minesweeper the unfortunate distinction of being the last ship to be sunk in the war.

However, areas that were heavily mined proved to be a threat long after the war ended and *Cupar*, another minesweeper, was to end up a victim six months later, in May 1919.

Those ships shown here as being lost beyond that date are those that were involved in the North Russia anti-Bolshevik activities, when the Allies decided to support the so-called White Movement against the Bolshevik faction led by Vladimir Lenin. There was no great enthusiasm for the British intervention at home, and this coupled with a general war-weariness and a lack of clear strategy on the part of the White Movement led to the Allied withdrawal from North Russian and Siberia in 1920.

Royal Marine Barracks, Durnford Street.

PER MARE PER TERRAM

'The Royal Marine Barracks, as all Plymothians know, are pleasantly situated in Durnford Street, cover a very large portion of land, and are admirably adapted for the training and housing of such a large number of men. On either side of the entrance archway are imposing quarters for the colonel-commandant and his officers, the trim lawn and window boxes of which deserve a passing notice. Indeed, the whole establishment looks quite a garden, the square being surrounded by trees, and the principal block covered with a mass of beautiful creepers.

It is past noon, but there are now on parade probably the largest muster of any which takes place in the barracks, "No absentees today," our guide smilingly observes; "the Friday mid-day parade is a real 'labour of love'." Different companies of men fall in, in front of their respective company rooms, and after answering to their names (under the circumstances seeming a somewhat unnecessary formality) are marched to the divisional pay office. Long lines of men in Indian file pass through the office, where each man in turn receives his due, and the task of paying some 1,400 to 1,500 men is quickly performed.

The weekly Friday pay day, which disburses approximately £2,000 is over in about half an hour, the accounts being made up by a staff of clerks under the supervision of a paymaster and warrant officer. The Marine system of weekly payment without stoppages has long been a model of neat management, and has latterly been adopted to a great extent in the line regiments, the only difference being that in the latter each company is paid by its own officer and colour-sergeant, whilst in the Marines the whole division is settled with one big parade by a specially retained accountant branch. It goes without saying that this is an extremely pleasant function, judging by the faces of all concerned' (Life of Our Gallant Marines, William Crockett, Doidge's Annual 1906).

The pay queue inside Stonehouse Barracks.

Royal Marines' Sergeants Mess, Stonehouse - 1905.

Although it was written a few years before the war started, Crockett's account of life in RMB Stonehouse was an interesting insight into service life at the time and he was keen to stress the various on-site institutions open to the uniformed inhabitants:

The coffee bar: 'Here the soldier may take his ease and "the cup which cheers and does not inebriate" at the same time amidst the most pleasant of surroundings. If he doesn't want to buy tea, coffee, sandwiches, or anything which is on sale, he need not, and can amuse himself by playing billiards on either of two large and completely equipped tables.'

The dry canteen: 'Stored with something of everything – ham, tea, coffee, groceries of every description used in a household – in fact a more than miniature Lipton's, where everything from potatoes to a man's woollen jersey is to be purchased at competitive prices, and the profits devoted to various divisional institutions.'

The 'wet' canteen: 'Here we find an excellent bar for the use of the men, where John Barleycorn holds his sway. Beer, stout, and mineral waters of the best and purest kinds are purchasable. The place is really a public house of the best type, governed strictly under military law by military men ... and at the same time that men enjoy the greatest possible freedom no drunkenness is permitted.

A large hall for entertainments adjoins the bar on one side and on the other there is a comfortable retiring room for the junior non-coms, who can enjoy their smoke and glass of ale, or play billiards, apart from the privates, from whom their promotion, in the interests of discipline, naturally separates them.'

Our commentator also singled out the Plymouth Division of the Royal Marine Band, which he noted had 'attained front rank, not only as a military band, but also as a very fine string band.

Through its ranks have passed some very fine performers, who have attained very good positions in private life on retirement. Three ex-sergeants are professors on the teaching staff of the portion of the Royal Naval School of Music which is attached to the Division, and which in part supplies the instrumentalists of the navy.

The veteran clarionettist Mutton, of concert renown, Elford (and who has forgotten his Lost Chord and Better Land?) and Isaacs, the well-known performer on the string bass.'

Top: 'Retreat at Sunset.' Buglers sounding Retreat. Bottom: The Band at Ceremonial Parade.

1913: The First Lord of the Admiralty, Winston Churchill, pays a visit to the Royal Marine Barracks in Stonehouse.

There was, of course, a lot more to the life of a Royal Marine than his down time and his training was across the board, both as a seaman and an infantryman.

It may be surmised that our Marine has been thoroughly trained as an infantryman at Deal – the depot of the corps – and that he is, for all intents and purposes, fit for duty as such on arrival at the headquarters of the Division in which he has elected to serve, and to which he always returns after his period of sea service. He has learnt to swim; can pull a boat, and take part in its management; he has learned knotting and splicing, and is versed in the mysteries of a reef knot, single sheet bend, sheepshank, cat's paw, and the many other knots and splices required in the art of seamanship. The laying out of a hammock also requires some study on his part, and as he is not served out on board ship with an iron cot, he has to learn to sling his evening's resting place with all the adroitness of an old tar.

Before, however, his gunnery instructors finish him off as ready for sea service, he undergoes a course of military training, during which he learns how to build and take to pieces a trestle bridge useful for the crossing of men and material across a ravine; to make shelter trenches; survey country; pitch tents – and for a month sleep in them; and to build ovens of sods, and to cook his meals in the open; in fact to perform every duty required of an infantry soldier, with the exception of slaying his enemies – and this duty, no doubt, he would welcome for the sake of variety.'

At the end of his tour Crockett was left pondering the difference between the Bluejacket and the Marine, 'knowing that in these days of steam the line of demarcation between the two is not as great as in the days when sail drill was almost everything.' His guide replied that he 'didn't really know but supposed that the Marine is cheaper.'

Certainly his life was no cheaper and many Plymouth Marines were lost in the Dardanelles Campaign in 1915, on board various vessels lost at sea and during the gallant and daring raids on Zebrugge, in April and May 1917, when attempts were made to curtail the U-boat activity in and out of the port that the Germans had adopted as a base to tackle Allied shipping, particularly those operating in the English Channel.

Top: *Field training – bridging.* Bottom: *'Action Front' A Field Gun and Maxim at Drill, Longroom, Stonehouse.*

The Royal Garrison Artillery firing a 6-inch gun from the Citadel, Plymouth. Opposite page: Citadel entrance and Officer's Gunnery Course, February 1916.

ROYAL GARRISON ARTILLERY

Before, during and after the war the role of the Royal Garrison Artillery was essentially to man the coastal artillery batteries that were vital to the protection of the port. Major-General Penton (General Officer Commanding, Plymouth Defences) was based in Government House, at Mount Wise and there were six companies of the RGA (Royal Garrison Artillery) in the area: Nos. 36, 38, 45 and 41 Companies; three Fortress Companies of Royal Engineers, whose headquarters were at Elphinstone Barracks; three companies of Army Service Corps – one motor transport and two horsed – at Granby Barracks; a section of the Army Ordnance Corps at the Gun Wharf; and one company of Royal Army Medical Corps at Devonport Military Hospital.

The line regiments then stationed in the Garrison was made up of four battalions of the 8th Infantry Brigade, a regular unit of the home service commanded by Boer War veteran Brigadier-General Beauchamp John Colclough Doran.

Those four battalions were: The 2nd Battn. The Royal Scots (1st Foot), Crownhill Barracks; 1st Battn. The Gordon Highlanders (92nd foot), Crownhill Hutments (later Seaton Barracks); 4th Battn. The Middlesex Regiment (77th Foot), Raglan Barracks and the 2nd Battn. The Royal Irish Regiment (18th Foot), who were also based at Raglan Barracks. The two Raglan battalions were under the command of Lt-Col Charles P Amyatt Hull and Lt-Col St JA Cox.

At that time the Garrison strength was estimated to be around 3,000.

The Devon RGA was part of Britain's part-time Army and had evolved out of the old Plymouth Volunteers. In 1913 there was a major parade on the Hoe with the corps band leading the way.

Following in their wake were the different coast defence companies, commanded by Major HP Moon. Individual companies were

Officers' Course of Gunnery, Citadel, Plymouth, February, 1916

The major parade of 1912 was the King's Birthday Parade at the Brickfields, with all of the armed services represented as well as the Three Towns via the Mayor of Devonport Edward Blackall and the Mayor of Plymouth, James Godding. Opposite page: Taking the salute.

commanded by Captains 'Tommy' Vosper, AO Ellis, Stanley Rogers and Humphrey Davy. There was also a detachment of Devon Fortress Engineers under Captain H Stone.

The largest unit there on the day was the 5th Devons, led by their own band and commanded by Lieut Col EB Hawker. They were followed by the 7th Devons (cyclists).

It was a grand affair and the ranks were further swelled by the presence of the Devon and Cornwall ASC and the Wessex Field Ambulance.

The Salute was taken by Major General Penton, and with him were a number of dignitaries, among them the Mayors of Plymouth and Devonport and the Chairman of the Stonehouse Urban District Council – all of whom he would be persuading to unite the following year.

Meanwhile one of those actually on parade was 18-year-old Robert Victor Walling, the only son of the local newspaper editor, Robert Alfred Walling.

Assembling in Citadel Road *'the men marched around by the Grand Hotel to reach the Hoe Promenade'*, wrote Walling.

'Officers were in blue patrol jackets, with swords – and they wore white cap covers. They did not wear full dress because the men were not issued with helmets. The 'other ranks' were in blue or scarlet walking-out dress, with caps, and carried rifles with fixed bayonets. Because the wheels of its 4.7 inch guns and the hooves of its horses would damage the tarmac, the Plympton battery of the RGA could not parade on the promenade, but it was drawn up at the foot of the slope, near the Citadel sally-port.'

The parade attracted a big crowd who *'gave the citizen soldiers a vociferous welcome,'* said young Walling, adding:

'The parade was later declared to have been a great success as a recruiting effort, many young Plymouth men rolling up to the headquarters of the various units to join over the following weeks.'

Men joining the RGA were generally chosen for their strength, because of the heavy duties involved, notably lifting hundred-pound shells and exercises involving mounting great gun barrels that could weigh up to 28 tons.

A few years earlier, the various local RGA units had been inspected

Three views of Fort Picklecombe.

by Major-General Dalton, who noted that each Company was under-manned, by around thirty men, and that the aim and efficacy of each battery was inconsistent: some fired their rounds quicker, but less accurately, while others were slower, but more accurate. Lentney (towards Renney Point), Watchouse (above Bovisand), Grenville (above Kingsand), Maker, Eastern, Western Kings and Devils Point were among the defensive points inspected and Picklecombe was singled out as the examination battery of choice – previously it had been at Penlee Point, but Picklecombe was judged to be a better place to look out for potential unwelcome intruders.

When war was declared, on 4 August, the 5th Devons were with the 4ths and 6ths on their annual training exercise on Woodbury Common, near Exmouth. On receiving their orders to mobilise they hastened back towards Plymouth and took up residence in the various coastal defence stations around, but it was only a week or so before they were summoned up to Salisbury Plain to join the Wessex Division (to which they belonged).

Not all of the men were experienced however:

'For many of us,' recalled FCAE sometime later, *'our journey began at the old Drill Hall, Millbay, where we passed the doctor and were sworn in: our initiation into the complexities of infantry training took place on the football field there: most of us were still wearing civvies when we were issued with our first rifle and bayonet (proud moment this).'*

The situation in Plymouth was mirrored elsewhere – the British Army was comparatively small and largely made up of reservists.

'In due course we were fitted, or should I say ill-fitted,' continued FCAE, *'with uniforms and felt that our emulation of the Guards was almost complete. Our food was plentiful, though unvaried – stew, stew, stew every day.*

The sleeping accommodation in the Drill Hall was not so good though. Some of us slept on the concrete floor, while others managed to squeeze themselves between the seats of the balconies at either end of the building, but still, we were all healthy and keen youngsters, anxious to learn our new "trade".

But first, we had to join the battalion which had been mobilised and was under canvas on Salisbury Plain and after a few weeks intensive training in field work, we were granted a short leave and on our return left for Southampton, to board the Nevasa.'

While at Perham Down on Salisbury Plain the men were inspected by the King and Lord Kitchener, and prepared for transfer to India where they would replace Regular Army units, who, in turn, were on their way to France.

There were 828 in the Plymouth contingent of the 5th Devons that sailed out of Southampton on 9 October, with another 832 from Exeter who made up the 4th Battalion – there was also a further 803 north Devon men who sailed on the slightly smaller *Galeka*.

The journey out was relatively uneventful although at Suez the Division was detained for several days because by that stage Turkey had joined the war and there were concerns that the men would be required to serve in Egypt. The arrival of an Australian contingent in Aden soon obviated that need, but the threat of being sunk by a German cruiser, *Emden*, that was known to be operating in the area caused further delay, until news broke of the sinking of the *Emden* by HMAS *Sydney*. Thereafter the 9,000-ton *Nevasa* continued on her way, this time without an escort, all the way to Karachi.

The final destination was Multan, a very hot cantonment (British Military Camp) in the Punjab:

'We settled nicely in this strange yet charming land. Everything was new to us, the food especially so, though there never seemed to be enough of it. We supplemented our meals with tea and buns from the old "charwallah", who would squat just outside the bungalow from long before daylight, with his tea-urn kept heated with a small charcoal fire.

Cash however was not plentiful, the rate for privates being 1/- per day (5p), and from this princely sum I personally had 4d per day deducted, this being my allotment to my mother.'

The 5th Devons remained in India until March 1917 when they were posted to Egypt, *'and to Palestine, where the battalion fought in the battle of El Jib, which contributed to our capture of Jerusalem,'* wrote local military historian Godfrey Wycisk, adding, *'It was then almost continuously engaged in fighting the Turks until May, 1918, when it was sent to France. There it came into action on 9 June and fought in various engagements, including the Battle of the Second Marne, until the Armistice. This was followed by duty with the Army of Occupation in Germany.'* They were, incidentally, the only Territorial formation invited to enter Germany.

Top: *The 5th Devons in the Drill Hall Grounds, Plymouth, waiting for marching orders.*
Bottom: *The 5th Devons leaving for India – Scene at Friary Station.*

Plymouth may have been one of the farthest British garrison towns from the front line, but it wasn't long before many of the full-time soldiers who had been stationed here were in the thick of it.

The Gordon Highlanders, under Lt-Col Francis Hugh Neish, and the Royal Scots, under Lt-Col H McMicking, had been on exercises on Dartmoor, but they were instantly rushed back to do sentry duty as the RGA were detailed to man the coastal defences. Within ten days however the Highlanders had left the hutments at Crownhill having been mobilised for action and landed at Boulogne along with the 1st Battalion of the Royal Scots (Lothian Regiment), who had been based alongside them at the main Crownhill Barracks.

By 22 August they had reached Mons and helped to line the Conde–Mons Canal near Nimy Bridge. There they sustained the brunt of the German onslaught and were forced to retreat, regrouping at Le Cateau, where they made a famous stand before back-peddling yet further. By now reduced to just one company they reached a line behind the River Marne and, under the command of the French General, Joseph Joffre, struck out at the German flank and managed to deflect the invading forces away from Paris.

The Highlanders had sustained great losses, and would encounter a great many more: during the course of the war over 50,000 men served in 21 different battalions raised by the Gordon Highlanders, over half of whom would be killed or wounded.

The Royal Irish Regiment raised several extra battalions too and between marching out of Raglan in August 1914 through to November 1918 would lose over 3,200 of their number, in divers war zones like Le-Pilly, Gullimont, Ginchy, Salonika, Mesopotamia and Palestine.

Also striking out from Raglan in August 1914 were the 4th battalion of the Middlesex Regiment, who like their Irish and Scots colleagues were to make up part of the 8th Brigade, 3rd Division, in France.

Meanwhile, as the 5th Devons were being shipped out to India, so the 1st Battalion of the Nottinghamshire and Derbyshire Regiment (the Sherwood Foresters as they were generally known) were making their way from Bombay to Plymouth.

On 2 October they arrived in the port and marched to Cattedown School where they were temporarily billeted before being marched across to Friary Station later that same day and being steamed up to Hursley Park, half way between Salisbury Plain and Portsmouth, where they were to be mobilised and trained for war.

By Bonfire Night, 1914 they had been landed at Le Havre, and were about to witness fireworks on a scale the world had never seen before.

Top left: *Raglan Barracks.* Top right: *2 October 1914, Sherwood Foresters march to Cattedown.* Bottom: *Dinner time in the playground of Cattedown Road school, with dinner served on desks.* Opposite page: *far left; Colonel William Gordon rides at the head of the Gordon Highlanders from Mutley Station though Plymouth to ship for the Continent.* Top: *Crownhill Barracks.* Bottom: *Royal Irish marching through Lockyer Street to entrain for France.*

Norman Horne: Devon RGA, promoted to Sergeant 1914.

However, to go back to that summer's day, when news that Britain was at war was first announced, 28-year-old Norman Horne, a local member of the Devon Royal Garrison Artillery (396 Seige Battery), was sent to Devil's Point to watch for signs of enemy activity at sea.

Promoted to sergeant that same year, Norman had joined the RGA some years earlier and would come to see wartime service in Italy, Egypt, Salonica, Basra, Bagdad and Mesopotania, but not straight away.

He witnessed the Gordon Highlanders leaving Plymouth a few days later and on 14 October 1914, out at Devil's Point, Western Kings, he witnessed:

'one of the most glorious sights of the war – the arrival in Plymouth Sound of the Canadian Army, safely convoyed across the Atlantic.

We saw all the transports pass our battery of guns at Devil's Point, being quite close in the narrows. As each troop ship passed we cheered and cheered, day after day. They were taken into Devonport Dockyard where they disembarked for the training on Salisbury Plain, etc., for France.'

Of course Norman wasn't the only one to be impressed by the incredible spectacle of troop-ships. The convoy had been aiming to disgorge their passengers at Southampton, but a submarine threat prompted them to put into Plymouth. The Germans had evidently got wind from their agents in New York that a troop-carrying convoy had set out from Quebec on 8 October and submarines *U8* and *U20* were dispatched to deal with it. Happily, *U8* was spotted by the French off Cape Gris Nez and *U20* was encountered off Culver Cliff and so the Admiralty initially ordered the convoy to shelter in Plymouth, but in the end, once disembarkation had begun it was decided to carry on.

It was, the largest single convoy ever seen in the port: 32 liners, escorted by five warships, carrying ammunition, stores, 1,000 tons of coal, around 100,000 sacks of flour and more importantly for the war effort, some 33,000 men, 7,679 horses, 127 field guns and an aeroplane. It was a massive movement of manpower that temporarily created a major logistical problem of where to billet the men, and their horses, and how to move them out of Plymouth and up to Salisbury Plain.

It was almost certainly the biggest 'invasion' (albeit a friendly one) of troops on to English soil since the Norman Conquest almost 1000 years earlier. Small wonder, therefore, that they received such great interest and a warm reception. Not that many members of the Canadian Expeditionary Force were Canadian born, only about half were – the rest being mainly Scots, English, Irish, Welsh and French.

In the event, it took 92 trains to transport the Canadian influx to Salisbury Plain, with convoys of military vehicles taking a slower road route through the county.

Top: *Friendly invasion –14 October 1914: over 30 liners, plus escorts head for Plymouth carrying over 32,000 troops.* Middle left: *Troops disembark.*
Bottom left: *Sunday 18 October 1914 Church Service for Canadian troops on the Hoe Promenade.* Bottom right: *Canadians exiting via Plympton in left-hand drive Renaults.*

The Canadian maple-leaf motif was to herald the first of a number of friendly invasions from different outposts of the Empire across the course of the war.

Later that same month a number of South African troops arrived on the *Kildonan Castle*. In January 1915 HMAS *Australia* called at Plymouth and throughout 1916 and 1917 there was a steady flow of troop ships arriving in the port from down under, principally from New Zealand, among the first being HMNZT (His Majesty's New Zealand Transport) *Tahiti*, which set out in convoy with *Maunganui* on 26 June 1916 and arrived in Plymouth two months later (22 August) with 2,123 troops on board. With names redolent of the South Pacific, New Zealand transport ships were regularly disembarking troops for the front in the port: *Tahiti, Willochra, Tofua, Ruapehu, Aparima, Navua, Ulimaroa, Corinthic, Mokoia, Pakeha, Pork Lyttlelton, Devon, Waitemata, Turakina* and, from Australia, *Omrah*. The last three, sadly, were all to be sunk by U-boats before the end of the war, while *Turakina* just a few weeks after unloading her human freight in Plymouth, having gone on up to London, was hit making her way, full of ballast, for New York.

Opposite page: *'Arrival of Australians in England. The men's faces show how cheerfully they have answered the call of the Old Country.'* Above: HMNZT Turakina which arrived in Plymouth on 20 July 1917 and which was sunk by U-86 a few weeks later on 13 August 1917. Right top and bottom: *'That the Empire is determined to stick together is shown by the way that India has respected the Call to Arms. The picture shows some of our Indian warriors at a recent landing'* which like the Australians, was at Millbay.

Top: 1914, Lancashire Royal Engineers Camp at Staddon Heights.
Bottom: With little in the way of transport, marching was the main way to get men from one point to another.

In January 1916 a contingent of West Indians, almost all of them Jamaicans, arrived in Plymouth. They were led, like most of the West Indian soldiers, by white men, in this instance, 29-year-old Lt-Colonel Charles Wood Hill. Wood Hill was to stay with his men throughout the war and was perhaps more sympathetic than most to his charges, for whom the overseas adventure had not started well.

'Many West Indians lost their lives from pneumonia on board ship from the West Indies to England,' noted Wood Hill later, *'and this was entirely due to the fact that they were unsuitably clothed – no warm underclothing, no overcoats and sick accommodation totally unsuitable.'*

On arriving in Plymouth he and his men were stationed at Withnoe Camp, near Millbrook.

'The camp was composed entirely of huts and, once again, the men suffered from the cold.

As soon as possible I went to London and saw Colonel Sir Edward Ward, Bart., who was acting Liaison Officer between the War Office and the Colonial office, with reference to the Overseas Forces, and implored him to bring pressure to bear to have the British West Indies Regiment removed from England as soon as possible to some warmer place where the men could start training in earnest and where there would be less wastage from disease.'

Within three weeks of Wood Hill's plea, the 1st and 2nd Battalions who had arrived in England at the end of 1915 and who were based in Seaforth in similarly parlous conditions, were removed to Egypt, followed by Wood Hill's 3rd Battalion.

'Unfortunately, misfortune still followed in their wake, for various outbreaks of measles, mumps and cerebrospinal meningitis occurred. The 3rd Battalion was especially unfortunate with respect to this latter disease, for they were stationed in a camp at Plymouth in which there had been an outbreak of this disease before and within a few yards of their camp there was another camp in which some British troops were suffering from mumps.'

Although seldom allowed to fight, and mostly confined to menial labouring tasks – digging trenches, loading ammunition, laying phone lines – the casualties were high: of the 15,000 or so black West Indians who served in the Great War, 185 were killed or died of wounds, but a further 1,071 died of illness and some 697 were wounded.

Another foreign contingent that passed through Plymouth during the Great War was the first assignment of Chinese Labour Corps (CLC). By 1916 the Allies were in danger of losing the war, human resources were very stretched and the British Trade Unions were against importing workers from outside the country to work in the UK. And so it was Winston Churchill, who, taking a leaf out of the French Government's book, hit upon the idea of employing Chinese workers, not in Britain, but behind the lines in France, where they could carry out tasks that Britons had been doing (working as engineers, repairing tanks and equipment, cooking, cleaning and general labouring) without incurring the wrath of the unions.

However in order not to directly involve the War Office, or compromise Chinese neutrality (they came into the war later) the men were recruited by a civilian trading company, Forbes & Co., who operated out of a small port in Weihai.

The beauty of this was that Weihai was a British-leased territory so the men could be signed up as nominally being British, thus obviating the need to inform the Chinese Government. By the end of the process some 96,000 Chinese civilians were absorbed this way into the CLC on three-year contracts that saw them being paid around half of what the British soldier was receiving (this was nevertheless around four times what they might be getting at home).

And so it was that on 18 January 1917 the first 1,000 'coolies' (as they were somewhat disparagingly referred to) in their peasant-style blue-padded jackets and military greatcoats set out from Shandong, only to arrive in Plymouth many weeks later, on 11 April 1917, before going on to France.

It was a long journey, particularly for men that had never left home before. Many struggled with the crossing and in Efford Cemetery there are the graves of eight Chinese Labour Corps men who never made it to France and who died at various points between 28 June and 22 August 1917.

Of those that did make it to the battle zone, even working behind the lines did not guarantee safety and although no exact figure is available it is estimated that between 10,000 and 20,000 CLC workers died in France over the next three years. Those that survived were not always paid in full, nor were they treated with respect instead, like the black soldiers from various corners of the Empire, they were regularly subjected to racial abuse.

Top: *Recuperating West Indian servicemen (from a local collection).*
Bottom: *Chinese Labour Corps workers.*

July 1915: Potential recruits on the tramlines outside 104 and 105 Old Town Street, the ground floors of which the War Office had taken over as recruiting offices.

Britain desperately needed manpower, not just to help behind the lines, but on the front line too. In August 1914 the British Army numbered only 730,000, most of whom were serving overseas. The German militia, by comparison, numbered almost two million and both the French and Russian armies totalled in excess of a million.

At that time, all the other three countries operated some kind of compulsory military service, Britain, however didn't and it relied on volunteers - either full-time soldiers or reservists (the Territorial Army).

It was clear from the outset that more men would be needed and within 48 hours of the start of the war the newly appointed Secretary of State for War, 64-year-old Lord Horatio Kitchener, started working on recruitment. A massive country-wide poster campaign ensued with the most enduring image being Alfred Leese's image of Kitchener that had first appeared on the front cover of the *London Opinion* magazine on 5 September 1914.

The Government were hoping for 100,000 extra men by the end of the year, but by the end of September, some 750,000 had enlisted and by the end of January 1915 more than one million men had taken the king's shilling.

In Plymouth the local Recruiting Committee had made full use of its MPs Waldorf Astor and Arthur Shirley Benn, arranging for them to address the crowds at Home Park, at Plymouth Argyle's home fixtures, and during the intervals of productions

at the Theatre Royal, the Palace Theatre, in Union Street, and the town's newest picture house, the Cinedrone (opened in 1913) in Ebrington Street.

Isaac Foot, local solicitor who had narrowly lost out on winning the Bodmin parliamentary election, in 1910, added his weight to the debate, as did the leader of the Suffragette movement, Emmeline Pankhurst, who spoke passionately in the Guildhall, urging men to uphold the honour of the country and women to push their menfolk into enlisting.

On 1 February 1915 a more specific local 'Call to Arms' was issued by the Devon Parliamentary Recruiting Committee – An Appeal to Devon Men and Women.

I CAN'T GET OFF AS I USED TO DO
BUT THE KHAKI BOYS ARE QUITE IN CLOVER
SO I THINK I'LL JOIN THE ARMY TOO —
WHEN THE NASTY HORRID WAR IS OVER!

" THIS LITTLE PIG STAYED AT HOME "

"It's the clothes that make the man!"   "C'est l'habit qui fait l'homme!"

Men who stayed behind were often portrayed as somewhat effete, whereas a man in uniform, was truly a man! In 1917 (through to spring 1919). Dartmoor Prison was turned into a camp for Conscientious Objectors - many of whom were worked on a new road near Two Bridges - 'Conshies Road'.

Targeting those yet to enlist, the over-arching question was simple: 'why haven't you?' But it was broken down into five more subtle enquiries:

1 If you are physically fit and between 19 and 38 years of age, are you really satisfied with what you are doing today?

2 Do you feel happy as you walk along the streets and see **other** men wearing the King's uniform?

3 What will you say in years to come when people ask you – 'Where did **you** serve' in the great War?

4 What will you answer when your children grow up and say, 'Father, why weren't you a soldier, too?

5 What would happen to the Empire if every man stayed at home **like you**?

Inside, the twelve-page document was steeped in rhetoric and reason: 'Think what the British Army is doing, and why it is doing it: It is fighting to save the honour of England and the very life of Belgium.

It is fighting on the Continent of Europe in order to keep the horrors of war away from our own land.'

Drawing on the recent horrors in Scarborough the authors brought their point home, quite literally by stating that:

'Already German guns have spoken on our shores. German shells have burst in our streets. The blood of English women and of English children has been shed by Germans ... it is the duty of all who have not enlisted to join at once and avenge them.'

The powerful prose juxtaposed short and pithy sentences alongside longer, linguistic passages:

'Your Country is calling you to come now, quickly, to her assistance, so that all these things and worse may not befall the English countryside, that our streams may never be tinged with the blood of innocent children, that our women may never pass through the bitter valley of shame and woe as the women of Belgium have passed, that our towns and villages may never be put to the sword and the torch, that our churches may never be desecrated, and our fields may never be ploughed into trenches and sown with death.'

Arguing that the war was both just and righteous the authors reiterated how 'By beating Germany on the Continent we prevent her from crossing the Channel.'

By this stage a number of issues had been raised here and elsewhere:

certain jobs, notably many of those in the Dockyard, were 'reserved *occupations,'* where jobs were deemed crucial to the war effort and men were given to understand that if they left their job voluntarily that that job might not still be there for them at the end of the war. Indeed giving up their job, albeit to serve their King and Country, might even see them forfeit the chance to get their old job back again. Understandably men in this position were soon issued with a badge to indicate their status.

But what of the others, those who had no badge either to indicate a reserved occupation or that they might have been a discharged serviceman. Clearly, a blue hospital uniform indicated a soldier or sailor recuperating, but what of those badgeless and un-uniformed young men?

Women were encouraged to hand these individuals white feathers to indicate cowardice and men who were of military age, but without work and who were entitled to Poor Relief, had their payments withheld by the Board of Guardians.

Some claimed to be Conscientious Objectors – against war on religious or philosophical grounds – others may have tried to enlist only to be assessed as unfit. Remarkably only about a third of men who tried to enlist were adjudged fully fit for service, while four out of ten men were found to be totally unfit for service – not surprisingly these men wanted badges too, to prove that they had tried to join up. Oddly enough, within the County there were those who felt that Plymouth men were more reluctant to come forward than in other towns around Devon, however, it should be remembered that a good percentage of Plymouth's working male population were employed in the Dockyard. As the Mayor, Thomas Baker, noted 30 percent of the male population of Plymouth were engaged in HM Services before the war – there was inevitably, proportionately, a smaller potential pool to recruit from.

But that didn't ease the pressure on the menfolk, or the womenfolk:

'Women of Devon! We appeal to you to help the great and sacred cause by giving your consent and your blessing to the men who are willing to go, and to show in this vital matter the same patriotism and same fine self-denial that you have shown in succouring the wounded and distressed.'

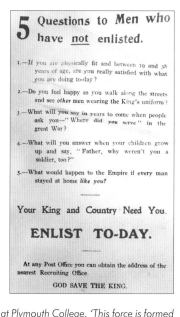

5 Questions to Men who have not enlisted.

1.—If you are physically fit and between 19 and 38 years of age, are you really satisfied with what you are doing to-day?

2.—Do you feel happy as you walk along the streets and see *other* men wearing the King's uniform?

3.—What will *you* say in years to come when people ask you—"Where did *you* serve" in the great War?

4.—What will you answer when your children grow up and say, "Father, why weren't *you* a soldier, too?"

5.—What would happen to the Empire if every man stayed at home *like you?*

Your King and Country Need You.

ENLIST TO-DAY.

At any Post Office you can obtain the address of the nearest Recruiting Office.

GOD SAVE THE KING.

WOMEN OF BRITAIN SAY – "GO!"

Top: *Members of the Plymouth Defence Force at Plymouth College. 'This force is formed of men who, though over the age at which they can enlist, still feel themselves capable of military duties, and are undertaking drill and training in order to place themselves at the disposal of the Plymouth Fortress authorities for local service.' Doidge's Annual.*
Above: *Men of Devon back page.* Right: *Women of Britain say – Go!*

HOSPITALS

Anticipating major demands for treating the sick and wounded, Salisbury Road School was taken over as a wartime hospital on Wednesday 5 August 1914 – the day the news that we were at war was announced in the press.

It was a hot summer's day and the 4th Southern Territorial Force was mobilised: *'The Company "fell in … move to the right in fours" and were off to Salisbury Road Council School, while the billeting party proceeded to Garrison Headquarters for the necessary order. All office stores, books, papers, etc., were loaded into the C.O.'s car and disappeared in the same direction.*

On arrival billets were at once appropriated, and the task of conversion of a board School to a Hospital commenced. And it was a task … for the school was precisely as the rising generation of Plymouth had left it the previous afternoon, every class room contained its allotted quota of desks and forms, and every desk and form was effectively screwed to the floor. The quartermaster's equipment of tools had not yet arrived, but that mattered not. The 4th Southern is only mobilized once in a generation – we hope. Screw drivers appeared from somewhere and the job started. All the rest of that day and all the next, hot and dusty men strained at fixtures, struggled with screws, and slipped on stairs with school furniture.

The result! On the third day the building was cleared and cleaning commenced.

Batches of equipment now kept dropping in all day and half the night. Messrs Spooners Ltd., the contractors for the ordnance supplies were indefatigable in rising to the occasion, and, as the materials arrived, "stores" nonexistent as such a few days before, began to take shape, to set up counters, etc., and to issue notices in more or less bold type:
'As for instance – "This store will be open at 6.30am and close at 12.30pm" "Orderlies will not pass this barrier" and "Please wipe your feet"! Four days previously children were taught washing here!"
The above extract is taken from the *4th Southern General Hospital Gazette*, June 1916 edition, it continued:

'Or, take the linen store, the largest, most responsible store of a hospital. In the basement was a carpenter's shop containing a dozen

Lt.-Colonel HW Webber: Administrator - 4th Southern General Hospital from August 1914. Opposite page: Salisbury Road School in its role as a hospital, the red cross on the roof a precaution against attack by enemy air ships.

Miss C. A. Tait McKay, joined the Territorial Force Nursing Service (4th Southern Unit) in 1911 as Sister, and was appointed Matron in August, 1912. Miss McKay was trained at Guy's Hospital, after a year's maternity training at the Plaistow Maternity Charity, and subsequently had six months' training under Queen Victoria's Jubilee Institute. She is a certified midwife, and holds the massage certificate of the ISTM and the certificate of the Royal Sanitary Institute as a Sanitary Inspector.

or so tool benches. At first, and until the contractor's men got to work, the "store" was set up by ranging the benches round the wall and piling the clothing on them. But it opened and kept open in spite of all difficulties.

On August 11th, the members of the TFNS arrived: Matron, 22 Sisters, 68 Staff Nurses. They travelled from all parts of the United Kingdom and introduced themselves to the C.O. on arrival.'

One of those Staff Nurses was the young Ethel Eastwood from London. Ethel was working in East Dulwich when she received her marching orders.

A letter arrived from the War Office ordering her to go direct to the 4th Southern General Hospital, at Salisbury Road School, Plymouth.

The letter, was one of many sent out that month to hospital staff in the capital and it said, in quite matter of fact terms:

'Madam, you are requested to join your unit of the Territorial Force Nursing Service at once.

A railway warrant is enclosed which entitles you to travel free and should be surrendered to the Booking Clerk in exchange for a 1st class ticket. A travelling claim is also enclosed.

Will you kindly fill in both carefully, with the date, line and route by which you travel.

On arrival you are to report yourself to the Administrative Medical Officer of the 4th Southern General Hospital, and also to your principal Matron, Miss Smale.

The sum of £8 will be issued to you for your TFNS uniform, which you must obtain as soon as possible if you have not already done so, and in the meantime, wear your own uniform.

It will not be necessary for you to have any plain clothes so you need not bring much luggage.'

The missive continued: 'In accordance with para. 21, TFNS Standing Orders, you will receive pay and allowances according to your rank, and a month's pay will be issued in advance.

When joining your unit, you must wear your badge and bring your copy of TFNS Standing Orders with you.'

Another recipient of a similar request was a young nurse who later wrote under the name Modestia: 'I remember how important I felt when I left that busy town in the Midlands and how envious my colleagues were that I had been "called up".

'The uppermost thought was that I should soon be back; and as the train rolled out of the station I lolled back in my carriage, content that we would soon have the Germans "done in."

It was the first time I had ever travelled in a first-class carriage, and I was so overcome with the feeling of wealth and luxury that I'm afraid I didn't behave myself according to that "state of life to which I had been called."

The journey to Plymouth was one of the pleasantest I have ever had. Everyone made a great fuss of us (I had joined six more "Terriers" at Birmingham) and they gave us flowers and boxes of chocolates. I thought it great to have a war, but, alas! how soon did I learn that it meant sorrow, suffering, and death.

When we arrived at the 4th Southern we were presented to the Commanding Officer who said a few kind words to us, and then we passed on to the Matron.

I was the second to report to the Matron, and I remember when she asked me my age and I murmured 24, she expressed satisfaction that "someone knew her age."

I learned afterwards that the Sister who reported before me was so terrified (she couldn't have seen Matron's humorous smile behind her glasses) that she forgot everything, even her age, and ever after was regarded (not least by herself) as not all there.

After leaving the Matron, we were interviewed by the billeting Sergeant, who marshalled us off to our respective billets where we were regaled with tomatoes and tea.

Having been promised " 'am and heggs" for breakfast, I retired to my room, and after duly thanking the Lord for "all His mercies" turned in. So ended a perfect day.'

As it transpired the Matron mentioned in the original dispatch was not in post at the opening of Salisbury Road, rather it was Alexandrina Tait Mackay and, writing in the *Queen's Nurses Magazine*, Matron Tait Mackay picked up the story:

'The business of transforming Salisbury Road Schools and the adjacent Baptist Church into a War Hospital of 520 beds was completed on August 20th and patients were admitted from the adjacent forts.

The first batch of 120 wounded warriors arrived from the Front on August 31st, forty of those were stretcher cases, and as soon as the news leaked out considerable excitement prevailed.'

Ethel Eastwood a Staff Nurse at Salisbury Road, formerly at East Dulwich, London.

Scene outside the MIlitary Hosptial, Salisbury Road. One of the cases being removed from the ambulance van – a London General Omnibus.

The 31 August 1914 was a Sunday, it was little more than a week after the Battle of Mons, everyone had bedded down for the night, when, at 1.15am the Commanding Officer, received a telegram: *"Prepare to receive 120 wounded."*

One can imagine the sudden burst of activity that followed, and the word quickly spread. However, it wasn't until 5.30pm, by which time a large crowd had gathered, that an ambulance train pulled into Friary Station with its precious cargo of tired and dusty men from Northern France.

Crowds gathered in the streets to watch their arrival in the impromptu ambulances: one of them was a converted London Omnibus – very much a novelty here at the time as the Three Towns were serviced only by trams.

Among the arrivals were many men of the Middlesex and Royal Scots regiments who were stationed in Plymouth at the outset of war.

'Many who were able to walk to the ambulance cars,' reported the *Illustrated War News*, the following week, *'were in cheerful spirits, and gaily answered the hearty welcome of the crowd. Their chief hope, like their comrades' elsewhere, is to recover quickly and return to the front.'*

Plymouth, of course, wasn't the only destination: by 31 August 1914 there were 300 wounded men in a hospital in Woolwich, 316 at the London Hospital, and 140 at Bishop's Stortford. On the next day 300 arrived at Brighton, and about 120 each at Portsmouth and Birmingham.

Less than a month into the war the impact of the fighting had already started to hit home. As they arrived many of the soldiers had wound dressings that had not been changed for days, and their wounds were oozing pus and often full of maggots – it was not a pretty sight. However, after a hot bath, some chicken broth and *'the kindly attentions of the nursing staff the men were soon revived.'*

Interestingly enough, as the number of servicemen admitted to our local military hospitals started to rise so shortages of key items – fruit, eggs, flowers and confectionary – that were regularly taken in to the men to make their incarceration more comfortable, began to hit home. Thus it was that Nancy Astor, the wife of local MP Waldorf Astor, proposed setting up a central supply depot in Plymouth to create a fairer distribution of gifts being donated for the welfare of the wounded.

Top: *Another serious 'cot' case being carried from Friary Station to the waiting ambulance van.*
Bottom: *Slightly wounded Highlanders having a joy ride to the Hospital. General Penton is on the left.*

Salisbury Road Baptist Church replete with its ad hoc red cross.

On 25 September, a second batch numbering 132 in all, including 14 Germans, arrived. Not surprisingly the presence of the enemy aroused even more interest, although clearly these walking wounded servicemen were, at the end of the day, just regular men like our own.

The wounded Germans left in October, as did some 30 other patients who needed special eye surgery. The men were taken from the hospital in brakes and transferred to a special coach attached to the train. A report in the press suggested that they all were looking much better for their stay at the hospital and only one was walking with the aid of crutches.

That same month the first contingent of wounded Belgian allies reached Plymouth, about 300 of them arrived in the town on Thursday 15 October, after a railway journey from the Kent coast that had taken almost 12 hours. These men were delivered to North Road Station and were taken off to the Royal Naval Hospital.

A week earlier, 125 of our own wounded servicemen, mainly Devonshire regiment men, from the Battle of Aisne, had arrived at Friary. Major General Penton was there on the platform to receive them. The delightfully named Miss Pleasance, a VAD (Voluntary Aid Detachment nurse) was there with a group of ladies providing refreshments.

Many of the men were suffering from bullet wounds.

'They speak in glowing terms of the French,' a report noted.

Elsewhere, writing in an autograph book circulated around the men at Salisbury Road, Private Pyle of the 1st Somerset Light Infantry wrote that he *'was wounded at Aisne on the 14th September and did not get a chance to come home until 4th October.'*

As the war progressed these autograph books became more commonplace and tended to feature little rhymes and dedications, but Sister Eastwood's little book handed around the wounded in Salisbury Road, was one of the first and many men took the opportunity to detail their circumstances:

'No 9109 Corporal Church 2nd Battalion Highland Lt Infantry. I arrived in Boulogne at the beginning of the war, marched through France to Belgium, experienced my first baptism of fire at Mons. Was in the retire from Mons down country; had narrow escapes while retiring from the enemy. Had it proper hard during the Retirement, pretty hard marching and forced, of course, for our own good as we

Top: *October 1914, German prisoners leaving Salisbury Road.*
Bottom: *Not all the patients pulled through - a Military Funeral procession from Salisbury Road.*

Top: *A ward in Salisbury Road Hospital.* Bottom: *In the playground, one of the Middlesex and a member of the King's Own Light Infantry.*

were drawing the enemy down country for the French troops to get in. Was at St Quintin, then took over trenches at a place called Suppe. After 9 days got relieved by French troops then marched 5 miles and and relieved troops on the right wing. From there we went to Arras and Ypres and I left there wounded by what they called a Sniper. He is a good shot, sent out to shoot any Tommy he sees going messages or knocking about. He is found either up a tree or in a burned village or on a roof anywhere he thinks he won't be seen and I can assure you it's pretty hard to find him in fact, he conceals himself that well that it's pretty near impossible to see him. So you see the Germans are as cute as ourselves, no doubt we have sold them a pup many a time, hiding our guns and putting up dummies, and you would laugh to see them firing at the dummies and our artillery about 500 yards off, but it is terrible to see the damage done by the Germans to France and Belgium. Horses lying dead, pigs knocked out and villages in ruins. In fact it was sad to see the refugees leaving: old men and women hardly able to crawl, also a mother with her babe in her arms getting out of the road for safety. I can tell you it touched us a bit, but no doubt they have done their worse. Now we are just started to do ours and I can safely say we are not forgetting to do it and uphold the honour of the poor people of France and Belgium whom they ill-treated. The Germans are all for Wine and Lager, but Britian (sic) is not forgetting to lager them with ammunition.

'It's very seldom the Kaisar (sic) is away from the Trenches as he is giving orders to his Generals what to do with the Contemptable (sic) Little Army, but he is beginning to see that the Contemptable Little Army is going to wipe his out.'

The above was written as one sentence with no punctuation whatsoever, it was also one of the longer pieces to have been penned for such a 'souvenir' account. Indeed in comparison with other books circulated by other nurses it was remarkably frank and detailed, as were a few other entries:

'I left Dublin on the 13 of August for France and arrived their (sic) on the 16th of August and fought on our way to mons and we had a very rough time of it their and we had to leave mons after to or 3 weeks and we had a few small fights and we got to Asine (Aisne) on the 9th September 1914 and we had a lot of fighting their and I got wounded on 15th September in the battle of Asine in the forehead and Eye while I was Bandaging up my Mates which got wounded and I was getting up I was wounded and I had to stop their for 3 days in the rain.

'When I was picked up I was sent strait home and I got to the 4th Southern General Hospital Plymouth the 25th September and I stop their (sic) for 2 weeks. Then I was sent to No.1 VA Hospital Exeter and went under 10 operations and had my Eye taken out ...'

No.1 VA Hospital, Exeter was the West of England Eye Hospital and was mobilised on 4 October 1914, making the author of the above, W Jose, one of the first intake.

Like the entry before it, this too was written as one continuous piece, with no punctuation, nevertheless it detracts not a jot from its impact and its ability to convey something of the horrors of what had started to unfold in France and Belgium.

These first-hand accounts were far more graphic than anything that appeared in the press at the time and one wonders if orders subsequently issued from on high as later entries in similar books across the long years of the war were far less revealing.

To take one more example from Nurse Eastwood's archive, Private T Law, 6914 of the Royal Irish Rifles wrote from his hospital bed in Salisbury Road:

'Arrived at Mons on August 23rd at 3.30 o'clock, commenced to dig trenches, got about 18 inches down when the first shell burst over us. Happily it done no harm. Were under shell, rifle and maxim gun fire for four and a half hours.

'Our losses were very small. 4 killed and 9 wounded. Great praise was given to our maxim guns for the great works done at Mons. Retired at 2.30am Monday. Got in touch with the enemy on 26 August, had it very rough fighting a rear-guard actions, went to Valley where we were 9 days in the trenches, it was very wet weather and had to hold the trenches against great odds, Left there and went to Reckbourne (?). Arrived on Monday 12 at 1.30pm, got into action same day at 2pm. Got wounded on Thursday 15th, bullet through 3 finger left hand.'

Like the other entries this was written with no commas, full stops or other punctuation but, nevertheless doubtless conveyed more information than his superiors may have wanted.

Certainly later in the war the standard issue postcard from the front was designed to convey little more than the absolute basics, and offered but little comfort to the recipient.

One of the longer entries in Nurse Eastwood's autograph book. Right: A field Postcard with little opportunity to personalise.

NOTHING is to be written on this side except the date and signature of the sender. Sentences not required may be erased. If anything else is added the post card will be destroyed.

I am quite well.

I have been admitted into hospital { sick } and am going on well. { wounded } and hope to be discharged soon.

I am being sent down to the base.

I have received your { letter dated_____ { telegram „ _____ { parcel „ _____

Letters follows at first opportunity.

I have received no letter from you { lately. { for a long time.

Signature } only. }

Date_____

[Postage must be prepaid on any letter or post card addressed to the sender of this card.]

(6464) Wt. W3497-293 1,000m. 12/14 F. T. & Co., Ltd.

The insights contained within the pages of these early autograph books, however, often contained quite shocking revelations:

'My worst experience was a case in which the Germans showed the white flag, our men rushing out to bring them into our lines. Immediately some hidden batteries of artillery commenced shelling us and the enemy picked up their rifles and started firing.

'It was just awful, the whole Brigade being practically wiped out.

'The worst of it was that we were unable to bring our wounded in for 2 days as the Germans continually shelled our stretcher bearers.'

So wrote Private HJ Watts of the 2nd Grenadier Guards after his experience at the Battle of Aisne. Like other early arrivals at Salisbury Road, Watts had been shipped back from the Continent on the requisitioned Royal Mail Steam Packet (RMSP) *Asturias* on 25 September and delivered into Southampton prior to entraining for Plymouth.

Watts was undoubtedly one of the more fortunate members of his regiment; one who was decidedly less fortunate was Second Lieutenant Godfrey Paget.

Twenty-three-year-old Paget had joined up sometime before the war had started and had assumed his new rank a week or so later on 14 August. One of the first wave of soldiers to see service in France, he sadly met his end at Aisne on 14 September.

We can only imagine the impact of the news when it reached his fiancée, Phyllis Martin, who was then living with her parents in No.7 The Esplanade on Plymouth Hoe.

Lieutenant Godfrey Paget, killed at Aisne, September 14, 1914. Inset: RMSP Asturias.

Phyllis Martin was no stranger to service life, her grandfather had been a very distinguished Naval Admiral and her great grandfather, Sir Thomas Byam Martin, had been Admiral of the Fleet and an MP for Plymouth.

Whether it was in the blood or whether it was a reaction to losing her young partner, Phyllis lost little time, after receiving the tragic news, in signing up as a Voluntary Aid Detachment. Throughout the rest of the war she would serve as volunteer nurse, in Plymouth, Plympton, Exeter, Longleat, Derbyshire and Ireland.

Her first appointment was with the South Devon and East Cornwall Hospital (later known as Greenbank). With the advent of hostilities, the War Office provided grants to allow a number of beds to be allocated to sick and wounded service personnel – Phyllis spent the first three months of 1915 working the wards.

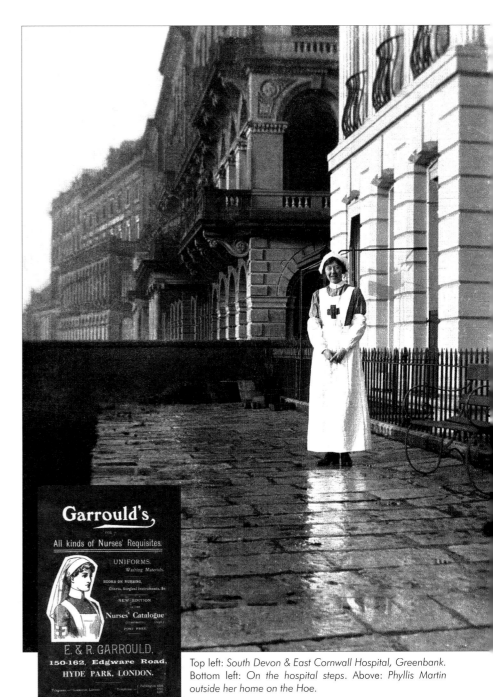

Top left: *South Devon & East Cornwall Hospital, Greenbank.*
Bottom left: *On the hospital steps.* Above: *Phyllis Martin outside her home on the Hoe.*

161

Phyllis had responded to a nationwide appeal for Voluntary Aid Detachments, VADs as they were called. Many of these unpaid workers were fast-tracked into nursing (much to the disapproval of many regular nurses) while others were recruited as cooks, clerks, kitchen-maids, house-maids, laundry-maids, and ward-maids, and drivers and any other work women could usefully be considered for. Certainly as the war intensified and everyone realised that it wasn't going to be over by Christmas, the need for men and women, whether fit for war or not, to turn to and do their bit for King and Country became more and more pressing – as did the demand for hospital beds as the wounded were brought home in their thousands.

In May 1915, to help cope with the situation, a Voluntary Aid Hospital opened up in Plympton. This was Mount Priory House, then owned by the 53-year-old Major Edward Henry Archer Tolcher, who also held Harewood House as his main residence. Tolcher allowed the house and grounds to be used primarily as a place for convalescents, most of whom came down from the Town Hall Hospital in Torquay.

Earlier in 1916 a recreation hut had been erected in the grounds, the funding coming principally from subscriptions and the proceeds of a jumble sale. Initially there were just 21 beds here, but over time that was increased to 50, plus another ten emergency beds. In July of the following year an additional wing was erected on the side of Mount Priory. Built at a cost of £720, the new facility was to serve as a recreation hut and messroom. At the same time the old recreation room of the house was converted for use as another hospital ward.

Nurse Phyllis Martin, photographed with various wounded soldiers in the grounds of Mount Priory - note St Mary's Church in the distance (above left). Far right: Mount Priory, wounded in a wheelchair. Middle: Opening day, May 1915, Mount Priory VAD Hospital. Right: Recruitment poster for VADs.

While every wounded serviceman had his own story to tell, the authorities were keen to ensure that information being sent back from the front was limited – partly to ensure that there was no leak of strategically sensitive details, and partly to prevent graphic accounts of the horrors of war reaching home. At a time when morale needed to be high, and fresh supplies of the nation's manhood were so crucial to the ongoing war of attrition, the truth was bound to hurt, not just the participants, but the war effort itself.

That didn't stop soldiers wanting to share their circumstances with their loved ones. On 28 December 1915, Frank Bowden wrote a letter that he hoped one of his chums, who had been given leave to attend a family funeral, would be able to take back to England and post.

Frank was the Head Gardner on the Port Eliot Estate, St Germans and had been with his battalion serving in France, living in trenches around La Basse and Givenchy:

My Own Dearest wife…

I shall remember this Xmas as long as I live if it's 100 years.

We went in the trenches on the 22nd for 48 hours. Came out on Xmas Eve and we had as rough a time as it's possible to have. I was (like all the rest) wet footed nearly all the time. Sometimes over our boot tops in water and mud. The first 24 hours was not so bad except for a heavy bombardment by the Germans. It was hell while it lasted. About 11 at night I was sent off to the front line to help carry one of our chaps who was wounded. He was a heavy chap and the trenches were narrow, knee deep in water and mud in places. I got back alright but had to throw away my socks and the socks in the bottom of my boots. Put on clean and was fairly comfortable again.

Next morning we were sent up to the frontline. Going up got wet again up to the knees but had to stick it… We watched the German lines through a periscope at night. We do one hour now and again looking over… just duck one's head when a machine gun pelts by, it wouldn't have been so bad but it rained hard the whole of the night. Every part of the trenches was flooded and falling in… One of our fellows was killed through a dry-out falling in when he was asleep. When we weren't on sentry we took turns at the pumps to try and keep the trenches from getting too bad.

The Germans were pretty quiet through the night… but about seven in the morning we were startled through the Germans blowing up

Two Tommies in a trench.

a mine on our left…They sent over shrapnel to help the work of destruction. We had orders to clear out, took what we could but we lost a bit, even some fellows losing their boots. An awful journey. I can't describe it.

We were plastered in mud, wet through and hadn't shaved for three days. We got safely back into reserve then our people let them have it firstly with the big guns.

What the use of it all was we don't know…

We spent a quiet time Xmas Day and Sunday till evening. Just as we were making ourselves comfortable for the night we were called out on parade. Went as we were. Marched off to the trenches as a fatigue party….

The trenches were over our knees with something thicker than soup. We got back to billets at 2 in the morning in a state I can't describe.

Wounded in the trenches and possibly about to get a 'Blighty'.

Up at 6.45am into one's wet clothes. No time for breakfast. On the march for about six miles to where I'm writing this and billeted for the night. A big barn I suppose. We may have a chance to get respectable again but it will take a few days…

To keep me going I had some cheese and chocolate. I hope you can read this. I am writing in a hurry but I have written it to show you a little more clearly some of our experiences.

It's better sometimes, but that's how we spent Christmas.

I have just received your letter. Send me a few shillings when you can. It's so useful in buying a few necessities. Don't forget candles. One pair of socks now and again. Don't send two pairs at once. I have to carry everything I possess everywhere, even up the trenches. I have plenty of tobacco, don't buy that, just a box or two of matches. The dozen mother sent went up the trenches. One of our fellows was carrying them in a sandbag with other things belonging to us which we thought would be useful. He fell under water with all the lot.'

The letter was never posted. It eventually reached Eva Bowden, with some other personal effects and family photographs, just before Christmas the following year, just weeks after Frank was killed in the last few days of the Battle of the Somme.

Less than a month after the new Plympton facility was opened, another Plymouth school, Hyde Park, was successfully converted for use as a hospital.

Practically identical to Salisbury Road, as it had the same architect, Hyde Park opened as another branch of the 4th Southern. Altered and adapted by the Royal Engineers, it opened on 13 June 1915 with 185 beds and was immediately filled with patients from Gallipoli, in the Dardenelles.

These were *'mostly men from our Australian Dominions'* and no sooner had they arrived than the Officer in Charge there, Major Fielding Whitmore (Royal Army Medical Corps) wrote to the Herald: *'Sir, Hyde Park General Hospital is now open and at present is filled with wounded from the Dardenelles. May I appeal to your readers for pianos, gramophones, games, a weekly supply of literature, none of which we have at present.*

'I have,' added the 37-year-old Major, who had grown up locally, in Stoke, *'only just been discharged from a French hospital myself, where I lay ill for several weeks and know how jumpy and nervy one is after the strain of fighting and how one longs for some music and for an interesting book, so I have no scruple about begging for these things on behalf of the wounded here.'*

Nurses and wounded at the 4th Southern Hospital - Ford, Plymouth.

Even with the extra space afforded by the new facility at Hyde Park it was still not enough to cope with the sick and wounded pouring in from the continent. The following month, the premises that had served for many years as Devonport Workhouse – Ford House *'a fine building on the Western border of the Three Towns'* – in Wolseley Road, was opened as yet another outpost of the 4th Southern.

Initially, in April 1915, the Guardians of Ford House had been asked if they could take in 150 wounded soldiers, but were unable to. However, in May it was announced that the War Office were going to take over the premises and in July, after structural alterations, it not only opened as a hospital but became the effective headquarters of the 4th Southern.

In the event, Ford was equipped with 436 beds, Hyde Park sported 223 with a further capacity for 22 in tents, while Salisbury Road had 280.

There was further bedspace at the Royal Naval Hospital and in September 1915, demonstrating their appreciation of the work being done 'for King and Country,' their Majesties, King George V and Queen Mary arrived in Plymouth and visited all three branches of the 4th Southern General Hospital as well as the Naval facility in Stonehouse.

Top left: *Male staff at the Hospital in 1916.* Top Right: *Ford Hospital – the former workhouse.* Above: *Men of the Colonial Forces, who were wounded in Gallipoli, arrive in England.*

King George V and Queen Mary visit Salisbury Road Military Hospital, September 1915.

'Many miles of streets in the Borough were thronged with enthusiastic and cheering crowds,' ran the local press report on the Royal Visit. 'The public were permitted to stand on the pavements and thousands were content to wait for hours to catch a fleeting glimpse of the Royal Party and to give testimony to their enthusiasm by waving handkerchiefs and in some cases small flags.'

Clearly details of the visit had not been made public, presumably in the interests of security, but 'by some means or other the public had obtained a fairly good idea of the day's programme and long before their Majesties had arrived at the Hospitals, densely-packed crowds gathered at the entrances.

'Their Majesties could not fail but to be impressed with the cordiality of their reception.'

After their whistle stop tour of the Hospitals their Majesties spent the afternoon in the Dockyard and the Royal Naval Barracks.

Meanwhile just a few weeks after their visit there was a major incident at Salisbury Road. A report published in the Western Daily Mercury on Tuesday 5 October suggested that the Military Hospital based in the school had been gutted by fire in the early hours of the morning. The alarm was raised by 23-year-old Bessie Denton of St Hilary Terrace, who was awoken by a strange crackling noise. Looking out of her window she then noticed a bright light under the scantling of the hospital roof on the southern side, almost opposite her bedroom. She roused her husband, Charles, who, as an insurance agent was doubtless more sensitive to such crises than most, slipped on some clothing and rushed around to the hospital gate and informed the guard. Meanwhile, Mrs Denton slipped on a mackintosh and rushed around to alert the caretaker, who had the keys to the playground. Throughout all this the flames spread and 'in a very short time practically the whole of the top floor was involved and it was soon apparent that at all events the upper portion of the building was doomed. Soon the fire seized the roof and the flames broke through. Between 3.30 and 4am the roof was aglow and the windows framed in jets of fire. Slates came rushing down.

Happily all the soldier patients were safely evacuated and there were no injuries, indeed thanks to smart actions of PC Damerell of the Plymouth Police Fire Brigade, the machines in the X-Ray Department were all saved. The intrepid constable evidently disconnected all the machinery himself and moved all the instruments to a place of safety.

October 1915, Nurses inspect the fire damage to the upper floor of Salisbury Road.

It was estimated that his actions saved the authorities about £1,200 - a significant sum. A subsequent report also suggested that PCs Bennett and Weeks worked particularly valiantly on this incident, along with rest of the Plymouth Brigade who *'worked like Trojans.'* Fortunately it would appear that all of the damage was repairable everything was very soon back to normal.

'Who comes and greets us at the door,
Who gives out cigarettes galore,
Who signs the passes - what a bore? –
The Matron

Who comes at noon just at our meal,
Uses the probe and makes us squeal,
Who does his best our wounds to heal? –
The Doctor

Who does the dressings all complete,
Who tries to make the men look neat,
Who counts their pulses every beat? –
The Sister

Who does the dressings all prepare,
Who makes the methylated flare,
Who doles out swabs with serious air? –
The Senior Pro

Who scrubs the lockers, dusts the chairs,
Who fills the bottles, mends the tears,
Who skips the ash-trays, if she dares? –
The Junior Pro

Who tear their clothes and wet their feet,
Who go to pictures every week,
Who ne'er forget their meals to eat? –
The Patients'

So wrote one of the war-time patients at Salisbury Road, giving just a slight insight into everyday life at the institution.

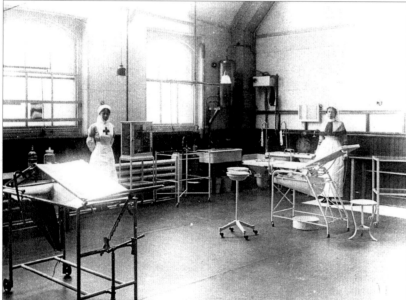

Top: *1916, members of Plymouth's Fire Brigade.*
Bottom: *Corner of the Operating Theatre.*

Various departments of Salisbury Road Hospital. Top: Medicine room. Bottom: Kitchen.

The Linen Store.

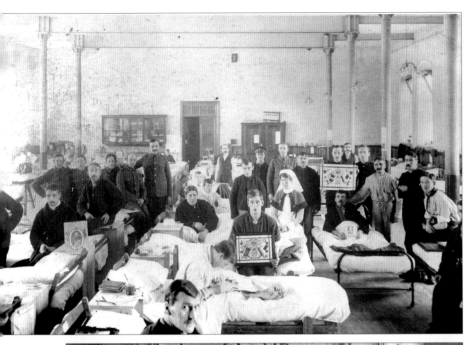

Top: Men display their handiwork in a packed ward in Salisbury Road.
Bottom: Medical Orderlies in Salisbury Road.

Clearly quite a few of the inmates had quite a bit of time on their hands and here, as in other hospitals around the town and around the country, they occupied that time as best they could.

Needlework – embroidery – was a popular solitary solution, as were reading, writing and sketching. Games were ever welcome and every institution was incomplete until it had a recreation room or, better still, a hut and in this the 4th Southern were very ahead of the game.

In the widely distributed in-house *4th Southern General Hospital Gazette*, an anonymous scribe wrote: *'the absence, from the wards, of men who are well enough to be "up" leaves perfect quiet for the bad cases, and only when you have been ill in a ward do you appreciate the value of this, though it has never been necessary to ask the patients to be quiet.*

They have always been "gentlemen" and their gentleness is never better seen than in helping a helpless comrade.

Imagine what a depressing effect it would have on the men if they were never able to get away from the wards. In the Hut, the crack of the billiard balls accompanied by hearty laughter helps give a more helpful outlook and consequently, a more rapid recovery.

Men who can and do play their games within range of the guns are going to be very miserable if deprived of their amusements when "sick".

In the Military Hospitals of days gone by a dining-room was provided, but no real Recreation Room and during the present war there has been no better work than the provision of Recreation Huts. Anyone who has still a lingering doubt as to their value should come and see for the themselves.

The 4th Southern General was the first Territorial Hospital to take the lead in Recreation Huts and since their erection they have been recognised as The Military Model Huts, and have been visited by many in order to get a general idea of their construction, and how they are run.'

The huts were generally the gifts of the local great and the good, and Major General Penton, Commander of the Plymouth Garrison was a great champion of the development.

'No words,' he once said, 'could ever express my thanks on behalf of the Hospitals to the Ladies and Gentlemen who so generously built and equipped these magnificent huts.'

The Mildmay Recreation Hut, Salisbury Road 4th Southern General Hospital.

Top: *Wounded soldiers being entertained by the Plymouth Press Bowling Club and magician Professor Johns.* Bottom: *Tea Party in the playground of Salisbury Road School.*

The Salisbury Road Hut was consequently known as Mildmay Hut (after the Major and Mrs Mildmay of Flete – they also sponsored a hut at Hyde Park) and at Ford it was the Lady Jackson Hut (after wife of the local MP, Sir John Jackson). Mount Priory at Plympton had a hut funded by cash gifts and various fund-raising activities.

The area's more affluent residents were also able to help out in other ways: Miss Bayly, of Torr, a great house then standing in isolation at the top of Hartley, gave at least one splendid 'Strawberry Tea' to the patients as well as organising weekly drives; there was a garden party at Mount Tavy, arranged by Colonel Fox, which included a Croquet Tournament for patients and visitors, another at Mount Gould Farm and many more besides.

The Press Bowling Club also organised events for the wounded, as did a number of other organisations, including The Plymouth Friends' Adult Group.

These diversions were not just for convalescing servicemen either. Earlier in the war Lord and Lady Seaton, of Beechwood, Plympton, had thrown a party for the first wave of refugees from Belgium.

Tea Parties were also arranged in the Hospital grounds, the erstwhile school playgrounds of the various institutions.

The cinema was another source of relaxation; the Hyde Park Hospital had its own projection team, but there were local cinemas too.

And then there was inhouse entertainment, some of it quite special; in May and June 1916, Lady Maud Warrender gave 'excellent concerts' at Salisbury Road and Hyde Park. On both occasions the celebrated amateur contralto, Lady Maud (who was a friend of Edward Elgar and had a song written for her by him) was accompanied by Mrs Mildmay of Flete and the Admiral's Band.

The concerts appear to have been a regular feature and in August 1917 we read that *'thrice during the month we were entertained by the Concert Party from Efford Camp, who also came on July 26.'*

The 'outstanding' concert that month, though, was *'that of Miss Phyllis Dare and her party on 17th. Miss Dare, besides singing herself and delighting everyone with her charming presence, also introduced Miss Pickup, the accomplished violinist, and Miss Warwick, the equally accomplished pianist. Two gentlemen also assisted with humorous songs and patter. Shall we ever again eat onions without remembering Mr Harry Farmer's amusing song? Major Wilson voiced our thanks and voiced them ourselves with three cheers.'*

The entertainments didn't just rely on outside talent, however, and as the occasion demanded nurses would turn themselves into 'Nigger' Troupes or Morris Dancers or whatever.

'The Morris Dancers went with great go and now we know what a disgraceful set of Flirts we have amongst us when caps and aprons are laid aside.

'Miss Davis, niece of Major Wilson, OC, charmed us all with her graceful dancing,' on that same evening.

On another occasion, Sister Fang and Nurse O'Byrne delighted their audience with Scottish and Irish dances.

Clockwise from top left: *Lady Maud Warrender; Phllis Dare (a national treasure); the nurse's 'Nigger' Troupe; Nurses in costume dress, at Ford House, 12 January 1917, nursing staff Morris Dancers at Salisbury Road.*

Top: *D Ward, Salisbury Road, Christmas 1916.*
Bottom: *Camel's Head School with tram lines being installed outside.*

'We ALL felt proud of ourselves at the end of the evening' wrote one, in-house, reviewer after the 1916 Salisbury Road Christmas concert, 'proud of our Hospital and everybody and everything in it, and if we are all here next year, we shall "Try Again".'

The reality was that no one knew how much longer the war would last. Going into the war in 1914 the Government had anticipated that it would be over by Christmas, while in Germany the Kaiser had told his troops that it would end before the trees lost their leaves.

Now already three Christmases had come and gone and there was still no end in sight, and all the while the casualties mounted on both sides. So did the number of facilities open to deal with them and the quality and quantity of transport used to ferry men from the field hospitals at the front to more solid and silent resources at home.

In May 1916 one of the latest generation of Great Western Railways' ambulance trains was put on display at Millbay. With 16 coaches the train could accommodate a team of 45 medical staff and almost 600 patients: 102 lying down, 472 sitting, with room for a further 18 infectious cases.

Built at GWR's Swindon Works, the train's gangways were wide enough to allow the movement of stretchers from a ward carriage to a treatment car and came with hot shower-baths and opening windows.

Guiding Plymouth's Mayor, Alderman Thomas Baker, and his deputy, Edward Blackall around the mobile unit the divisional GWR superintendent said a complete train could be built in just six weeks. As if to demonstrate the need for such a facility, the greatest strain on resources to date came at the end of 1916 as the costliest battle the world had ever seen was played out in the muddy fields of France.

The Somme Offensive began on the first day of July. A concentrated effort on the part of the Allies to drive the Germans back, it's estimated that following the instruction to leave the trenches and walk towards the German lines some 19,240 members of the British Fourth Army were killed and a further 38,230 were wounded.

All in all, over the course of the 141-day offensive, over 300,000 men were lost in the fighting, and a further 750,000 wounded, of whom almost half a million were British or Commonwealth servicemen.

As part of the attempt to deal with the influx of the 4th Southern, on 17 January 1917, a new outpost was created in what had been Camel's Head School.

Maristow Ward, South Devon and East Cornwall Hospital, Christmas 1914.

The patients come in ill one day,
And silent go to bed,
But when they go away they say -
"Three cheers for Camel's Head." '

Miss Laura Dack was the first Sister in Charge and in no time at all it was up to a full complement of staff and *'a comfy homely kind of feeling increases day by day.'*

Camel's Head School was newer even than Salisbury Road or Hyde Park, it had opened just five years before its conversion as a hospital and the tram route to it was created around the same time. It's very newness made it even more suitable as a medical facility, particularly as it came equipped with internal bathrooms.

Just five or six weeks after Camel's Head was commissioned, another local school, Paradise Road Elementary School was taken over as a section of Devonport Military Hospital, which was only a matter of yards to the east on the other side of the road.

The school had opened in 1907 and was immediately requisitioned on the outbreak of war in 1914. However, it was soon handed back to the Education Authority who re-opened it. But as the war intensified and more and more bed space had to be found, so the school was taken over again. The children were moved out to temporary accommodation in neighbouring Sunday Schools at St Barnabas and Belmont and on Monday 19 February 1917 the Paradise Road building became yet another hospital facility.

Just like the 4th Southern was forced to expand so too was Devonport Military. The school at Keppel Place (later Stoke Damerel High School), had been put into use as the 1st Sectional Hospital under the Red Cross, on 21 August 1914. Woodland Fort, the Durnford Hotel and Peverell Park Villa (in Outland Road) were also pressed into service, the latter as a hospital for Officers.

Johnston Terrace Elementary School was also taken over, as an extension to existing availability in the Royal Naval Barracks on the other side of the road.

There was also a Military Convalescent outpost at Derriford – essentially a canvas camp – men accommodated in tents.

This was in service by November 1917 and clearly was not ideal in winter: *'The men under canvas feel the bleakness of the weather and tents have been blown down,'* ran one press report.

Keppel Place Military Hospital, taken in the lower playground of the school. Hannah Bladon, Chief Cook, is in the centre of the group.
Opposite page top: Keppel Place School with a Red Cross flag superimposed by the publisher. Bottom: Paradise Road School/Hospital.

Passing the time, convalescent servicemen playing cards on the grass at Millbay VAD Hospital - note the Duke of Cornwall Hotel and Millbay Station in the background.

1917 had already seen a number of tents go up at Millbay as, on 22 May a new VA Hospital opened there.

Instituted at the request of the Military Authorities, Millbay was officially blessed by the Mayor of the newly amalgamated Three Towns, John Goldsmith.

Sited in the old Drill Hall, across the road from the Duke of Cornwall Hotel, the 'new' facility had 200 beds, divided into a number of wards created by the judicious use of partitions. There was also a kitchen and a recreation room.

During the summer of 1917 additional bed space was created by the erection of marquees on the spacious Recreation Ground alongside. There were, in total, 69 women listed as full-time, part-time, half-time, or occasional pantry staff. There were a similar number of ladies recorded as being nursing staff and at least 19 cooks. There were also ladies in charge of linen, two male orderlies - also volunteers – and a handful of female clerks and stewards, many of them bearing names that suggested that they were the wives and daughters (most of them were Misses) of the leading local figures of the day, including Lady Helen Murray, Miss Lopes and Miss Strode.

Certainly the Hospital was made ready and equipped with funds made available from local dignitaries, and established businesses, among them Lord and Lady St Levan, Sir Henry and Lady Alberta Lopes, the Earl and Countess of Mount Edgcumbe, Messrs Dingle, Spooner, Yeo, Popham, Tozer, Coryton, Bayly, Winnicott, Wakeham and Waring. The local papers also contributed, as did the Plymouth, Stonehouse and Devonport Tramway Company and the Australian Red Cross Society.

Well over 150 Voluntary Assistants helped out at Millbay during the two years it was operational. In that time 1,965 patients were admitted, with the most present on any one day being 253. Major George Sydney Strode Strode OBE, was the 57-year-old commandant of the operation. A former High Sheriff of Devon, Strode's family seat was the nearby Newnham Park. His main senior medical officer was Dr Edgar Down, while Mrs Unwin was the sister in charge.

Among the many VAD nurses who worked at Millbay, was Phyllis Martin, who arrived in June 1917, having enjoyed spells at Plympton and Exeter since she'd last operated in Plymouth. Phyllis had now completed at least two year's service and had just (4 June) been elected as an 'Associate' of the British Red Cross Society.

The contribution of the Australian Red Cross Society to Plymouth's latest ad hoc hospital reflected the fact that it was largely occupied by servicemen from the Southern Hemisphere. Among them 22-year-old Private Francis Murray Kay of the 21st Battalion of the Australian Imperial Force.

Kay, who was from Woolloomooloo, had signed up in Sydney in the summer of 1916, and left his homeland on 3 November, along with many of his countrymen, sailing for Europe onboard the HMAT (His Majesty's Austraian Transport) *Afric A19*.

The journey took many weeks and sadly, but fortunately for Kay and his comrades, the ship was sunk soon *after* reaching its destination, in February 1917.

Meanwhile Kay and his compatriots were soon at the heart of the action at Bullecourt, near the French city of Arras. Alongside them were units from Britain, Canada, Newfoundland and New Zealand. The battle of Bullecourt raged from 9 April to 16 May 1917, and minor gains were made at the expense of major casualties, in the region of 100,000 of them, with Private Kay, seemingly among them. The young, married, serviceman made multiple entries in Nurse Martin's autograph book, the first dated 11 July 1917. It read, somewhat enigmatically: *'He who would hit the mark, should aim higher, Every arrow that flies feels the attraction of the Earth.'*

A couple of weeks later, Nurse Martin, Private Kay, and two of his fellow Australians, Messrs Robin and Dunn, enjoyed a day out in the country, visiting the family home of one of two other young ladies – 'AW' and Violent Collins – who had also ventured out that day. Violet was an old friend of Phyllis Martin and her family home was a grand residence just outside Callington, named Newton Ferrers.

As convalescent excursions go this clearly was successful and a week or two later Private Kay added another entry in Nurse Martin's book, it read: *'Think of me now, think of me ever. Think of the days we had together.'*

Beneath it was stuck a second square of fabric, two half triangles, the colours of the 21 Battalion of the Australian Imperial Force.

As it happened Francis wasn't the only one of the three young Australians to fall under Nurse Martin's spell – another rhyme in her autograph book was entered by Private Robin, Kay's comrade from the Australian Imperial Force: *'Phyllis Martin is your name. Single is your station. Happy be the man, that makes the Alteration.'*

Top: *Staff and patients at Millbay VA Hospital, 1917, with Millbay Rinkeries building in the background.* Above left: *Francis Kay and Phyllis Martin at Newton Ferrers, 23 July 1917.* Right: *Messrs Dunn and Kay with Violet Collins and 'AW' on the same outing, at Callington.*

COMRADES IN ARMS

Not in the Prescription.

Not to be outdone, Dunn, who was a Corporal in the Australian Engineers, weighed in with his contribution, dated 14 August, it ran thus: *'Love is like a woman's glove, just a bit of kid!'*

Romantic attachments between patients and nurses were nothing new and while they weren't perhaps as frequent as many a patient has ever imagined or hoped for, they were certainly commonplace enough to spawn many a wartime picture postcard. And while Nurse Martin never married one of her convalescing comrades, one of her contemporaries, the aforementioned Sister Ethel Eastwood, who was at Salisbury Road when it opened as a hospital August 1914, did.

Fred Bladon was a Cornish boy who had joined the Devonshire Regiment, but was subsequently discharged through ill health. Relieved of front-line duties he was working as a medical orderly at Salisbury Road when he met Ethel.

The couple enjoyed a whirlwind romance and were married, in Newton Abbot, in October 1915. Two years later, in October 1917, the first of their three sons, Frederick, was born in Devonport. The couple were still in Plymouth in August 1919, when their second son, Geoffrey, was born.

Above: *Fred Bladon, medical orderly at Salisbury Road.*
Left: *Fred and his newly wedded wife Ethel Eastwood.*

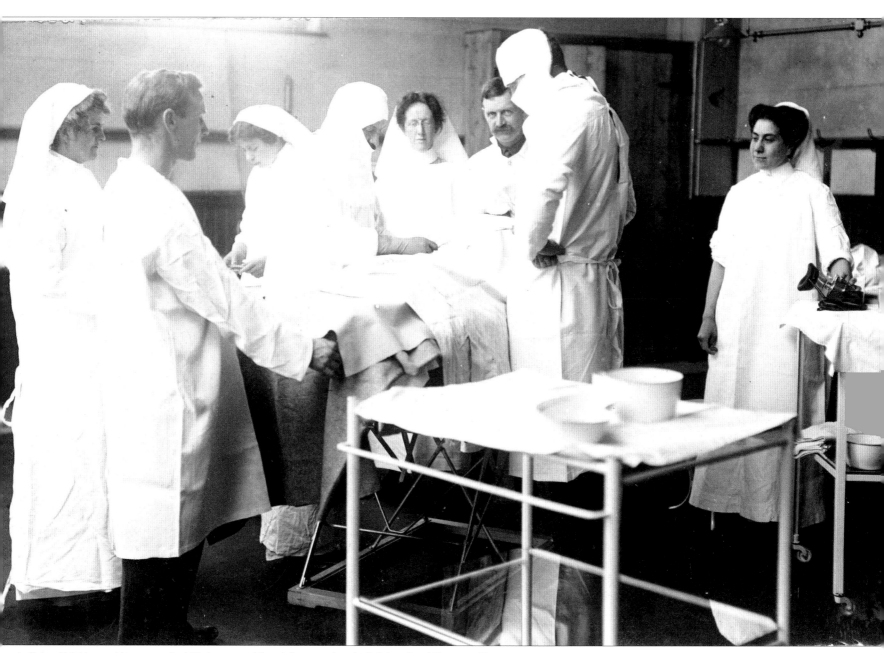

Lt-Colpnel Webber and his team – Fred Bladon, second from left – at work in the Salisbury Road Operating Theatre.

Top left: Col. Charles Faunce, who came to Plymouth District in 1916 as Assistant Director of Medical Services (ADMS). Faunce had gone to France with the original Expeditionary Force and took part in the retreat from Mons, the Battles of the Marne and Aisne, and in various actions in Flanders. Top right: Devonport-born, Edinburgh-educated Maj. Cheyne Wilson. Above: The 4th Southern NCOs on mobilization in 1914.

Romantic liaisons are nothing new at the workplace, whatever the circumstances, nor is the need to relax, and sport was actively encouraged among the medical staff.

In the summer of 1916 Sergeant Major Griffiths came up with the idea of holding 'Sports in Connection with the Hospital' and duly invited all the sections of the 4th Southern to send representatives.

A number of meetings followed and culminated in a successful afternoon of sport in the grounds of Plymouth College.

Each section was well represented and rivalry between them was keen. The RGA band provided a 'soothing influence' and the event was 'favoured with the presence of the Garrison Commander and Mrs Hickman – who kindly distributed the prizes.'

Major General Hugh Palliser Hickman had succeeded Major General Penton as Garrison Commander in Plymouth that year and from their earliest days here: '... showed a keen and devoted interest in the work of the hospitals.

'The Hospitals are frequently visited by General Hickman and he has been instrumental in having improvements made for the benefit and comfort of the wounded,' said the Gazette editor, adding, 'Mrs Hickman has been most energetic with the aid of her daughters, Mrs Kennedy and Mrs Stuben, in arranging concerts and entertainments for the wounded.' In particular 'she has organised a system of supplying comforts for the sick and wounded Australians.'

Lt-Col Webber, introducing Mrs Hickman, referred to the fact that it was 'the first meeting of the kind in the history of the unit, and all will agree with him in wishing it might not be the last, did that not involve the continuance of the war.'

Continue it most certainly did and early in November 1916, at a meeting held just to the east of Hyde Park Hospital in Mutley Barracks, a decision was taken to organise a joint Hyde Park/Salisbury Road football team:

'A subscription list was opened, and a liberal response to same was made by the officers of each section, giving the club a good send-off. Major W Cheyne Wilson was elected President and Captain EG Smith Vice-President.'

William Cheyne Wilson had been Company Officer of the 4th Southern since Salisbury Road had been set up, indeed he'd been with the 4th Southern since inception of the Territorial Force in 1898. Following the removal of the HQ to Ford House he became Medical

Top left: *Major General Hugh Palliser Hickman and his wife Beatrice Helen. Hickman succeeded Penton as Commander of the Plymouth Garrison in 1916. Above: Officers in charge and nurses from Hyde Park.*

Top right: *Major Reginald Henry Lucy and his wife. Lucy had come to Plymouth as House Surgeon to the S Devon & E Cornwall Hospital in 1891 and was in the first wave of 4th Southern Officers on the formation of the unit. Above: Camel's Head nurses.*

Top: *The Royal Army Medical Corps football team from Hyde Park and Salisbury Road.*
Bottom: *In the grounds of Devonport Military Hospital.*

Officer-in-charge. A popular and inspirational figure, the 50-year-old bachelor lived with a cook and housemaid in Wentworth Villas and had long been a significant figure in Plymouth's medical fraternity.

Described as *'a stickler for military etiquette'* he *'spent all his spare energy enthusing football matches, cricket especially, being an expert at same and a favourite "umpire".'*

It's not clear what other teams the newly established RAMC AFC played but the club managed to fulfil 16 fixtures before the season *'was abruptly brought to a close, owing to the majority of its playing members having to go on draft.'*

The team would appear to have been mainly made up of privates, with Pte Ricketts scoring 11 of the team's haul of 31 goals – of the rest only three were scored by a man of higher rank – Corporal Bray. The club's demise reflected the ever-increasing need for any fit young men to join the war effort.

By the late spring of 1917 the Americans had at last been persuaded to enter the war and on Tuesday 26 June the first contingent of American servicemen arrived in Plymouth.

As part of a bid to create a home from home the Americans opened a YMCA in Foresters' Hall and a Military Hospital at Laira under Colonel Dutcher.

As it happened the new facility turned out to be relatively short lived, unlike the Military Hospital on the northern bank of Stonehouse Creek, which had already been standing for over 100 years.

In use throughout the nineteenth century, it was extended during the Boer War, but would probably have closed soon afterwards had it not been for the outbreak of war again in 1914.

Among the many casualties to have been convalescing here during the Great War was the remarkable Reginald St John Battersby. Anxious to do his bit for King and Country Battersby had, like many young men, lied about his age in order take the King's Shilling.

Claiming to be a 19-year-old draper, when he was in fact four weeks shy of his 15th birthday, Battersby managed to secure an early commission and on 1 July 1916, the 16-year-old led a platoon into action at Serre, on the first day of the Battle of the Somme.

Wounded in the wrist and right thigh he was soon back at the front and in March 1917 he was wounded again and sent back to England a second time. On this occasion his left leg was amputated and, while convalescing at Devonport Military Hospital, he was told

Royal Naval Hospital c.1900 showing Zymotic blocks in the course of construction, with the Military Hospital (left) on the other side of the Creek.

he should resign his commission on the grounds of ill-health and wounds. However, Battersby, who was still under 18, replied that he would be getting an artificial leg sometime around Christmas and was *'quite fit in every other way,'* and *'wished to remain in until the end of the war.'*

He won the day and in March 1918 was passed fit for office work, which he did for the Royal Engineers in London for the remainder of the war.

Curiously enough, just as there had been a question mark over the old Military Hospital, so too had there been over the building on the southern side of the creek.

Regarded as the finest institution of its kind, and long-used as a template for hospital design, the Royal Naval Hospital at Stonehouse had been in use for over 150 years when war was declared in 1914. But at the end of the nineteenth century a site at Torpoint had been considered for a replacement facility; however, those plans hit *'technical difficulties'* and instead the decision was taken to upgrade the entire site. The old laundry was demolished and a new £8,000 steam laundry, fitted with state-of-the-art equipment, replaced it.

In 1900, a further £14,000 was invested in a series of Zymotic Blocks to deal exclusively with infectious cases, while another £15,000 was spent on the construction of two new blocks *'for the treatment of officers' cases only, one for surgical and the other for medical cases.'* Meanwhile, *'to meet the requirements of the sick berth staff a new block is to be erected on the south side of the hospital'* (*The Naval and Military Record and Royal Dockyards Gazette* 1898).

The journal also reported that around £3,000 was going to be spent on renovating the existing wards.

As part of that process the ward blocks were reconstructed and steel escape stairs and sanitary annexes were added; dividing walls between the wards were removed and the continuous colonnades linking the blocks were glazed over with upper corridors added on the north and part of the south side.

A few years later, around 1912–13, electronic lifts were built on to all of the blocks, all of which meant that at the start of the Great

Top: Sick-Berth attendants photographed at the back of Trafalgar Block c.1916.
Above: Royal Naval Hospital Medical Officers photographed outside the chapel c.1916.
Inset top: Reginald St John Battersby.

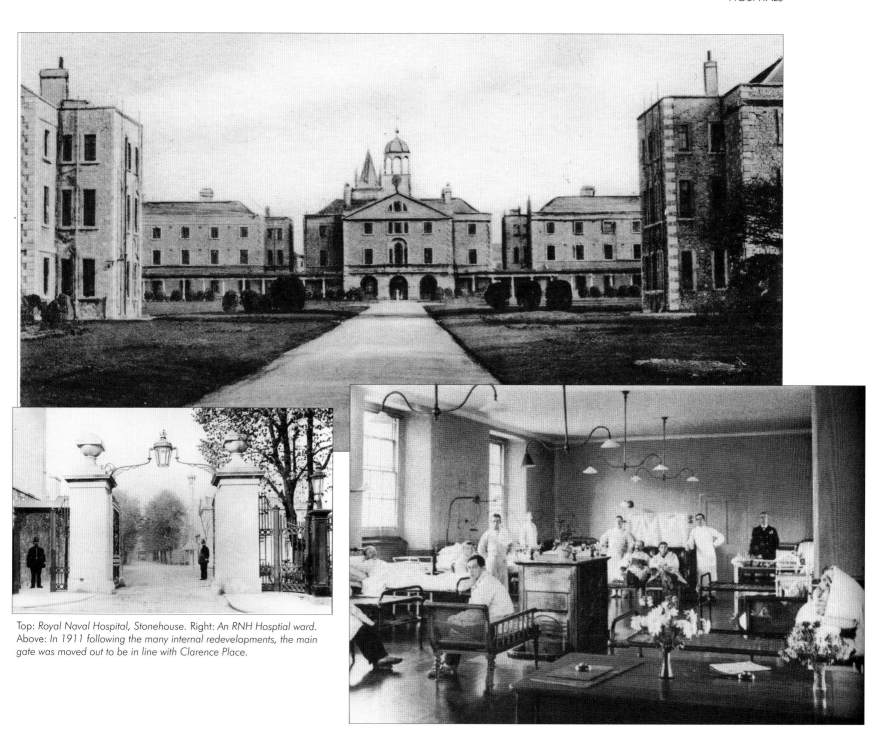

Top: *Royal Naval Hospital, Stonehouse*. Right: *An RNH Hosptial ward.*
Above: *In 1911 following the many internal redevelopments, the main gate was moved out to be in line with Clarence Place.*

Top: *Phyllis Martin with recuperating Australian servicemen at Millbay.*
Above: *Late summer 1917 - Messrs Dunn, Kay and Robins, three convalescing Australians, are entertained outside Miss Martin's home, No.7 The Esplanade.*

War, the Stonehouse complex, far from being an outdated Georgian development was as ready to deal with the demands of war as almost any other hospital in the country.

A large number of Belgian soldiers made up the first wave of incoming wounded in 1914 and the hospital was to remain fully occupied throughout the conflict. Indeed, the neighbouring school, in High Street, was used as an overflow for sleeping accommodation and two residences within the walls were taken over to provide additional accommodation for medical officers and nursing sisters.

In 1915 Nancy Astor presented the hospital with an Astor Hut and two years later a further building – the Canada Gift Hut – was donated by the British Sailors' Relief Fund, Canada.

William Henry Norman was the Surgeon-General in charge in 1914 and on completion of his three-year term he was succeeded by the first in a long line of Surgeon Rear-Admirals, William Wenmoth Pryn.

Pryn, in turn was knighted when he retired in 1919.

Such appointments tended generally to be relatively short. In 1917 Lt-Colonel Webber – the Administrator of the 4th Southern – was called away to do duty in the 56th General Hospital in France, where he was to have charge of a 100-bed facility.

"It is an open secret,' reported the *Gazette*, 'that he had applied for a transfer abroad some months ago, feeling that he would like to do more active work in the service of his country. The call came on August 8th and in a few hours he reported at Southampton and soon found himself on the shores of our great Ally.'

In the same issue of the *Gazette* we learned that Sister Macauley, Staff Nurses Murphy, Nightingale and Rich and VAD Nursing member Chamberlin had also all left the 4th Southern in Plymouth for Foreign Service. Meanwhile, Sister Button, Staff Nurses Beedle, Brown and Dickson, from Salonika, and Lewis, Murdoch and Pericho, had arrived in their stead, along with VADs Miners, Seabrook and Whitaker.

It was by no means an unusual month and just as there were comings and goings of wounded and convalescing servicemen there were comings and goings of staff. Plymouth certainly saw plenty of uniformed movement across the war years: although it was barely open for two years, the temporary hospital at Millbay saw almost 2000 patients pass through its ad hoc and canvas quarters, 253 of them arriving on one day alone!

Even the much more modest outpost at Plympton, with not much more than 50 beds, accommodated over 1250 patients between May 1915 and March 1919 when it finally closed.

Factor in the other Hospitals open across the Three Towns during the war and it's no great leap of arithmetic to work out that tens of thousands of servicemen spent time here recuperating in their Convalescent Blues.

The idea of creating a bespoke uniform for servicemen recovering in hospital was not new in 1914, it had been adopted in the Boer War for men returning from South Africa. However, because of the numbers involved, it became a far greater problem during the Great War.

Men in what were virtually outdoor ill-fitting pyjamas were a common sight in Plymouth.

Handed out to the men in place of what could often be lice-infected, muddy, mouldy, manky front-line battle-dress, these blue flannel/flannelette combinations had a pale collar, and came with a white shirt and red tie. The effect was undoubtedly distinctive, and clearly indicated that its wearer was back from the battlefields and was not a candidate for the white feather of cowardice that some handed out to men of a certain age if they weren't in uniform. It also helped to maintain discipline.

Little variation was permitted, apart from being allowed to wear your own hat – something that instantly distinguished certain of our colonial cousins and allowed for differentiation between regiments.

However, the uniforms did have a number of drawbacks: Firstly they were fairly uniform in terms of size – although not quite 'one size fits all', they were a long way from being individually tailored and men frequently had to 'flap' or 'cuff' their trouser legs and jacket sleeves to get them to a sensible length.

Secondly, rather like most pyjamas, convalescent blues had no pockets, partly an economic measure and partly because the men weren't supposed to hold money while in hospital; it was assumed they had adequate food, drink (strictly non-alcoholic) and entertainment. This, of course, made socialising difficult, although it couldn't be denied that the outfit also attracted a great deal of sympathetic admiration from all sections of society.

Hosting, entertaining, feeding and fund-raising on behalf of these battle-scarred heroes were popular pastimes for those anxious to do their bit on the home front.

Top: *Boer war casualties at Devonport Military Hospital in their Convalescent Blues, in 1901.* Bottom: *Wounded men being treated at the Press Bowling Club in 1915.* Right: *One size fits all!*

"POOR MAN! AND HAVE YOU BEEN WOUNDED
AT THE FRONT?"

"NO, MA'AM—— AT THE BACK!"

"Pauvre homme, c'est sur le front que vous
avez été blessé?"

"Non, Madam——au contraire!"

A popular picture postcard from Donald McGill. Many such cards were captioned in French and English.

Officers, however, were exempt from the requirement to wear the blues, head to toe, they were instead provided with an armband emblazoned with red royal crown. Even so this didn't make them exempt from certain indignities - as a humorous piece in the *Gazette* purporting to have been written many years into the future, noted:

'The excavations of Professor Widdel on the site of the medieval town of Plymouth proceed apace' and discoveries were made a "Schospital" – so called because of the difficulty of determining whether it was an educational or medicinal establishment.

Among the documents found was a 'set of Penal Laws, entitled "Rules for the Guidance of Convalescent Officers".

The old word "convalescent" has become obsolete in the mists of time. From various indications it was presumed that it applied to men injured in and broken in the tribal conflicts that raged from 1914 onwards, and for whom, it is believed, the large number of establishments called "Hospitals and Homes" were built. But in the light of new discovery we see that "convalescent" was a term synonymous with criminal, or evil-doer.

Let us examine the penal code itself. At once we realise the savage brutality of those black days. The wretched 'convalescent' was outlawed and forced to wear a blue band as his badge of shame. Professor Widdel believes that is was marked on the bare arm with woad, or perhaps tattooed in. Thus branded, the unhappy creature was deprived of drink. This is most clearly stated. We may picture him limping along begging of passers-by for a taste of beer, or a nip of whisky, but everywhere being harshly repulsed by reason of his unmistakable band. We may imagine his pale, drawn face, pressed against the window of some public-house where within are people happily drinking, oblivious of his agony. We may see him staggering alone, everywhere refused until he is compelled to quench his thirst with water or some equally noxious liquid, drinks that our wiser times have for centuries stigmatised as unfit from human consumption. Well were those days called the "Dark Ages".

To increase the rigour of the punishment, these "convalescents" had to walk barefoot! For regulation 2, distinctly forbids the use of footgear, shoes being particularised. Held in universal detestation they were compelled to wear gloves lest respectable citizens be contaminated by their touch. This survival of caste law is of great interest to archaeologists.

At this point we come upon a portion of the code that makes us realise, as nothing else can, the unbelievable cruelty of the time, For these convalescents were compelled to carry with them the instrument of their own chastisement.

"Officers must carry canes." With what a thrill of horror do we read this. Think of it! An outlaw is peacefully walking along enjoying the air and doing harm to no one. Suddenly a brutal warder sees him smoking a pipe, or wearing a soft hat, or some other trivial offence against the harsh law. He springs on the man, takes his cane and in a few moments the quivering air resound with the appalling shrieks of his helpless victim! Probably his chastiser was one of the dreaded VADs, (Buttu translates this as Vengeance And Discipline) the sinister records of which Society occasionally darken the records of the early XXth century.

We live, thank Heaven, in a happier age today and our hearts go out to those miserable souls, the "convalescent officers", whatever their crimes and these must have been great, we cannot but feel that by their inhumanity, their oppressors placed themselves in an even lower level of wickedness.

Well was it that the great cataclysm of AD 1920 wiped out the civilization of the period with its darkness, its crime, and its deep shame as evidenced in these inhuman laws.'
'R'

The piece was written in the summer of 1917 and it's interesting to note that 'R' didn't foresee an end to the war until 1920.

Clearly there were drawbacks to wearing evidence of the Convalescent Blues during the daytime for officers and for men, some more serious than others, however by night, Officers had a distinct advantage: they were entitled to a personal clothing allowance and could choose from silk pyjamas gifted by members of the public and aid-agencies.

Whether the men were wearing silk night attire or ill-fitting flannelette one thing was certain – a night in the hospital was far more comfortable than a night on the battle-line.

PEVERELL PARK OFFICERS' HOSPITAL, PLYMOUTH

An interesting group of officers who are in the Peverell Park Hospital at Plymouth. The names, reading from left to right, are: Back row—Lieut. S. F. Shingleton, R.F.A.; 2nd Lieut. R. A. Shedden, Leicester Regiment; 2nd Lieut. W. Dingley, D.C.L.I.; 2nd Lieut. C. V. Rouse, London Regiment; Lieut. H. Binks, Sherwood Foresters; 2nd Lieut. H. A. Mohen, R.F.A.; Lieut. W. Collet, Leicester Regiment; 2nd Lieut. H. Jeacock, Worcesters. Middle row—2nd Lieut. E. J. Davis, R.F.A.; Captain Brett-Young, R.A.M.C.; Captain A. Walker, R.A.M.C. (O.C. Hospital); Sister Hobhouse; Captain G. W. Fry, Gloucesters; Captain A. E. Legg, Worcesters; 2nd Lieut. A. T. Brooks, Devons. Seated on ground— 2nd Lieut. A. C. B. Wellacott, Royal Inniskilling Fusiliers; 2nd Lieut. N. E. Farr, Seaforth Highlanders; 2nd Lieut. J. R. Stopford, Rifle Brigade

Above: Wounded Officers of Colonial Regiments on the bridge of a tender being landed 'somewhere on the South-West Coast' (i.e. Plymouth).

Top: *Plymouth Friends' Adult School entertaining wounded soldiers and sailors.*
Bottom: *Plymouth Nurses parade for the Mayor in Guildhall Square.*

'It is Winter again in England,
As usual, beastly cold,
But I wouldn't change my quarters
For one hundredweight of gold.
I am lying snug in hospital,
A "Home away from Home,"
And back to muddy Flanders,
No more I wish to roam.

Gee! It's great to be out of the trenches,
Away from the shot and the shell,
Snug in Hyde Park Hospital,
Praying you won't get well.
Yes, it's fine to think you're out of it,
And it's good to be able to say
"Though you're swinging the lead in Blighty,"
You've done your bit in the fray.

Now this apology for poetry is finished,
I've had my little say
About the finest place I've been in,
For many and many a day,
And should I return to the trenches,
Back to the same old grind,
I'll remember Hyde Park Hospital,
And the friends I've left behind.'

So wrote DGW in early 1917, expressing sentiments echoed across the world. The Great War was a truly bloody conflict in which more than 10 million servicemen were killed, more than 20 million wounded and goodness knows how many mentally scarred for life. Of that number over one million of the fatalities were from Britain and the Empire with over two million wounded.

Shell-fire and shrapnel were the main destructive elements, accounting for over 1.5 million casualties. Over 40,000 of these casualties lost one or more limbs and some 65,000 suffered head, eye and facial injuries. Meanwhile, the psychological damage from witnessing these horrors and living under the relentless assault of booming high explosives was incalculable.

As early as September 1914, just weeks into the war, wounded servicemen at Salisbury Road, who had seen action in the Great War and the South African conflict: *'assured the younger soldiers that the "Boer business was nothing in comparison with that we have had in France".'*

There was no comparison with anything that had taken place anywhere on the planet before, hence the initial difficulties the authorities had coming to terms with what would come to be known as 'Shell Shock.'

Symptoms ranged from extreme tiredness, to speech difficulties, to uncontrollable shakes, and often came with no sign at all of physical injury. At first doctors thought that the condition may be due to shock waves being sent out by the exploding shells, damaging the nerves and brain tissue, hence they dubbed it 'Shell Shock.' A few doctors, however, began to think the damage may have been more psychological than physiological.

Not everyone was that understanding however. Sympathy was rare and given that the main role of the medical staff was to get men back in action as quickly as possible, typical methods of dealing with 'Shell Shock' victims included solitary confinement, electric shocks, disciplinary treatment, shaming and generally appealing to a man's sense of masculinity and urging him not to be so weak.

Women, even those working at the front and exposed to the noise and horrors at close quarters, were not even considered as potential victims themselves.

Meanwhile among the regular local advertisers in the *4th Southern General Hospital Gazette* there were ads for various products that were clearly targeting 'Shell Shock' sufferers: Bynogen *'Recommended in Mental and Nervous Exhaustion, for all Enfeebled Conditions,'*; Fry's Cocoa *'It is the most resourceful beverage at all times - resists exhaustion, stimulates immediately and is a permanent strengthener'*; Allenburys Diet made with boiling water - *'Enfeeblement of nervous energy is produced by overstrain rendering the sufferer incapable of sustained effort during the day and sleeplessness at night'*; and most pointedly of them all Virol: *'War Nerves, Are you "run down," "jumpy," irritable, and always anxious about the future? - Virol is nerve food with no added chemical "whips".'*

The use of emotive terms like *'enfeeblement'*, *'mental exhaustion'* and *'war nerves'* was of little solace to the sufferers of Shell Shock and it's small wonder that many struggled to cope with society's view of them.

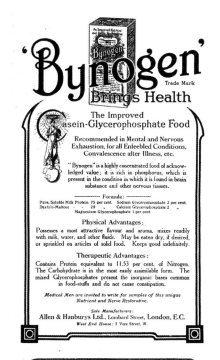

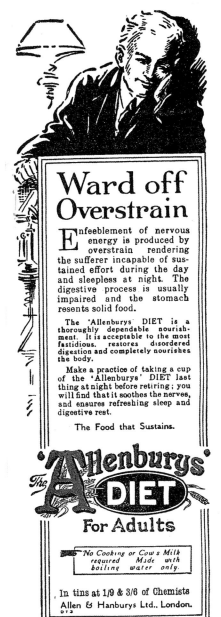

From time to time there were distressing reports in the local papers of men who couldn't cope, some quite early on in the war:

Mind Unhinged by Experiences at the Front

'An inquest was held at Devonport yesterday on the body of Andrew Burgoyne, a Private in the 1st Devon Regiment who cut his throat in a London and South Western Train between Exeter and Plymouth. The deceased, before re-joining his regiment, was a skilled worker at Devonport Dockyard and resided in Plymouth. The jury returned a verdict of suicide and that his mind was unhinged by his experiences at The Front' (2 January 1915).

A fortnight later 45-year-old George Thompson, a retired naval stoker who'd been called up for service on 4 August 1914, but was subsequently invalided home with paralysis, spent a month in the Royal Naval Hospital, and was suffering from depression; he also cut his own throat. He left a wife Rosina and two daughters Beatrice 21, and Winifred 16.

Even after the war had ended there were still cases:

Ford Hospital Tragedy: Shell Shock Victim's Death

'Gunner Inglin RGA was found dead in the bathroom at Ford Military Hospital last night. He had a wound in the throat and a blood stained razor was discovered by the side of the bath. The deceased came from France and was admitted to the hospital a few days since. He was suffering from shell shock.' (22 February 1919)

It's been estimated that by the end of the war over 80,000 servicemen or ex-servicemen were struggling to cope with everyday life. Fortunately for many in Devon there was one pioneering doctor, Dr Arthur Hurst, at Seal Hayne, Newton Abbot, who took a different view to most of his contemporaries and through a sympathetic programme that included hypnosis, massage and dietary adjustments was said to be able to 'cure' 90 percent of the cases that came to him, in just one session.

Hurst's progressive treatments not only included those administered in the hospital, but also, on one occasion, saw him involve a number of patients recreating a full-scale battle scenario on Dartmoor.

The 4th Southern sent most of its 'Shell Shock' victims out to Mount Tavy Auxiliary Hospital on the edge of Dartmoor near Tavistock.

Those men who didn't respond well to treatment and who were lucky enough not to be Court Martialed for cowardice – a rare occurrence – tended locally to be sent to somewhere like the Plymouth Lunatic Asylum at Bittaford, just beyond Ivybridge.

Post war there was also the former wartime Army camp at Wearde Farm which became the Saltash Hardening Centre in 1923 – after a period as a Queen Alexandra Convalescent Centre.

In addition to a variety of roles as a training/recreation area, Dartmoor proved useful in another capacity during the war - as a significant source of sphagnum moss.

With so many walking wounded, supplies of cotton and gauze dressings were quickly stretched and, in 1915, after a little experimentation, sphagnum moss was found to be useful as a dressing as typically the dead plants can hold around 20 times as much liquid as their dry weight.

Volunteers recruited to collect the moss were given special badges and large quantities were cleaned and thousands of dressing each week were prepared at the Prince of Wales' factory at Princetown (the Prince gave the buildings and bore all costs involved).

Of course the Great War saw a great deal of improvisation and innovation, and although he didn't practice in the county, the pioneering work of the man widely regarded as the father of plastic surgery certainly benefitted at least one local man.

Harold Gillies was 32 when he joined the Royal Army Medical Corps and while in service in France witnessed a couple of medics skilled in dealing with facial injuries. On his return to England, Gillies managed to persuade Sir William Arbuthnot-Lane, RAMC's chief surgeon, to set up a reconstructive surgery in Aldershot (Arbuthnot had operated on many prominent figures, including politicians and members of the Royal Family and was the top surgeon of his day).

That facility was soon outgrown and in June 1917 Arbuthnot oversaw the opening of Queen Mary's Hospital in Sidcup and it was there that Gillies performed the first example of plastic surgery on 26-year-old Warrant Officer, Walter Yeo, from Plymouth.

Yeo had sustained terrible facial injuries at the Battle of Jutland on 31 May the previous year, while manning the guns on HMS *Warspite*. In August 1917 he had a skin transplantation, with a novel 'tubed pedicle' flap. It is thought to have been the first of more than 11,000 operations that were carried out on over 5,000 men over the next few years.

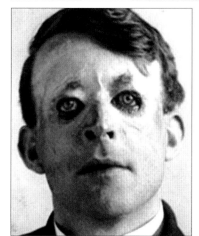
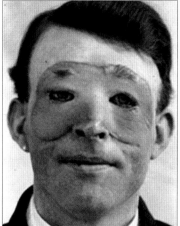

Top: *Mount Tavy*. Middle: *Sphagnum Moss cleaning at Princetown*. Bottom: *Walter Yeo from Plymouth with (right) his pioneering skin transplant.*

HMS Warspite laid down in Devonport Dockyard in 1912, launched in November 1913 and commissioned in 1915..

DOCKYARD AND WARSHIPS

Laid down in Devonport Dockyard in October 1912, the Queen Elizabeth-class battleship, HMS *Warspite*, was launched a little over a year later, on 26 November 1913 and commissioned in 1915 under the command of Captain Edward Phillpotts.

Designed by the celebrated naval architect, Sir Philip Watts, *Warspite* followed in the tradition of HMS *Dreadnought*, the ground-breaking vessel that Watts had been encouraged to produce by Admiral Sir John 'Jacky' Fisher some six or seven years earlier.

Warspite was itself particularly innovative, in that she was oil, not coal, fired and, in response to rumours that the Germans were producing warships with 14-inch guns, was equipped with hitherto untested 15-inch weapons.

The First Lord of the Admiralty, Winston Churchill, personally approved the changes: *Warspite's* oil-fired engines were said to confer a distinct 3-knot advantage over her peers and made her one of the fastest, and most fearsome, battleships in the world.

Meanwhile, to give an idea of just how fast technology was moving, it had only been a couple of years earlier that the Admiralty had spent £40,000 on a new coaling depot in the Keyham Extension.

In the grand scheme of things however that was small beer compared to the more than £4,000,000 the Admiralty had spent on the Keyham Extension overall at the dawn of the twentieth century.

This page and opposite, work in progress, North Yard Extension takes shape – 1902–05.

The Keyham Extension did much to enhance Devonport's national and international reputation. This colossal project involved almost 3,500 men and led to the development of a new residential area at Weston Mill. All told it took ten years to complete and incorporated over two million cubic feet of Cornish and Norwegian granite and over 200,000 tons of cement. It also saw a great deal of shingle and sand taken from the beaches of Hallsands and Beesands on the South Devon coast, a move by the contractor that ultimately undermined those villages and saw many of the houses there being swept away. At one point, over 1,000 tons of material was being dredged from Hallsands and landed at the Dockyard every day.

Not surprisingly this was the greatest extension ever in the Yard's 200-year history: encompassing an area of over 110 acres, it effectively doubled the size of the Devonport facility, being more or less equal in area to the existing Keyham Yard and the original Dockyard together.

Two new basins were created: one a 10-acre tidal facility, the other a 35.5-acre closed basin with a 240-yard-long entrance lock that could double as a dry dock. There were also three further dry docks, or graving docks, of similar length, between the two basins.

It was a truly major feat of engineering and in order to create the sprawling new complex a giant coffer dam, extending almost one and a half miles along the tidal side, was created to allow the men to work the muddy floor and eastern bank of the Tamar.

Sir John Jackson, who at the age of 25 had won the contract to build part of Stobcross Docks in Glasgow (in 1876), was the successful tenderer for the work. Jackson was a remarkable man. In 1894, having won another contract to work on the Manchester Ship Canal, he managed to complete his part of that undertaking in two-thirds of the contract time, a feat that led to him being awarded a knighthood.

The first vessel to be docked in the new Extension was HMS *Hibernia*. Devonport-built and launched on 17 June 1905, the *King Edward VII*-Class battleship – named after the Roman name for Ireland – was eased into No.9 Dock by three Dockyard tugs on 10 August 1906, although the new facility wasn't formally opened until Thursday 21 February the following year when the Prince and Princess of Wales entered the basin in the Port Commander's ship, *Vivid*.

The Royal Navy put on the best show it could, as the Royal couple were conveyed up the Hamoaze from Royal William Yard:

'As the *Vivid* approached the Dock, the caisson or bar to the entrance to the lock slowly receded and left the way clear, with the exception of a guard rope which was ornamented by red, white and blue ribbons, the cutting of which, by the *Vivid*, was the first part of the Opening Ceremony.

'Amid the booming of guns the vessel passed smoothly and majestically through the ornamental barrier at 12 noon, going through the entrance lock into the great enclosed basin by the side of which a reception Pavilion had been prepared, where the principal ceremony of the day was to take place.

'The Royal Party were received by the Commander in Chief - Sir Lewis Beaumont. A large number of distinguished guests had already assembled, including the Lords of the Admiralty, the Lord Lieutenant of the Country (Earl Fortescue), the Bishop of Exeter, and Sir John Jackson.

The Lord Lieutenant welcomed the Prince and Princess of Wales, and Sir John Jackson, the contractor, gave a brief account of the works.'

Jackson also presented the Prince with a gold casket containing an illuminated plan of the extension on vellum.

The Prince of Wales, concluded his reply by thanking the Lords of the Admiralty who had invited him, with the King's permission, to name the basin, the 'Prince of Wales Basin'.

In the evening there was a grand MIlitary Tattoo at Mount Wise with the massed bands of the six battalions that were in garrison, along with 200 sailors from HMS *Cambridge* carrying lighted torches.

Conspicuous by their absence however, were the Mayor and Corporation of Devonport who had snubbed the event, on the grounds that the Admiralty had deemed it 'impracticable' for their Royal Highnesses to drive through the streets of Devonport.

Top left: *Launch* of the Hibernia. Bottom: *Vivid sails into the new Keyham Extension.*
Opposite page: Vivid *entering and leaving the newly named 'Prince of Wales Basin.'*

It had been quite a different story almost four years earlier when the couple came to inspect the work in progress on the great Extension. On that occasion *'thousands of flags waved in the breeze, stretching along and across the roadway'*, as the Prince and Princess were driven across Stonehouse Bridge, *'and thousands of people shouted and waved their hats and handkerchiefs in welcome'*.

Their programme stretched across several days culminating, on Thursday 23 July 1903, with the launch of HMS *King Edward VII* - the battleship that had been named after Prince George's father who had laid the keel for the vessel the previous year.

The ship was the largest ever built at Devonport: *'and the biggest battleship ever constructed for any navy. The weight of metal which the Princess sent gliding down the ways into the harbour was no less than 6,100 tons. From the royal platform, over which the huge ram projected, the bulk of the ship seemed enormous.*

'The scene was dazzlingly brilliant, the platform and enclosures being crowded with officers in uniform and ladies in gay costumes, while every ugly detail of the yard was hid by a profusion of bunting.'

The Prince and Princess arrived at 3.15 and were received by Admiral Henderson, superintendent of the yard. Christening the ship with a bottle of colonial wine, the Princess cried, "Success to the King Edward VII".'

Top: *The Prince and Princess of Wales at the launch of HMS* King Edward VII *- 23 July 1903.* Middle and bottom: *the ship slips into the Hamoaze.*
Opposite page: *'From the royal platform, over which the huge ram projected, the bulk of the ship seemed enormous'* (Doidge's Annual 1904).

King Edward VII and Queen Alexandra at the launch of HMS Queen. Opposite page: HMS Queen slides into the Hamoaze: 'The noise of the cheering and the whistling was even more deafening than usual; and beneath the shrill scream came the majestic roar of a royal salute from the port guardship.'

When King Edward VII visited the Three Towns in March 1902 with his Queen, Alexandra, it was very much an event of local and national interest, as it was the Royal couple's first major public event since the end of the mourning period after the death of his mother in January 1901. Furthermore, the King had yet to enjoy his official Coronation (the event planned for June 1902 was postponed until August on account of the King's indisposition). That, of course, had no bearing on the rapturous reception the Royal couple enjoyed when they arrived in Devonport at a densely crowded King's Road (re-named in honour of the royal visit).

The King was introduced to the Mayor of Devonport, Edgar Leest, by Lord St Levan. The outburst of enthusiasm from the crowds packed on the hillside was extremely hearty and unanimous, and seemed to impress their Majesties, as a silver casket with the official introduction was presented to the King.

In his formal reply the King said: *'It has interested me much to see the vast dockyards, arsenals, and barracks of Devonport, which are of such importance to the strength and welfare of my naval and military forces, and give employment to so many inhabitants of the town, which has grown rapidly around them.'*

He added, *'I pray heartily that your municipality may continue to grow in efficiency and prosperity.'*

The following day, Saturday 8 March 1902, Queen Alexandra, with the King at her side, launched the dockyard's latest warship:

'The Queen looked radiant as she advanced to name the ship,' ran one contemporary report. *'She raised the bottle once and flung it against the bow of the ship, but failed to break it. A little more vigour in the second instance was successful. The wine ran down over the steel plates; the Queen said, "I name this ship the Queen. God speed her and bless all who sail in her".'*

Launch of HMS Minotaur, 1906.

Devonport Dockyard at that time was very busy. Of the Admiralty bases only Portsmouth came close in terms of building battleships and somewhat remarkably they were all to survive the war.

HMS *Minotaur* however, launched in 1906, almost didn't make it. During trials in the Sound there was an explosion on board and five of her crew were injured.

A few years later, on Saturday 24 August 1907, HMS *Temeraire* slipped into the Hamoaze in what *Doidge's Annual* described as 'one of the most successful of all the series of ship launches that have taken place since the Dockyard was established over 200 years ago.' The Countess Fortescue performed the Christening Ceremony, taking a 'flower-encircled bottle of wine' which was dashed against the bow of the vessel with such vigour that it was smashed to atoms – 'and as the wine fell in a shower on the ground the Countess named the vessel "Temeraire" and wished "Success to her and all who shall sail in her".'

The Dockyard Choir under the command of the organist, Mr Hele, were present and led the singing of the hymn *Eternal Father, strong to save.*

'The Battleship, which was laid down on January 1st, had taken 7 months and 24 days in the course of construction. She represents the most up-to-date specimen of naval architecture afloat, and, what is especially significant, the launching of the *Temeraire* places Great Britain in the unique position of having three of the Dreadnought class afloat.'

Right: *Three images taken at the launch of the Temeraire, 1907, with Countess of Fortescue (photograph on left) officiating in the presence of Earl Fortescue, Admiral Beaumont, Admiral Barlow, Major-Gen Sir John Leach, Mr EA Richards and the Rev GH Marwood.*

Top: *Dockyard fitters.* Bottom: *RNEC students in the Smithy.*

'Her construction,' continued the *Doidge's Annual* report, 'reflects great credit on all engaged in building this great "Leviathan of the deep. Most notably, the Constructor, Mr A E Richards, and Messrs JT Ottewell and WT Mason, Foremen of the Yard".'

An obvious consequence of all the Dockyard expansion and the building of ever bigger battleships was that more and more men were taken on to work in the Yard, necessitating the construction of new Central Offices in 1911. This move was soon followed by the erection of three new dining-halls, the largest of which could seat over 1,500 men and serve up a main course – meat and two veg – plus a pudding for the princely sum of 5d (about 2p).

The new dining arrangements were to prove invaluable during the war as they were able to serve many thousands of troops either embarking or disembarking at the Dockyard, as well provide servicemen's wives and children with free hot meals.

There were many other improvements made to working conditions as well, notably with regard to communication across the whole of the yard as well as with the internal travel arrangements and the Dockyard railway: eight new locomotives were delivered into the Yard between 1914 and 1919 and in April and May 1915 new platforms, each around 400ft long, were constructed around No.5 Wharf.

'Some indication of the usage of these platforms is gained from instructions on the handling of horses by train issued in June 1915. Water troughs were provided and at No.6 Wharf a rail for tethering 100 horses. Troops returning from combat required Hospital trains, and these also used the platforms, but were followed by a water tank wagon from which disinfectant was sprayed onto the track.' (Burkhalter)

The Dockyard was undoubtedly undergoing massive transitions in every department. By the 1890s the Yard had gone over entirely to making steel vessels – and not wooden hybrids – and in the five years up to 1910 the total tonnage of ships built at Devonport was an impressive 144,000 an increase of 57,000 tons on the previous five-year period, which in turn was considerably more than the 61,000 tons and 64,000 tons up to 1900 and 1895 respectively, and an enormous increase on the 32,000 tons of metal up to 1890.

By 1914 the number of men working in the Yard had risen to around 12,300 men. During the course of the war that figure grew to over 20,000 men and some women too.

Not since the Napoleonic Wars 100 years earlier had the Devonport money-go-round been so well oiled. However, just as there had been a shortage of servicemen back then, so there was again now. Previously, Press Gangs had been the Government's preferred instrument of recruitment, now it was Moral Pressure and, from May 1916 onwards, Conscription.

Before that, and indeed after that, there were many angry fingers pointed at some of the younger fitter, Dockyard workers – among those pointing was Sergeant Spencer John Bent, who, in the first few months of the war, was awarded the highest and most prestigious award for gallantry – the Victoria Cross.

The 23-year-old East Lancashire Regiment drummer, had taken command of his platoon when his commanding officer, platoon sergeant and various other colleagues had been struck down. Having taken charge, Bent and his platoon held their position in heavy fighting near Le Gheer in Belgium and he was hailed a hero. Sergeant Bent was subsequently paraded around the country to help with the national recruitment drive and it was at a rally at Millbay Drill Ground that he suggested that there were many men in the Dockyard wearing war badges who could enlist if they desired to do so.

The statement was received with much applause which suggested that *'many in the town share Sergeant Bent's opinion'*.

Clearly there was a common perception at the time that the men in the yard were earning good money, working long hours of overtime, in warm, dry conditions and able to go home at night. A far cry from the men who were stuck in damp, wet, rat-infested trenches, their feet rotting in their boots, their bodies alive with lice and their lives on the line on a daily basis.

The situation, however, was far from simple, as CH Petty was keen to point out in a letter to the local press: *'Let me assure Sergeant Bent, as one who is in a better position to judge Dockyard men than he is, that, since the outbreak of war, hundreds of these men have applied for permission to enlist. This they have been refused and others have been deterred from making similar applications. In the event of compulsory military service being adopted by this country I am convinced that any in the Dockyard who are called upon to serve would do so willingly.'*

The correspondent went on to add: *'Does Sergeant Bent realise*

12 NOON AT DEVONPORT DOCKYARD GATES.

that since August 1914 the Dockyards have added many fine ships to our glorious Navy and they keep others in repair and ready for action. But for the strength of this Navy our Dockyard men are maintaining and increasing, Sergeant Bent and others would perhaps have had an opportunity of winning their distinctions on British soil instead of the Continent.

Does he realise that in the event of a large Naval engagement, which is always a possibility, thousands of those he accuses of shirking, would be required to make good the damage which the enemy would inflict on each ship and that the men are really being held in reserve by the Admiralty in view of this possibility.'

Clearly it was an uncomfortable situation for many, which was precisely why the war badges were issued in the first place – to show that these were men in reserved occupations and that they were indeed *'doing their bit for the country.'* Furthermore, if they ignored the Admiralty dictate and took the King's shilling they were almost certain to jeopardise their chances of ever getting work again in the Dockyard in the event of their safe return.

As it transpired, a great deal of the Dockyard's resources were given over to repair and renewal rather than new building, although there was a certain amount of submarine work undertaken, as well as the conversion of a number of so-called Q Ships.

H.M. SUBMARINE A7.
SUNK OFF PLYMOUTH WITH ALL HANDS JANUARY 16TH 1914.

Above and inset: The ill-fated submarine A7.

Submarines were new to warfare in 1914, but by no means new to the Navy or to Devonport. Indeed, *Holland 1*, the Royal Navy's first submarine had only been launched some 12 years before war was declared, but curiously enough was already on her way to the breaker's yard in 1913 when she foundered off the Eddystone and sank.

Eight years earlier, *A4*, one of the subsequent class of naval submarines was sunk at Devonport after her ventilators had been flooded by the wash of a passing warship. That same year, 1905, *A8* was on a routine training exercise in the Sound when four of her crew, who had been standing on the vessel's casing, were swept into the water when the submarine's stern suddenly kicked up and the craft swiftly slid below the surface of the water.

The conning tower had been open and although tugs and divers were soon at the scene, rescue operations were abandoned after an hour or so as two major underwater explosions indicated that there was no hope of survivors.

Remarkably the *A8* was later raised, and repaired, and sent back into service. Meanwhile, the bodies of the crew were given a huge send off, thousands turning out to see the funeral procession wend its mournful route from the Dockyard Chapel to Ford Park Cemetery. Brave were the men who signed up as submariners in those early days, and intense was the reaction, in January 1914 when a fourth of 13 A-Class subs was sunk (the first *A1* had gone down in 1904 after being struck by a luxury liner).

The tragedy occurred in the middle of an exercise in Whitsand Bay: six subs were involved in a series of dummy attacks on surface ships when *A7* dived ready to take the offensive, but nothing more was seen of her. There was only enough air on board to give the men six hours before surfacing, but despite a major search operation it was six days before she was found.

None of these craft were actually built at Devonport, and it wasn't until April 1915 that the first locally constructed craft were laid down in the Dockyard. Five months later, in the presence of King George V and Queen Mary, submarines *J5* and *J6* were launched. On 31 May of the following year, 1916, they were joined by *K6* and *K7*, the Navy's first steam-powered submarines.

Devonport's fifth and final wartime submarine, *J7*, joined the fleet in 1917, slipping into the Hamoaze for the first time on 21 February.

Top: *1905, funeral procession of the unfortunate crew of the A8 submarine passes Stoke Damerel Church.* Above: *A6 and another A-class sub in dock.*

Gordon Campbell VC

Only seven J-Class submarines were built, the K-Class being faster and D and E-Class being easily the most populous classes with 38 of the former and 58 of the latter being launched between November 1912 and June 1916.

At the start of the war the German Navy had just 29 Untersee Boots (Under Sea Boats or U-Boats), but they quickly became the scourge of the British fleet, sinking five cruisers in the first 10 weeks of the war. Determined to try and undermine the supremacy of the Royal Navy, the German high command were quick to realise the potential threat that their U-boats represented and 360 had been built by the end of the war, almost half of which (178) were lost, but which between them accounted for over 11 million tonnes of mainly Allied shipping. With much of that shipping lost in the English Channel, Plymouth became very much a centre of anti-U-boat operations.

RNAS Cattewater (later RAF Mount Batten) was developed as an aerial submarine-spotter base, while in the Dockyard, alongside general refitting and repair work, there was a lively campaign to create what were originally known as Decoy Ships.

These were essentially regular merchant ships that were equipped with well-concealed heavy armaments. The idea was to lure U-boats into range, at which point a number of surplus personnel, constituting a kind of 'panic party' would abandon ship in lifeboats and then the remaining gun crew would throw off their camouflage covers and take aim at the unsuspecting enemy.

After a number of ships had been thus converted the Admiralty began identifying them as Q1, Q2, Q3 etc. and before long they had become known generally as Q-Ships. Foremost among the names associated with these 'Mystery' or Special Service Vessels was 29-year-old Gordon Campbell, who fitted out his ships at Devonport. In October 1915 Campbell commissioned a tramp steamer – *Loderer* – which was restyled HMS *Farnborough* (Q5) and in which he would go on to sink two U-boats. He was also responsible for the sinking of *UC-29* while commanding (with his crew from the no longer seaworthy *Farnborough*), the former coastal collier HMS *Pargust* and possibly another while in charge of HMS *Dunraven*.

All three ships were awarded the VC, Campbell accepting the first for himself and allowing the two others to be drawn by ballot among his crew who were men mainly recruited from the Mercantile Marine and the Royal Navy Reserve.

A happy band aboard HMS Cordelia which was attached to the Devonport Gunnery School in the summer of 1919.

Top: *Crew of Submarine Chaser 354.* Bottom: *Six USSC vessels in Devonport, both images post-war and prior to their return to the United States.*

Further honours were awarded, by the American authorities, to the commanders of a small fleet of Submarine Chasers based in Plymouth.

The United States had remained largely neutral throughout the early years of the war: there had been a certain amount of pressure from the Anglophile contingent, but a large number of Irish and German Americans were in favour of neutrality, as were a large number of other US citizens. However, the German barbarism in Belgium, followed by the sinking of the British passenger liner *Lusitania* in 1915 started to change some of those opinions. The loss of the *Lusitania* saw some 1,200 civilians drowned at sea, a figure that included 128 Americans. The act – perpetrated in defiance of International Law – sparked a growing movement in support of the Allies – a movement that became unstoppable at the start of 1917 when the Germans decided to step up their all-out warfare against any shipping heading for Britain, a move in some small part triggered by the deployment of disguised merchant vessels or Q Ships.

Having said that, the Germans further compounded the situation by offering Mexico a military alliance. Thus it was that the US President, abandoned his policy of neutrality and instead petitioned Congress for a 'war to end all wars', one that would make the world 'safe for democracy'.

The United States duly entered the war on 6 April 1917 and while it was true that the country had not been gearing its army up for conflict, America had been gently bolstering its navy and before long Plymouth's anti-submarine activities had been enhanced by the arrival of the aforementioned fleet of Submarine Chasers.

These small, swift vessels operated in groups of three with two wing boats and a central craft listening on hydrophones for underwater activity. With a crew of 20 or so and a couple of officers, there were dozens of submarine chasers stationed here.

Plymouth was Sub-chaser Detachment 1 and the man in charge was 43-year-old Captain Lyman Atkinson Cotten. Based in Japan as the naval attaché at the American Embassy in Tokyo at the start of the war, Cotten was promoted to Captain in 1918 and sent out to what was considered, in terms of responsibility, an admiral's billet in charge at Plymouth. Besides larger vessels like USS *Parker, Alywin* and the repair ship *Hannibal*, there were anywhere between 36 and 72 subchasers in the port and Cotten's job was the training and

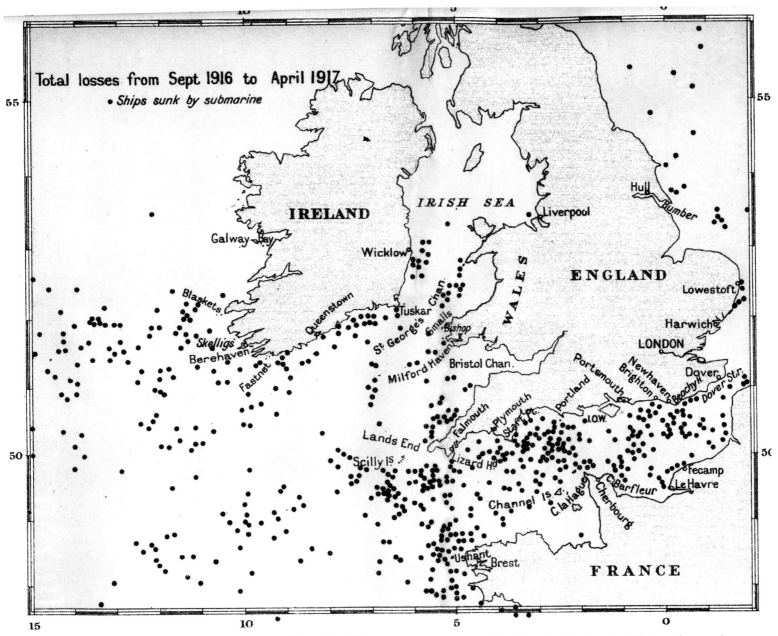

Total losses from Sept 1916 to April 1917
• Ships sunk by submarine

Map charting Allied losses to U-Boats between September 1916 and April 1917 – by that stage one in every four ships attempting to get into Britain was being sunk.

operations of his men and their ships, as well as looking after any American troops, stationed locally, who were awaiting transfers to various field units.

It was the US naval men though who cut the most distinctive figures: *'The tall sailors in their white caps walking in the streets seemed to bring a breath of assurance with them: a great Ally, sound in limb and fresh of wind, with infinite resources to hand, had come to join us,'* recorded the man, who, at that time was a local newspaper editor, Robert Walling (*The Story of Plymouth*).

Walling also spoke of the *'swarming flotillas of little ships in Plymouth Sound, and its harbours, flying the Stars and Stripes – mass-produced submarine chasers which flitted into the Channel and back at all hours of the day and night. They had a gay and saucy look, for all their grey paint, and their ships' companies became popular in the town. Officers and ratings made innumerable friendships, many of them enduring.'*

Top right: *Some of the crew of SC 181 – Pat, Salty, Tim, Dav, Hal, Joz, Don (Donald Huntley) and Ben.* Middle: *Donald Huntley.* Left: *Radio operator on SC 83.* Opposite page: *Submarine chasers on the US Naval Base at Victoria Wharves, on the Cattewater, looking across to Turnchapel.*

That Captain Cotten was successful is evident from the fact that during his command of the subchaser squadron, not a single Allied merchant ship was lost within his area of responsibility – furthermore not a single mine was laid there either. Not surprisingly therefore Cotten was awarded the Distinguished Service Medal for establishing and commanding the Plymouth base, while a large number of the men in charge of the subchasers were awarded the Navy Cross, among them F Allerton Read jr, Halsey L Ford, Lieutenant Garrison Payne, Fred Beckman, Cornelius Evans and Archie Vanderwall.

As so many of their endeavours went unseen, well below the surface of the sea, it was difficult to quantify their success in actually eliminating U-boats, as a typical, official, diary entry testifies:

'At 10.55 am Group 20 made sound contact with Submarine about 5 miles Southeast of Saint Anthony Head. This sound was followed through considerable interference and at 1.10pm was fixed as being at a distance of 200–250 yards from the Group Leader. Attack was delivered by the 3 boats of the Group in line abreast; 7 Depth Charges being fired; then all stopped and listened and for about 30 seconds the sound of a Submarine was heard, but as though the engines were damaged. No further sound contact and no evidence of damage having been done to Submarine' (US Naval Forces - Operating from Plymouth, England).

After the war 24 American submarine chasers were overhauled in the Dockyard before heading back across the Atlantic. Jobs in the Yard were fast evaporating however and redundancies were inevitable.

In the early years of the twentieth century Batten Bay, accessed via Mount Batten, was a popular destination with day-trippers.

MOUNT BATTEN

In the pedestrian-friendly, pre-omnibus days, when land-based public transport was principally limited to tram routes, watermen and ferryboat operators provided popular cross-water alternatives to what could readily be accessed on foot.

Mount Edgcumbe, to the west, and Mount Batten, to the east, were particular favourites for the residents of the Three Towns. On a good day it was not unknown for 10,000 passengers to avail themselves of the services of the various ferries that regularly plied to and fro across the Cattewater. On days like that the two pubs on the headland, the 'Castle' and the 'Breakwater', thrived, as did the hut near the coastguard cottages, the large, weekends-only, bell tent at Batten Bay and the many other stalls and side-shows set up to entertain and amuse the day trippers.

In 1908 a pontoon and bridge were set up so that steam ferries like *The Little Pet* and *The Favourite* could connect with the landing stage at low tide, but nine years later the directors of the Oreston and Turnchapel Steamboat company were forced to shelve plans to create a new pier at Mount Batten because *'the Government has taken possession of the field and cottages'*.

There had already been a hint of official intervention some years earlier, when, in 1903 (the year Wilbur and Orville Wright had first successfully pioneered flight) a nine-hole golf course had been laid out on the headland. Stretching from the narrowest part of the peninsula right out across to Jennycliff and up to Fort Stamford, the club was created for the United Services, with the Commander-in-Chief, the ex-officio President.

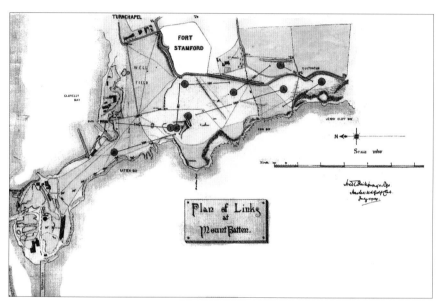

Mount Batten Golf Links 1904.

Primarily designed for officers, the club was financed by a levy on all of the Officers' Messes in the area and although non-commissioned servicemen could play the course they weren't allowed to use the club house overlooking the Cattewater. It was possible for certain civilians to join the club, however, but only if they were successfully elected by officer members and, of course, as long as they were not members of the fairer sex!

The Golf Course opened in 1904 and little could any of the United Servicemen then have anticipated that the institution of a fourth arm of the Services, a decade or so later, would ultimately prompt the closure and subsequent relocation of the facility.

Top: Colonel SF Cody – rear of picture in cowboy hat, demonstrating his man-lifting kite to the Admiralty in Plymouth Sound, April 1904.
Bottom: A signed Cody picture from the year before his death.

In the meantime, however, there was another challenge to the accessibility and to a certain extent, the desirability, of visiting Mount Batten, namely the ever-increasing stench emanating from the Plymouth Fish Guano and Oil Company that started manufacturing fertisliser from a long, limestone building on the edge of the quarry beneath the Mount Batten tower. Processing large amounts of dogfish waste from the relatively new Fish Market on the Barbican, this was, indeed, a very smelly business and in 1912 an injunction was served to close the premises, and a by-law was passed forbidding the gutting of fish at the market.

The injunction wasn't enforced, however, and the work carried on … until the Admiralty decided that Mount Batten would be better deployed in a different role altogether.

The idea of an 'aquaplane' – an aircraft that could land on water – was still relatively novel in 1913 when 'the Cattewater, which is sheltered from the prevailing South Westerly winds, was used for seaplane trials with the aircraft being pulled up onto the shore line' (Dennis Teague).

Plymouth had already logged several interesting aerial experiments prior to this, most notably with the American Colonel SF Cody demonstrating his man-lifting kites to the Royal Navy in Plymouth Sound in April 1904, and, on 11 September 1911, when 47-year-old Hilda Hewlett flew a Henri Farman biplane, the Blue Bird, at an airshow at Chelson Meadow.

A former Wild West showman from America, Samuel Franklin Cody became a British subject in the early years of the twentieth century and was given the honorary rank of Colonel by King George V. Cody was an early aviation pioneer and the British Army had recognised the potential of his man-carrying kites before the end of the Boer War. Four years after his display to the Admiralty in the Sound, the charismatic Cody made the first official powered flight in Britain, travelling 500 yards across the Laffans Plain at Aldershot. Tragically, in August 1913, during a trial of his Cody Floatplane, Cody and his co-pilot, cricketer William Evans, were both killed when his machine broke up in the air in Farnborough; he was 46. Four years later, in a situation that demonstrates how fast aerial technology was moving, his son, also SF Cody, who had joined the Royal Flying Corps, 'fell in action fighting four enemy machines.'

Hilda Hewlett was another remarkable character. She was the first woman in Britain to obtain a pilot's licence. Shortly before the war she set up a flying-school and then an aircraft manufacturing business with the French aviation engineer, Gustav Blondeau, in 1910, which, by August 1914, was producing ten different types of aircraft. During the course of the war the company made over 800 military aircraft and employed around 700 personnel. Her son, Francis, whom she taught to fly, won the DSO in 1915 and became a Group-Captain – not surprisingly perhaps, her husband, Maurice, who thought women would never be as successful in aviation as men, separated from the forthright Hilda in 1914.

Back in Plymouth, however, it wasn't until September 1913 that plans were drawn up to site an actual flying-base in the area and even then it wasn't until 1916 that those plans were finalised.

In the early days of aviation, not everyone could see the potential for flying observatories, let alone the prospect of aerial bombardment. A few years before the war one senior cavalry officer thought that aircraft would frighten the horses and therefore be more of a hindrance than a help. Curiously enough, the first commissioned aircraft seen in Plymouth would appear to have been the seaplanes that came down at the beginning of 1914 to help in what would prove to be the futile search for submarine *A7* that went missing off Rame Head shortly after leaving Devonport Dockyard.

It seems that two aircraft were involved in the search; one flown down from Kent, the other transported by train.

By that time the Government had embraced the potential use of the flying machine as a weapon of war and in 1911 had formed an Air Battalion. This move was consolidated the following year with the establishment of the Royal Flying Corps, an organisation that had both a military and a naval 'wing.'

On 1 July 1914, just a month or so before what was then the almost inevitable outbreak of war, that naval wing became the Royal Naval Air Service, however this did not initially herald the development of Mount Batten as an air base. The preferred site, locally, for the RNAS and the air*ships*, rather than air*planes*, was at Chelson Meadow.

At that stage of development airships were favoured over airplanes or seaplanes primarily because these giant inflatable craft could remain airborne for much longer periods – up to four hours – and could more or less stop and focus on one area if need be and if weather permitted.

The first woman to hold a pilot's licence (No.122) in Britain – Mrs Hilda Hewlett – who flew a biplane at Chelson Meadow in September 1911.

Top: *Airship SSZ-42 at Chelson Meadow - note the number of ground crew involved.*
Bottom: *Airship SSE-2 crashes in the Cattewater, attempting to land in a gale at Chelson Meadow.*

Submarines were the main concern and in order to try and combat the threat in the Channel, RNAS stations were set up along the southern coast and RNAS Laira was one of these.

The airship was an unreliable beast however, as their crews had no parachutes and worked in open cockpits, they moved slowly and their engines could be unpredictable: *'Airship SS Z14 stationed at Chelson Meadow, while on a flight, developed engine failure and ballooned over the English Channel and landed in France in the trenches at Montreivil. Another airship attempting to land in a gusty wind at RNAS Laira became unmanageable, floated above the ground and came down in the Cattewater close to Mount Batten'* (Gerald Wasley – Mount Batten).

More suited to observational duties than offensive operations, the Admiralty soon switched allegiance from the airship and found in favour of the flying-boat, opting to site a new base at the very entrance to the Plym at Mount Batten. Styled RNAS Cattewater, work on this new 30-acre seaplane station commenced in the early part of 1917. A couple of hangars close to the Batten Breakwater were quickly erected, together with some basic accommodation close to the old coastguard cottages. The two pubs on the peninsula were requisitioned by the Admiralty, the 'Castle' being adapted as the official residence of the base's Commanding Officer. Public access was inevitably restricted.

In April, after further building work that saw more hangars, workshops, storerooms and a smithy appear, the station was officially opened, although it didn't become fully operational until August. Mount Batten Breakwater was equipped with an impromptu set of railway tracks and a crane was borrowed from the Dockyard to run up and down its length pulling seaplanes out of the briny and parking them along the structure.

Before long there was the best part of 600 personnel working at the station, by no means all of them male: *'early in 1918 the largest contingent of the Women's Royal Naval Service arrived at Plymouth and were accommodated in wooden huts at Mount Batten'* (Wasley). Around the same time the Royal Naval Air Service and the Royal Flying Corps were united and refashioned as the Royal Air Force and the Mount Batten station was renamed RAF Cattewater. And a veritable hive of activity it was too, as anti-submarine surveillance and attacks were stepped up to try and counter the growing menace.

Top: *Mount Batten starts to take shape as an Air Station.*
Above: *Work begins on one of the smaller hangars.*
Right: *The completed hangar sits at the end of the Mount Batten Breakwater, the former 'Breakwater Inn' to the left.*

Top: *A series of Short 184 seaplanes line the Mount Batten Breakwater with the views to the left and above showing the same scene from different angles.*

It was dangerous work, engine failure was a constant concern and many craft crashed while on patrol – six in the first three months of the station being in operation. Furthermore, with their easily damaged wooden floats and flimsy fabric coverings the seaplanes required a lot of maintenance and air crews were heavily reliant on efficient ground staff: *'the fabric that covered the frame was easily torn, a ripped wing or tail-end could bring down a seaplane'* (Wasley).

Nevertheless the various state-of-the-art flying machines that breezed in and out of RAF Cattewater were a source of endless fascination to a generation too young to take the King's shilling and, more significantly, enabled Plymouth to stake a unique claim in the story of the Great War in that it was the only place in the country to support all four arms of the United Services in such close proximity – Royal Navy, Royal Marines, Army and Royal Air Force.

Top right: *Work is carried out on a damaged seaplane float.* Above: *1 April 1918 the Royal Naval Air Station becomes RAF Cattewater.*

Curiously enough, Plymouth enjoyed another unique claim to aerial fame the following year, on 31 May 1919, for that was the day that an NC4 flying boat arrived in Plymouth after completing the first ever aerial crossing of the Atlantic.

Lieutenant-Commander Albert Cushing Read USN navigated and led the six-man crew which included pilots Elmer Stone and Walter Hinton, flight engineers James Breese and Eugene Rhodes and radio operator Herbert Rodd. Three United States NC (Naval Curtiss) craft started out on the voyage – NC1, NC3 and NC4 – but only one completed the epic excursion out of America.

The race to complete the first crossing of the Atlantic had been the dream of many since at least 1913 when the *Daily Mail* offered up a prize of £10,000 for the: *'aviator who shall first cross the Atlantic in an aeroplane in flight from any point in the United States, Canada, or Newfoundland to any point in Great Britain or Ireland, in 72 consecutive hours.'* As well as the time stipulation, there was also an understanding that the feat had to be performed in just one aircraft. The challenge was put into abeyance during wartime, but in 1918 the *Daily Mail* renewed the offer and manufacturers and aviators started looking for partnerships.

Foremost among those to rise to the challenge was Glenn Curtiss a former bicycle racer, motorcycle manufacturer and flying boat pioneer.

Curtiss, who made the first officially witnessed flight in America, had started making engines for airships as early as 1904 and in 1908 had joined the AEA (Aerial Experiment Association) a group that had been set up by Alexander Graham Bell in Nova Scotia.

Curtiss flew his first successful 'hydro-aeroplane' in 1912 and soon afterwards was introduced to a retired British naval officer, John Porte, who had his eye on that *Daily Mail* prize. However, the war intervened and Porte was called up again and started commissioning Curtiss flying-boats for the RNAS and specifically for long-range anti-submarine surveillance.

Clearly the war saw spectacular advances in aviation and by 1919 there were several companies competing to make the crossing. In the event Curtiss was successful even though, to achieve that success the NC4 flew a somewhat circuitous route from New York to the Azores via Massachusetts, Halifax (Nova Scotia) and Trespassey (Newfoundland). The final leg to Plymouth came via Lisbon (Portugal)

From the top left: The NC4 touches down in the Cattewater after completing the first transatlantic crossing and is met by air crew from RAF Cattewater, then joined by an escorting, flag-bearing, RAF Felixstowe flying-boat.

and Ferrol (Spain). It was a tremendous feat of organisation and the route was also populated – every 50 miles or so – with American naval vessels, mainly destroyers, lighting up the way with searchlights and 'star shells.'

All in all the journey took 23 days. Curtiss was more interested in the crossing than the prize money and had never been aiming at a 72-hour flight. As expected the flight was roundly celebrated, although the British press did not give the feat proper recognition until the plane arrived in Plymouth.

'Now that the NC4 has reached England her crew has been overwhelmed with adulation by the British Press ... but no amount of slopping over can wash out the fact that the British Press did not appreciate the significance of the NC4's victory when that victory was won,' said the editor of British based magazine The Aeroplane, in June 1919.

'America must accept the apologies of the aeronautical section of the British Public, and one would merely ask that the remissness of our Press be set down to pure ignorance and not to malice.

It has never occurred to any of our newspaper magnates that the British Public will take the very best of anything as eagerly as it will swallow the very worst. They only know that it is not interested in what is merely clever. Consequently it has never occurred to them to build up a newspaper staff composed entirely of intelligent educated gentlemen.'

Further dismissive rhetoric followed and then nearing the end of the piece, the question was asked – 'And now what next ... After the first non-stop journey we shall begin to introduce an illimitable series of minor classes in the competition. We shall have the "the first one-man flight", then we shall have "the first flight with one engine," "the first flight with two engines," "the first flight with four engines," "the first flight with one passenger," "the first flight with ten passengers," "the first flight with fifty passengers," "the first flight with a woman passenger," and so forth and so on, ad infinitum. The first thing that really counts is being first across. And that honour has gone to America.'

And in Plymouth, where that journey ended, the crew were given a Civic reception at the Mayflower Stone on 7 June 1919. One week later, two British officers, Captain John Alcock and Lieutenant Arthur Brown, flew non-stop from Newfoundland to Ireland 'in less than '72 consecutive hours'. The British Press were ecstatic. Minister of Air, Winston Churchill, presented the men with the Daily Mail cheque, and King George V honoured them both with a knighthood.

The crew of the NC4 are given a Civic Reception after being driven to the Mayflower Stone on the Barbican's West Pier – from whence the Pilgrim Fathers had set sail some 300 years earlier.

Corporal Farmer and Captain Hall pose between the props of a Felixstowe flying-boat at Mount Batten.

All those who perhaps hoped that, at the end of the war, the Mount Batten peninsula would be returned to the public domain were almost certainly disappointed. While the scale of the operations there were significantly reduced – and the base became primarily a care and maintenance facility – the rapidly growing fourth Armed Service had plans to develop the seaplane station: plans that involved the purchase of more land rather than the relinquishing of any of that which had been recently acquired.

Thus it was that on the same day as Alcock and Brown completed their non-stop crossing of the Atlantic in Ireland, 14 June 1919, at Mount Batten the Air Ministry held a 'Cattewater Conference' with a view to discovering just how much of the headland they could afford to buy in their quest to make Mount Batten an operational RAF station.

The reasoning was simple: aircraft technology had advanced in leaps and bounds, quite massive leaps and bounds, during the course of the Great War and, as of 1919, the only country capable of launching an aerial attack on Britain was our ally – and our enemy of old – France.

France was, at that time, the only European country with a sufficiently strong air force: their airfields were in easy range of the south coast and we had no air defences of consequence in the South West.

A budget of up to £30,000 was approved and the main beneficiary would appear to have been the Earl of Morley, who owned much of the land under review, as well as a villa in Turnchapel and the 'Castle Inn', cottage and boathouse, which, along with 18 acres of land, was held by the Octagon Brewery on a 30-year lease from the Earl. Much of the Batten peninsula had been appropriated by the Admiralty under the terms of the Defence of the Realm Act, earlier in the war. Now, however, the public were perceiving a more permanent ban on their right to roam the headland.

'Public landing on the Batten's foreshore was forbidden, resulting in the Oreston and Turnchapel Steamboat Company claiming substantial amount of money for the loss of income' (Wasley).

Top: An early seaplane in the Sound. Above: Lt Colonel PA Shepherd, Commanding Officer at Mount Batten after the war. Right: RAF Cattewater Rugby Football Club 1918–19 season.

ONE OF THE LITTLE 'DUCKS' WHO'S HELPING TO HATCH THE SHELLS

Photograph of Plymouth Munitions Girls taken by the Novelty Studion, 184 Union Street.
Opposite page: Bull Point Munition Workers, Rooms 79 and 80.

WAR WORK FOR WOMEN

In May 1915 the introduction of Conscription was accompanied by the passing of the Munitions of War Act, which forbade munitions workers resigning without their employer's permission and which also paved the way for women to enter this particular workplace, although not without an element of reluctance on the part of the trade unions.

However, it had quickly become apparent in the first few months of the war that the conflict was going to get through munitions at an alarming rate and a shortage of shells on the front lines in the early part of 1915 was to contribute to the downfall of the last ever Liberal Government.

The much-publicised 'Shell Crisis' reported in *The Times* saw Lord Northcliffe – the owner of *The Times* and the *Daily Mail* – launch a direct attack on Lord Kitchener, the former blaming the latter for the death, in action, of his nephew.

Prime Minister Asquith (who had been in power since 1908), relying on information from Kitchener, had assured his audience at a speech in Newcastle, in April 1915, that there was no shortage, but this was clearly not the case.

A coalition Government subsequently saw Kitchener moved out of Munitions and Lloyd George moved in. In Plymouth a training centre was established in the Technical School, opposite the new Library and Museum building in Tavistock Road. Within a year or so over 373 women had been trained there and 335 of them had been placed on production lines in factories in Union Street, Prince Rock and Bull Point, amongst others. Shell cases were also produced at Devonport Technical College, while Andrew's Garage, behind the Athenaeum, started milling aluminium into fuse caps for shells.

Initially most of the women attracted into munitions were single, or at least childless, but as time went on and demand increased, wives and mothers were enrolled. However, no matter how efficient the women were, they were paid slightly less than half the wage of a man doing the same work – that is £2.2.4d (£2.11p) as opposed to £4.6s.6d (£4.32p) a week.

'Munitionettes were the largest group of women workers during WWI and by 1917 it was estimated that 80 per cent of all weapons and shells were being produced by women. By 1918 almost a million women were actively involved in the manufacture of guns and ammunition. They were proud to be called Tommies' Sisters' (Lawer).

The work was by no means easy and the yellow 'lyddite' powder involved in the process of making these explosive devices could turn the girls bodies yellow – earning them the nickname 'canaries'. Many were forced to take time off sick, and nationally over 100 were to die of lyddite poisoning. Two half-pints of milk were issued to the women every day, but there was no effective treatment, although, over time symptoms did eventually clear up.

There were, incidentally, similar male/female wage disparities in the Dockyard, where even though women were on piece-work they were paid significantly less than men doing the same work. It was even worse for girls under 18 who were on half the rate of their older workmates, although, even they were better paid than women in established female roles, like clerks, telephone operatives, tracers and indeed any job that did not involve manual industrial work.

The necessities of war were to have deep and far-reaching consequences in the workplace and in society at large. Before 1914 few women worked and those that did were mainly in textiles, retail or domestic service. Such employment was generally the lot of the single, working-class woman and in the event of marriage, she was generally expected to, or even required to, give up her job.

However the advent of war brought changes across the board. Thousands of men were suddenly taken out of the workplace; not only did those jobs have to be replaced, but with only a part of their husband's weekly incomes, many, servicemen's wives started to struggle; meanwhile, in the interests of patriotism, many well to do ladies stopped buying new clothes, putting thousands of, mainly female, textile workers, out of work.

The solutions were obvious, although not necessarily welcomed in all corners. For the Suffragette movement though, here was the perfect opportunity and they provided the Government with invaluable assistance in setting up the Women's Service Bureau, helping to place women into work where there were no men.

Munitions were top of that agenda and the so-called 'Munitionettes' soon demonstrated how successful this arrangement could be, although the new situation was not without its concerns. Foremost among them was the worry that there may be a degree of immorality between 'Munitionettes' and soldiers. Voluntary women police officers were put in place, largely to monitor the situation.

Plymouth was by no means unique, but here, where a large number of young women found themselves with financial independence for the first time, there were obvious additional grounds for concerns, particularly with thousands of young soldiers passing through the training barracks at Crownhill.

Two groups were at the forefront of monitoring the 'dangers': the Woman's Patrols set up by the Headmistresses's Association and the Federation of University Woman, and Margaret Damer Dawson's Women Police Volunteers.

Damer Dawson was a wealthy 40-something spinster who had been working towards establishing a female presence in the police force before the war. In 1914 she was prompted to join forces with Nina Boyle when the two were horrified at seeing Belgian refugees being recruited as prostitutes as they arrived at British railway stations.

A Voluntary service was established, but the two fell out over whether a curfew should be imposed on women's behaviour.

Boyle thought no, but Dawson's view won through and the WPV soon became the WPS, Women's Police Service – Britain's first uniformed women's police service – and together with the Women's Patrols, who were very active in public parks and cinemas (indeed they recommended that lights shouldn't be dimmed between films), they were evident in Plymouth.

The Chief Constable, in January 1916, indicated that he was prepared to give Women Police a trial, but did not make any strong recommendation, however at the same meeting it was agreed, by an almost unanimous vote, to stop the sale of intoxicating liquor to women for consumption on licensed premises at 6pm.

It was felt that the time had arrived when the Watch Committee should give their attention to what was known to be a growing evil. They could not shut their eyes to the fact that women were frequenting public houses when they ought to be in their homes.

Henry Vigurs Harris, addressing the Council meeting, asked if it was right that the whole care of the streets and parks of the borough should be left entirely to male constables. To which Councillor Willies replied that some 27 or 30 years ago a number of respectable ladies were employed on the Vigilant Committee of a Society for the Supression of Vice and 'they made no end of mischief'.

A few days later a Miss Hamley pointed out in the press that Women's Patrol Work had been quietly carried out in Plymouth for three years without the cognizance of many of the ordinary citizens.

'We are 20 busy women,' said Miss Hamley, 'at present engaged. In 1914 for the first three months there were 50, but several have left. Nancy Astor was among those who enrolled as a Woman Police Volunteer, but they were not entirely popular. The women were not sworn in as Constables and had no power of arrest. Their main duty it seems was 'to turn girls and lads out of the doorways' and there were frequent letters in the press, complaining about 'ancient spinsters following soldiers about with their flashlights'.

The WPS ladies were also expected to cut their hair short and volunteers were required to address their female superior officers as 'Sir.' After the war Dawson's request to have her volunteers made into police officers was turned down, ostensibly on the grounds that the women were too well educated and there would be friction; however the Police Commissioner apparently disliked Damer Dawson and a number of her fellow WPS ladies.

Sadly Damer Dawson died, of a heart attack, in 1920, the year the WPS became the Women's Auxiliary Service. It transpired that she had spent much of her small fortune on her police force and what remained she left to her WPS friend and companion, Mary Allen.

Officers of the Staff of the WPS; D Meeson Coates (Chief Inspector), Miss St John Partridge, M Damer Dawson (Chief Officer), MS Allen (Chief Superintendent), B Goldingham (Principal of Clerical Department).

WAR WORK FOR WOMEN.

Carrie the Cop Copping Coppers.

DRIVEN FROM HOME BY A WOMAN

PLATFORM Nº 3

HELD UP FOR INSPECTION

Concerns over the well-being of women, their morality and their sexual health promoted members of the Plymouth Watch Committee to suggest the local re-enaction of the provisions of the Contagious Diseases Act of 1866, a draconian measure which essentially allowed for the arrest of any woman who was merely suspected of being free and easy with her sexual favours.

The proposal met with a wave of telegrams against the notion and the the Women's Freedom League wrote to the Prime Minister requesting that he receive a deputation from them. Mr Asquith's secretary replied that Plymouth Town Council had deferred the proposal for further consideration and added that no local body had the power to take any action, of the sort that the League feared, without the authority of Parliament.

But the fears were there and the thought that the presence of women in the workplace would create problems extended across the professions and across the country.

As councillor Lovell Dunstan had already suggested, in relation to the appointment of women police, it would be likely to cause jealousy, as it had in other towns, between the wives of the men and the women constables. '*In some towns,*' he said, '*women had gone to the Chief Constable and complained of the attention their husbands paid to the women police.*'

However, as more and more men left for the front so more and more women stepped into their working shoes. Women became railway guards, postwomen, window cleaners and tram drivers and conductresses.

Plymouth Town Council even debated the uniform that such female tram staff should wear and what they should do with their hair while wearing hats.

It was very difficult for men to try and bury their prejudices when it came to redefining the role of women in the workplace and society at large, and the situation was not helped by the fact that the world of picture-postcard artists was equally chauvinistic.

The reality, however, was quite simple. With so many men removed from the labour market, the employment of women was inevitable. Furthermore, with the menfolk away the reaction of women was simple: on the one hand any additional income was not just welcome but necessary, and on the other hand, here was a section of society anxious to be seen to be doing their bit for King and Country too.

Unfortunately not everyone saw the situation that way, especially those men whose attitudes were more deeply ingrained than most.

'Farmers must not continue to break the hearts of women as they had been doing during the last two years,' ran one local report in 1917. 'They have not been receptive enough in welcoming the great patriotic efforts which women had made to work on the lands.'

Women had been working as agricultural labourers for many years before Lord Selbourne, in January 1917, decreed that 'women must take the place of men on the land so that men can be spared to fight.'

This marked the birth of the Women's Land Army, an outfit soon to be branded by some as the 'lilac bonnet brigade' because of the early rush of mainly middle and upper-class women who stepped forward.

Girls could enlist for a year or just half a year, and many couldn't wait for their contracts to expire – the work was hard and the pay was poor. While men could earn as much as seven shillings (35p) a day, some girls were on as little as two shillings (10p) a day, or a meagre 2d or 3d an hour (around 1p).

Towards the end of the war the importation of hundreds of American Fordson tractors helped alleviate the situation, but such is not to belittle the work of over a quarter of a million women who worked as farm labourers during the Great War, with some 20,000 in the Land Army itself.

These land girls are a bit up-ish, but I shall try to carry on with 'em!

You ARE some "Farmer's Boy!"

When women started to wear trousers.

THE GIRLS WENT ON THE LAND, AND BOYS WENT TO SEA!

NATIONAL SERVICE

Sunshine on the Land

A patrol of the 5th Plymouth troop in July 1911, with Leonard Squire, Harry Drew and Billy Mills.

TOO YOUNG TO FIGHT

'The Boy Scout, as you know him, is a bare-kneed, happy-go-lucky boy, with possibly an ugly face and probably a good heart, and at any rate with a hat and staff. But what has he got to do with the War?' Asked the founder of the movement Lt-General Sir Robert SS Baden-Powell, from 'somewhere in France' and somewhat tongue in cheek, in the early part of the conflict.

Baden-Powell was, of course, enormously proud of the movement he had set in motion, a movement that had grown out of a conversation he had had in Glasgow in 1907, when he had been there to inspect some 7,000 members of the Boy's Brigade. It was there that Sir William Smith, who as a 29-year-old army officer and Sunday School teacher, had founded the Boy's Brigade in 1883, asked Baden-Powell if he had ever considered refashioning his training manual for soldiers – Aids To Scouting for NCOs and Men – into something that might appeal to boys.

Later that year Baden-Powell, who had just turned 50 and was already an Army veteran of great distinction, held a camp for boys from different social backgrounds on Brownsea Island, in Poole Harbour. The camp, held during the first week of August 1907, prompted Baden-Powell to rewrite his manual which was then published the following year as Scouting For Boys. Inspired by British-born Ernest Thompson Seton's Birch Bark Roll of the Woodcraft Indians, it was an instant success and by September 1908 100,000 boys had enrolled as Scouts.

Six years later many thousands of lads, the length and breadth of the country, were enjoying their annual camps when the news that war had been declared first broke.

'The call,' noted Baden-Powell, 'could not have come at a more opportune moment for rapid response.'

Clearly there were issues with Scout Leaders being instantly required for military service, but the lads who were too young to serve quickly slipped into supporting roles. The Annual Report of the 5th Plymouth Troop from December 1915 provides a wonderful insight:

'Since the start of the war the activities of the Troop have been somewhat restricted, due, amongst other causes, to the absence on service of several of our officers and to the lack of spare time on the part of those remaining.

TOO YOUNG TO FIGHT, BUT NOT TOO YOUNG TO HELP THE FIGHTER.
(Belfast Boy Scouts' War Service Commemoration Picture.)

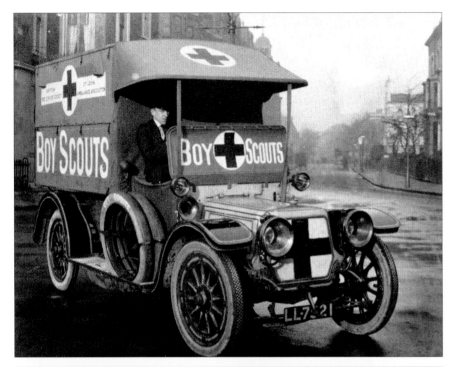

Local military conditions and regulations have also kept us under to some extent, especially in the case of our Sea Scouts, who unfortunately have been unable to do anything much in their line, as all the officers who looked after that branch of the Troop are away.

The total number from the Troop now on active service with HM Forces is 12 which includes two scoutmasters, two assistant scoutmasters, two acting scoutmasters, two patrol leaders, two scouts, and one SM and one acting SM who were only attached to the Troop.

Up to present they are all safe. In addition there are eight or nine ex-members whom we know are on service.

Mention should also be made of the scouts on coast-watching duties. It may not be generally known that since mobilisation the Admiralty has employed scouts to assist in coast-watching. Two stations have been supplied with scouts from this district and more than half the number are from this Troop. Altogether 12 from this Troop have been and still are, on this duty.

In other ways than this, scouts have been employed in the public service and a special War Service badge has been issued by London Headquarters to those scouts who complete 28 days, of at least three hours per day, voluntary public service.

At the time of mobilisation scouts were on duty as messengers at the various military offices, hospitals, etc and their services have also been requisitioned by the local recruiting committees, ambulance associations, relief committees, etc. Twenty-three of these War Service Badges have already been awarded to members of this Troop.

In March we held a concert at the Prince's Hall in aid of the Belgian Relief Fund. It was a great success and we were able to hand over the sum of £10.10s.0d to the fund.

Towards the end of the year the Chief Scout made an appeal to scouts all over the country for funds to provide a new motor ambulance car for the front, in place of the one which had been presented by the Boys Scouts Association and was getting worn out. To raise money scouts were asked to obtain a day's employment wherever possible and give their wages to the fund. By this means we were able to hand in £5.5s.6d, being the second largest amount raised by any one Troop in this District.'

At that point in time the Troop numbered 64 (including 10 Sea Scouts) and a further six on coast-watching duties.

Top: Ambulance purchased by the Scout Movement. Bottom: The 4th Devonport Wolf Cub pack 1916 – 'this was the year that this section was founded'.

Across the country some 20,000 scouts were called up in this way, their duties included beach patrols, salvaging wreckage, looking out for fishing boats that were working unauthorised hours, checking that boats that came ashore had valid permits and reporting on all vessels they saw.

As the Chief Scout (Baden-Powell) himself observed: *'The fellow-countrymen scarcely realise that these lads are watching and patrolling their coasts day by day and night after night in all weathers – doing their duty from sheer patriotism.*

The fact that they have been retained, and that from time to time more have been asked for, and supplied, implies that they are not without value in the eyes of the authorities.'

Cooking, cycling, signalling, and administering first-aid, were all part of the Boy Scout's training. It was a fine preparation for service, of course, but the Chief Scout was perhaps more concerned to think it was a fine preparation for life.

Not all Scouts, Scout Leaders and ex-Scouts were fortunate enough to survive the war. Many lost their lives in the conflict, including at least six of the 20 or so boys that had been at that first camp on Brownsea Island with Baden-Powell and four former members of the 5th Plymouth Troop: Leonard Squire, William Baker, Fred Temlett and Athelstone Holman.

Leonard was Scoutmaster of the troop and a sergeant in the Prince of Wales' Battalion of the Devonshire Regiment, with whom he would appear to have gone out to India in 1914 and then on to Suez in April 1917. An exemplary figure, who was 'mentioned in dispatches' Leonard died almost a year later, just before their return; he was 26 and is buried in Cairo.

William Baker, the son of a billiard table maker from Union Street, was Assistant Scoutmaster for the 5th and was serving with the 24th Battalion of the Royal Fusiliers when he was killed in action in France, in July 1916.

Fred Temlett and the wonderfully, regally, named Athelstone William George Holman were both too young to sign up for war service, but not too young to work and both were employed as merchant seamen. Their respective families both lived in Neath Road and the boys were doubtless mates as well as fellow scouts.

Tragically, Fred was just 16 when he died, while serving on board the SS *Treverbyn*. The *Treverbyn* was a seven-year-old, 4,000-ton, defensively armed British steamer that was travelling from Narvik to Manchester with a cargo of iron ore, when she hit a mine laid by a German U-boat (*U75*) in the Outer Hebrides. Fred was one of 27 who drowned or were killed in the explosion on 3 September 1917.

"LEAVE IT TO ME"

THE GREAT BOY SCOUT.

The Great Boy Scout: Jack Cornwell awarded both the Victoria Cross and the Bronze Cross - then the highest honour in the Scouting Movement. By the end of the war it was estimated that 250,00 members of the Scouting Movement went to fight and that some 10,000 lost their lives across the battlefields of Western Europe.

Athelstone, was the same age as Fred and he was serving on the slightly bigger SS *Galway Castle*, an 8,000 ton vessel that had been requisitioned as a troop ship in 1914 but had reverted to commercial service for Union Castle (she was the only one left), in 1915.

In 1916 the vessel was, somewhat unusually in the First World War, attacked by a German bomber. The bomb hit its target but failed to go off and *Galway Castle* sailed on. The following year she was accidentally grounded on the Orient Bank, East London, but again survived the ordeal without damage. However, on 12 September 1918, just two days out of Plymouth, the ship was torpedoed by *U-82*. The blow broke the back of the ship, raising concerns that it was in imminent danger of sinking. Sensing that the U-boat was lining up for a second strike, there was a scramble to abandon the ship – there were 204 crew on board, 346 passengers and some 400 wounded South African service personnel.

As it transpired there was no second strike and the ship didn't sink straight away, indeed it floated around for a few days before radio signals attracted destroyers to decant the survivors. Sadly, though, 143 persons had perished in the initial panic as the lifeboats that had been launched were swamped in the heavy seas. Seventeen-year-old Athelstone Holman was one of that number. It must have been a devastating blow for his 40-year-old mother, Annie, who had already lost her husband and who was living in Neath Road with her brother (who was himself a widower) and her two daughters, Rose and Wibo, and her brother's children.

Undoubtedly the most famous young Scout to lose his life at sea was 16-year-old John (Jack) Cornwell. A Royal Navy sight setter, serving on board HMS *Chester* at the Battle of Jutland, Jack died days after being wounded at his post alongside his 5.5-inch gun. Posthumously awarded the Victoria Cross for remaining at his post, awaiting orders, surrounded by dead and dying colleagues, Jack Cornwell was to be the youngest ever recipient of the VC in the Great War and every school in the country was sent a picture of him. Seven million schoolchildren subsequently purchased a special stamp that helped to raise money to fund a ward in Queen Mary's Star and Garter Home for war-disabled soldiers and sailors.

Boy Scouts and Wolf Cubs in Guildhall Square, Coronation Day 1911.

The American Ambassador, Walter Page, visits the Mayflower Stone with his wife and Nancy Astor.

AN AMERICAN IN PLYMOUTH

It was on the occasion of the third anniversary of the start of the war that the man who had been appointed as the American Ambassador in London in March 1913, came to Plymouth to make a speech that would resonate around the world.

Walter Hines Page was a 61-year-old journalist and publisher who had long advocated American involvement on the side of the Allies. A good friend of the President, Woodrow Wilson (who had taken office in March 1913 and who had first met Walter Page some 35 years earlier when they were both young men): Page helped to create pro-British sympathy on the part of the President and the American population. Not everyone was impressed, as many American businesses had strong links with Germany.

Undaunted, Page waged his persuasive arguments and found ready friends in Plymouth in the shape of the sitting MP and newspaper proprietor Waldorf Astor and his wife Nancy, both of whom had been born in America - Waldorf in New York, Nancy in Virginia.

In February 1917 Page sent Woodrow Wilson a telegram containing a transcript of a German telegram that British intelligence had intercepted and decoded. The British government were very anxious that their ability to decipher German correspondence was not compromised, but wanted to warn the American President of the content. The official line was that a copy of the telegram had been bought in Mexico. In the telegram, which was addressed to the President of Mexico, the German Foreign Minister, Arthur Zimmermann disclosed the German plans to commence unrestricted submarine warfare from 1 February: 'We shall endeavour in spite of this to keep the United States of America neutral. In the event of this not succeeding, we make Mexico a proposal of alliance on the following basis: make war together, make peace together, generous financial support and an understanding on our part that Mexico is to reconquer the lost territory in Texas, New Mexico, and Arizona. The settlement in detail is left to you.'

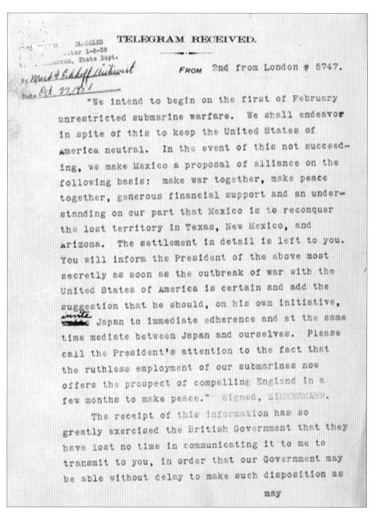

The original transcript of the Zimmerman telegram.

The telegram continued: 'You will inform the President of the above most secretly as soon as the outbreak of war with the United States of America is certain and add the suggestion that he should, on his own initiative, invite Japan to immediate adherence and at the same time mediate between Japan and ourselves. Please call the President's attention to the fact that the ruthless employment of our submarines now offers the prospect of compelling England in a few months to make peace.' Signed Zimmerman.

Within a month of receiving Page's message, Wilson asked Congress for a declaration of war on Germany, four days later, on 6 April, both Houses had ratified the decision and America joined the war.

Thus it was that Walter Page came to Plymouth at the beginning of August for a five-day visit to the city, during which time he went down to the Mayflower Stone with Nancy Astor, to commemorate the departure of the Pilgrim Fathers to found the United States. He dined with the Major-General Penton, had lunch with the Admiral Superintendent, viewed Drake's birthplace, played golf at Whitchurch Down, attended the United Services Sports at Home Park, reviewed the troops on the Hoe and made a major speech in the Guildhall.

In that speech Page made much of the similarities between the two countries and was at pains to point out that the USA today includes 'more English-speaking white men than the whole British Empire.

They have ... not only outgrown in numbers all the British elsewhere, but they have kept what may be called the faith of the race. They have kept the racial and national characteristics. They have kept British law, British freedom, British Parliaments, British character, and they are reared on British literature.

Politically two peoples, in all high aims and in the love of freedom we are one and must remain one forever. Not only have our warships come, but our troopships have landed an army on the soil of our brave Ally across the Channel, where the enemy yet keeps the wavering line of an invader. And more warships will come and more troopships laden if you need them till that line is for ever driven back until the submarines are withdrawn or for ever submerged.'

At that point the Guildhall audience broke in to spontaneous cheering and Page continued: *'There is coming the greatest victory for free government that was ever won, and the day of this victory which we are both fighting for may turn out to be the most important date in history.*

The necessity to win it has cleared the air as no other event in modern times has done, and but for the millions of brave lives it has cost this clearing of the air would richly repay all the treasure the war has cost. For it has revealed the future of the world to us, not as its conquerors, but as its necessary preservers of peace.'

It was a long speech and these are only extracts, but from the self-styled 'Guardians of Civilisation' the message was clear, as was the exhortation for both British and American people to get to know one another better: *'It is your duty,'* said the Ambassador, *'to learn all you can about the United States, about the country, about its people, their institutions, their occupations, their aims, and to make the acquaintance of as many Americans as you can. It may be you will not like them all. [Laughter] It may be you don't like all you own countrymen. [Renewed laughter]. But you will, I think, like most Americans. Certainly most of them like you'* [Cheers].

In pursuance of the above, Page recommended conveying such information via lectures, cinema, the press and school text books.

'There is no land so full and pleasant and full of useful information for Americans as your land and no people so well worth our intimate acquaintance as your people, and it is equally true that no other land and no other people are so well worthy of your sympathetic study as the United States and those that dwell there, for they have the spirit of the modern world as no others have it.'

And here Page made an interesting claim: *'I hope you will pardon me if I say that a visit to America and to your great colonies is an excursion into the future of human society.'*

The implication was clear, with the mighty United States on our side the war was now as good as won: *'Americans now here confer daily with most Departments of your Government, and your corresponding representatives in the United States confer with most Departments of the American Government, so that the greatest possible unity of action may be secured.*

Our highest naval and military officers are in command of our forces in your waters and on the soil of France. [Cheers]. Our fleets in your seas are constantly becoming larger and our advanced army in France secures constant additions. The most skilful American surgeons attend the Allied wounded of all our armies, and American nurses in ever-increasing numbers assist them. American engineers and labourers are laying railways behind the British and French lines. American scientific men are giving their skill not only at home but at the front to perfect scientific methods of making military activities more accurate. American lumbermen are felling your forests and cutting the trees for war uses. Labourers under American engineers are building and rebuilding military roads in France, and our money is pouring into the war coffers of all the Allies' [Cheers].

The speech was printed in full in newspapers and published by the American Government for distribution around the world, for propaganda purposes. In a letter to his son, describing his time in Plymouth, Page wrote: *'It's strange how very little the provincial Englander knows about what we have done and mean to do. They took the speech finely, and I have had good letters about it from all sorts of people in every part of the Kingdom.'*

After his five days in Plymouth Page returned to the Embassy in London *'dead tired'*. He was clearly not a well man. The following August he was invited back to Plymouth again, but was too unwell to make the journey. The Mayor and a delegation went instead to the Embassy to present him with the Freedom of the Borough on 20 September 1918. A few days later Page resigned his post and returned to the United States, where he died, at home, four days after Christmas 1918.

This page and opposite: *Dr Page salutes 1,000 soldiers and sailors on Plymouth Hoe beneath the 'Stars and Stripes.'*

ARMISTICE

'News of the signing of the armistice reached us this morning before 9 o'clock through the courtesy of the Admiralty Headquarters at Mount Wise. A veritable pandemonium arose in the Dockyard and district: scores of sirens rent the air with their shrill blasts and big steamer horns boomed out their deep-throated message. At last the world war had come to an end. School children demonstrated to their hearts' content, marching along the principal streets, singing and cheering and exchanging greetings on all sides. One procession had as leader the ubiquitous Charlie Chaplin replete with moustache, cane and preposterous boots.'

So ran the account in the Plymouth-based *Evening Herald* on Armistice Day, 11 November 1918. In what would soon become their sister paper, the *Western Morning News*, there was an account of nine-year-old Bernard Crock, who was hurrying down College Road, Mutley, late for school when he heard the sound of ship's sirens screaming in the distance. When he arrived at school he noticed that a number of pupils were already on their way home. *'There's no school today,'* his teacher told him, *'go home as soon as you can ... and put your cap on straight!'*

On his way home young Bernard noticed people appearing at open windows, pouring into the streets. In the centre of Plymouth crowds gathered outside the newspaper offices; people anxious for confirmation of what they assumed the cacophony coming from Devonport meant. They waited in their thousands outside the *Morning News* Offices in George Street, opposite the Theatre Royal, for official confirmation. Finally the call came from the Admiralty at Mount Wise, who telephoned the newspaper with an official statement, but it wasn't until 11am, ahead of the publication of the next edition, that formal notice was posted in the window. A public announcement was subsequently made by the Mayor, JP (Joseph) Brown, in the Guildhall Square.

By then the crowds had been further swelled by British and Australian servicemen and the roads became impassable.

'Scene in Plymouth when it was announced that the Germans had accepted the Armistice Terms.' Phyllis Martin is at the back of the throng with her brother-in-law Willie Knight.

Two lorries full of German prisoners of war, were brought to a halt by the impenetrable mass of men, women and children, but, according to the newspaper report the following day, even the prisoners appeared to be relieved, while for their part the crowd showed restraint towards their former foe.

It was a day that brought out the best in everyone. As one of the many Australian servicemen here that day recorded in his diary: 'Up at 7am shaved and had breakfast then got pass and went to Devonport Military Hospital to see dentist. On the way in buzzers, whistles on our ships all started blowing, terrific noise at 9.10am. It was the news come through of signing of Armistice terms by Fritz, great excitement. Saw dentist and had tooth filled and away by 11am. Stayed in Devonport for little while then went on to Plymouth, called in restaurant for dinner and was given glass of port wine and had dinner free. The place a seething mass of people all gone mad. Caught 10.30pm tram and in bed 11pm' (from the Diary of William Dalton Lycett, whose family had emigrated from Middlesbrough to Australia in 1910).

Inevitably there were mixed feelings in some quarters, especially for those who had lost close friends and family members, Will Lycett was one of those. He had joined up in September 1914, his father, Harry (who was 49 in 1918), had also served with the ANZACS (Australian and New Zealand Army Corps), as had three of Will's brothers, Harold, Harry and Frederick. Sadly, however, Frederick lost his life in Belgium, in 1917, on 'Hill 63.'

The statistic across the ANZAC contingent was consistent – one in five of those who served were destined never to return, in other words some 80,000 servicemen from Australia and New Zealand lost their lives in the Great War.

Across the British Empire, and particularly in Services' towns like Plymouth, there was barely a family that wasn't touched in some way by tragedy during the Great War. Over a million young men had been lost and over two million wounded, including around 800,000 from the UK alone (with over 1,600,000 wounded). Nevertheless Armistice was a time for rejoicing. The church bells rang and the lights stayed on long into the night. At last the time had come to allow for relaxation of the Defence of the Realm restrictions.

The war to end all wars was over.

Top: *Harry Lycett, front, with three of his sons, Harold, Will and Harry in Belgium in February 1918.* Opposite page and above: *Victory parades through George Street.*

Top left: *The two sides of the Plymouth Peace Medal.* Top right and above left and right: *Scenes from the rain-affected 'Peace Day' in Plymouth, July 1919.*

AFTERMATH

On 18 January 1919 the Paris Peace Conference was opened, 27 nations were represented with the main decisions being thrashed out between the 'Big Four' – France, Britain, Italy and the United States. Five major peace treaties were prepared with each of the main vanquished parties, the last being the Treaty of Sevres (with the Ottoman Empire and the Republic of Turkey) which was signed off in August 1920. The first was the Treaty of Versailles, with Germany, which was concluded at the end of June 1919.

The signing prompted a national 'Peace Day' which was celebrated around the country in July. A number of towns and cities struck a Peace Medal, Plymouth was among them. A figure of peace adorned one side and the Borough Crest the other, with the wording around it reading 'Peace Day 1919 – JP Brown Mayor, Plymouth'.

Unfortunately for all of those involved in that summer's day of celebration a heavy downpour somewhat marred the proceedings as various bodies marched past the saluting point outside the Municipal Building and raincoats were the order of the day, as dignitaries lay wreaths in memory of fallen comrades at the base of the Armada Memorial, on the wet and windswept Hoe.

The weather had been marginally better, if not a lot warmer, the previous month, when, on 13 June 1919 the Prince of Wales (later King Edward VIII and the Duke of Windsor), visited the area and planted a sapling oak on the new housing estate at North Prospect. The estate was part of the 'Homes fit for Heroes' initiative that followed in the wake of the war.

There had been widespread concern throughout the Great War over the poor physical health and general condition of so many young men living in urban areas and the Housing Act of 1919 was designed to address the situation.

Not everyone appreciated the significance: as the Prince dug his spade into the soil an onlooker jokingly remarked: 'better than digging trenches.'

For many returning servicemen a new home, or even a new life, was scant compensation for the horrors they had encountered in the trenches, the only saving grace perhaps was that they had, at least, made it home.

Right, top and middle: 13 June 1919, the Prince of Wales visits the new housing estate at North Prospect.
Bottom: Swilly Road, North Prospect, 1919.

Plymouth's Great War Memorial erected on the site of the former Hoe Lodge, the original entrance to the Hoe Park.

REST IN PEACE

There are over 2,000 war memorials commemorating those who fell and those who served in the Great War dotted around Devon. They take a wide variety of forms – crosses, columns, obelisks, plaques and even, in some instances, a building, most commonly a memorial hall or victory hall. By far the most common of these are the crosses, there are around 250 in the county, many of them modelled on Sir Reginald Blomfield's 'Cross of Sacrifice' – a simple angular stone cross with a downward-pointing sword – intended to 'speak of its own time'. There is one in each of Plymouth's major cemeteries: Ford Park, Weston Mill and Efford.

Plymouth's official Corporate commemoration took the form of an eight-foot-four-inch figure of Victory with a laurel wreath in one hand and a downward-pointing sword in the other.

Created by the established septuagenarian Scottish sculptor, Bernie Rhind, whose work is on display around the world, the Memorial which was designed by Messrs Thornely & Rooke, was unveiled by Lord Derby, the then Secretary of State for War.

Speaking at the ceremony at the original entrance to the Hoe where the memorial was sited, Lord Derby said that it was 'only partly in tribute to the noble men who died. It is also a reminder to future generations that war can be waged only at a great price and heavy toll of the best blood of the nation.

It should be a deterrent to war in the future that future generations should know what war means, and that each town and each parish should know the toll that war has made in our midst.'

The Memorial was to honour the lives of 2,000 local men and one woman, and a roll of honour, listing all the names, was deposited in a cavity at the base of the Memorial by the Lord Mayor, Solomon Stephens. The event was attended by a very large crowd and it was estimated that around 500 wreaths and bouquets were laid on the stonework.

The process of agreeing what form 'Plymouth's guerdon to the fallen' should take, and where exactly it should be sited, and how it should be paid for, had 'generated differences and difficulties which hampered the project at every stage'.

Above: *Large crowds attend the unveiling of the Plymouth War Memorial on the junction of Citadel Road and Lockyer Street.*

Various proposals had been put forward, including a major cenotaph structure running north/south across the middle of the Hoe Promenade. The idea was that the dates of the war would be recorded on the northern, shaded elevation, while 'Remembrance', should be etched into the south facing and hence sunlit side.

The proposal failed to win favour however, as did one or two other ideas. Of course the desire by communities up and down the country to have their own memorials erected put enormous pressure on local stonemasons and they struggled to cope. It didn't help that the profession was poorly paid, it also didn't help that there was no obvious mechanism for funding the construction of all these worthy projects – the average stonemason was being paid something like twelve shillings a day (60p) and when the Plymouth memorial was unveiled there was £1,000 still outstanding.

Nevertheless, in the first few years after the war memorials were unveiled at an impressive rate.

The most prominent of all the Plymouth memorials, indeed the most prominent of all of the Devon memorials, is the Naval War Memorial that fronts on to the Hoe Promenade, and sits between Drake's Statue and the Armada Tercentenary Memorial.

One of three identical structures commemorating the names 'of those Officers and Men who have no other grave than the sea' (the other two are at Chatham and Portsmouth), the Plymouth memorial records some 7,268 names of those lost at sea.

The impressive yet simple edifice was designed by another Scottish sculptor, the celebrated – and decorated – Sir Robert Lorimer, with individual sculptures by Henry Poole.

The massive stone obelisk is surmounted by four bronze figures representing the Four Winds of Heaven, supporting a representation of the world, while the base features four buttresses each sporting the 'sculpted figure of a lion couchant, looking outwards'.

Unveiled on Tuesday 29 July 1924 by one of George V's five sons – Prince George (who was later to die on active service in the Second World War), the memorial, like its Portsmouth and Chatham counterparts, was intended to serve as a 'Leading-mark' or 'Sea-mark' for ships entering the port.

An estimated crowd of 25,000 attended the unveiling, doubtless, many of them being sons and daughters, wives, partners and parents of those 7,000 or so in whose honour the memorial had been created.

Left: *Another of the unsuccessful proposals.* Below: *29 July 1923, the unveiling of the Plymouth Naval War Memorial by Prince George, attracts an estimated crowd of 25,000.*

Opposite page - top left: *Artist's impression of the proposed Cenotaph for the Hoe.*
Top right: *Another design destined not to be realised.*
Below: *Unveiling of the Plymouth Naval War Memorial on 29 July 1923.*

Devonport's Great War Memorial, Devonport Park. Inset: 14 March 1923 unveiling by Lord Methuen.

Remarkably, perhaps, the Naval Memorial was neither the first nor second Great War Memorial to appear on the Hoe, that honour going to the Royal Marine Memorial that sits in front of the Royal Citadel.

The Royal Marine Memorial was designed by a sculptor who had served in the Marines during the war, William Storr-Barber. An image of a model for the memorial was published in the *Illustrated London News*, in August 1919, but it wasn't until November 1921 that the prominently placed piece was unveiled.

The two figures either side of the plinth represent the dual nature of the Royal Marines – Per Mare, Per Terram – the former in shirt-sleeves wearing a sailor's hat, the latter in greatcoat and a helmet.

The figure surmounting the memorial is a naked man – St George perhaps – *'fighting the eagle of militarism'* (Gray, *Lest Devon Forgets*). Few major memorials were unveiled locally before the Royal Marine offering, but it is worth noting that before the official Plymouth Memorial was revealed and before the Naval Memorial was unveiled, Devonport had commissioned and completed their own monument to the fallen.

Although part of an amalgamated Plymouth since the start of the war, Devonport somehow contrived to erect their own obelisk which was sited near the middle of Devonport Park. They eschewed the offer of unveiling the Plymouth and Devonport memorials on the same day and even included a bronze plaque sporting the old Devonport borough arms on one side of the stonework. Another plaque, on another face, has the emblems of the Royal Navy, the Army and the Royal Flying Corps and, significantly, there was a fly-past of two airplanes from Lee on Solent at the unveiling.

Designed by Charles Cheverton of London and built by local sulptor James Hunt (of Sutton Road) and remembering over 2,000 Devonport men and women who died during the conflict, the poignant landmark again features a figure of 'Victory' at the base of its 33 foot-high pedestal, which in turn is surmounted by a large stone cross.

Unveiled by Field-Marshall Lord Methuen on 14 March 1923, fully two months before the Plymouth Memorial was ready, the event was attended by the Mayor of Plymouth, as well as Lord St Levan (the major landowner in Devonport, who was also chairman of the Memorial Committee) who said that he hoped that the memorial *'would serve to point the path of duty to those who come afterwards should they receive a similar call'*.

The Royal Marines' Memorial on Plymouth Hoe.

Top: *Plymouth tender Sir Richard Grenville meets Lapland in Plymouth Sound.* Above: *Surviving stewardesses at Millbay.* Top right: *Journalists try to get an early statement.* Middle: *Titanic crewmen on Grenville.* Bottom: *Surviving crew members of the Titanic 'quarantined' at Millbay Docks*

THEY PASSED THROUGH PLYMOUTH

On the morning of Sunday 28 April 1912 the Red Star Liner, *Lapland*, eased into Cawsand Bay bearing 167 surviving crew members of the *Titanic*. It had been thirteen days since the world's largest liner had met its icy end, and arrangements were made between the White Star Line and the Red Star Line, a related but rival company, for the *Lapland* to return the crew (many of whom, incidentally, had to work their passage) to England.

Plymouth's three tenders, the *Sir Francis Drake, Sir Walter Raleigh* and *Sir Richard Grenville*, went out to meet the impressive vessel - it was over 600ft long (remarkably the *Titanic* was nearer 900ft). *Drake* took the transatlantic post, *Raleigh*, the *Lapland*'s passengers, as well as those passengers who had been holding tickets for the *Titanic*'s second sailing, the return journey from New York, scheduled to leave on 20 April. Meanwhile, the *Grenville*, pulling up against *Lapland*'s bow, took all the crew, including 24-year-old Alfred Shiers. Devonport-born Shiers was a lucky lad and had been at sea for eleven years already when he signed up for service on the *Titanic* as a fireman on 6 April 1912. The 29 coal-fired boilers of the *Titanic* required a complement of 176 men hand-shovelling an incredible 600 tons of coal a day. On the evening of the 14 April Alfred was off-duty, reading in his bunk, when he felt a slight shock and rumble. He went up onto the well deck to investigate and saw the iceberg disappearing into a haze at the back of the ship. On returning to his quarters he discovered water coming up through the No.1 hatch, whereupon he went up to the boat-deck and was directed to lifeboat No.3, but there was no-one there so he went over to lifeboat No.7. However, having helped lower that boat he was ordered into lifeboat No.5.

In the event he was one of 212 crew (20 were women) who survived; 693 not so fortunate male colleagues (plus three women) perished, including 29-year-old Devonport-born Charles Hodge, an engineer, 27-year-old steward William Fox from the Rame peninsula, and 41-year-old Plymouth-born Ernest Hamblyn, a bedroom steward. All three were lost at sea along with many of the other 1,500 passengers and crew who perished in the freezing North Atlantic waters.

Curiously enough, Shiers was one of the comparatively few crew members to testify at the British Inquiry a few weeks later. However, all of those who arrived in Plymouth that day, signed statements at Millbay in the presence of a number of officials including 52-year-old Plymouth solicitor Harold Wolferstan who, together with another member of his firm, was representing the Board of Trade.

Clearly it hadn't been possible to take the sort of statement that was required on board the *Lapland* before its arrival and so Millbay virtually became an impromptu detention centre. The firemen-stokers and seaman were processed first and then 'released' to travel home that night, most to Southampton. The stewards and stewardesses were kept overnight and weren't allowed off site, until their statements had been taken. A train took them to them home the following day at around 4pm.

Not that that was the end of Plymouth's links in the *Titanic* story, as the *Mackay Bennett*, a cable ship which later spent many years in the Cattewater, arrived in Halifax, Nova Scotia with 190 bodies rescued from the scene of the tragedy. It had been a gruesome commission: there were only 100 coffins on board and in addition to those recovered 116 other bodies had been found, but had been buried at sea, half of them mutilated and unidentifiable.

They had, however, found the body of the wealthiest man onboard the *Titanic*, Colonel John Jacob Astor IV. Astor, an investor, inventor, writer and real-estate magnate was 47, and had recently remarried following a high-profile divorce. Much to the delight of the gossip press, his second bride was a year younger than his son William (incidentally, his cousin's son, 32-year-old Waldorf Astor, had, been elected MP for Plymouth less than eighteen months earlier).

And finally there was Mrs Jane Quick, a 33-year-old Stonehouse woman who had emigrated to Detroit a couple of years earlier, 'to start a new life' with her husband, Frederick, a Plymouth plasterer, and had come home, with her two young daughters Phyllis (eight) and Winifred (two), to visit relatives. All three survived and Jane spent many years travelling across America regaling awestruck audiences with her story.

Another British ship destined to leave these shores, never to return, was the Endurance and she was in Plymouth the day that war was declared – Tuesday 4 August 1914.

She had sailed out of London the previous Saturday and was bound for the Antarctic as one of the two vessels on Sir Ernest Shackleton's latest expedition.

Of course, the mobilization of men and the need to prepare for battle caused Shackleton to reassess his position and, having consulted the crew, he contacted the Admiralty:

'There are enough trained and experienced men among us to man a destroyer,' he wrote. In reply he received a very simple and succinct telegram from Whitehall – it said *'Proceed'.*

Winston Churchill was then the First Lord of the Admiralty, and in a follow-up missive he assured Shackleton that it was the wish of the British Government for the expedition to go ahead as planned.

On Friday 7 August Shackleton came down to Plymouth to see the ship off and to have a farewell meal with his men at the Duke of Cornwall Hotel. The following day, which proved to be a fairly wet and windy summer's day, Endurance set sail for the Weddell Sea and Antarctica where she would ultimately be crushed by ice and sink.

Plymouth, was of course, no stranger to such explorers and although he hadn't set out from here, Captain Robert Falcon Scott was a local boy and news of his loss, which had reached England the previous year, hit the town and the country hard. Curiously, although Scott and his men had been beaten to the South Pole by the Norwegian Amundsen, Scott's heroic failure almost outshone the success of his rival, at least in this country.

Top: Endurance trapped in ice.
Middle: Captain Robert Falcon Scott.
Right: John McCrae, medic, poet and soldier.

Among those others who passed through Plymouth between August 1914 and November 1918 was Lieutenant-Colonel John McCrae of the Canadian Artillery (he was here in October 1914). A leading Canadian physician, McCrae had distinguished himself in the Boer War and although, aged 42, he was initially turned down for service in 1914 on age grounds, he offered himself up as a 'combatant or Medical' and ultimately did both. His life-saving endeavours earned the respect of all who came into contact with him.

It was death from shelling of a promising young officer in his brigade, Lieutenant Alexis Helmer, a graduate of McGill University, where McCrae had been a lecturer in Medicine and Pathology before the war, that had prompted McCrae to write his poignant poem, *In Flanders Fields*, on the back steps of an ambulance behind the lines at the second battle of Ypres in May 1915.

It was by no means his first foray into poetry, but following it's publication in Punch in December that year, it instantly struck a chord and although it had appeared anonymously in the press, McCrae was soon identified with the piece and it not only made him famous but also led to the adoption of the poppy as the symbol of human loss in the Great War.

'In Flanders fields the poppies blow
Between the crosses, row on row,
That mark our place; and in the sky
The larks, still bravely singing, fly
Scarce heard amid the guns below.'

Tragically, McCrae, who had a history of

asthmatic attacks, was defeated by 'the old enemy' in January 1918. He had just learned of his promotion to Consulting Physician to the First British Army when he died in Boulogne of pneumonia – he was 45.

We have no record of how the well-travelled McCrae felt about his short stay in Plymouth, however Arnold Ridley, another author, who would later write the *Ghost Train*, an adaptation of which was the first film to be shown at the Gaumont Cinema in Union Street in 1930, and, who, later still would become even better known as Private Godfrey in the long-running television series about the Second World War, *Dad's Army*, had all too graphic recollections of his time in Plymouth.

He would later recall how, in 1916, he was marched three miles in a rainstorm to Crownhill where his battalion was based, and then, soaked through, waiting half an hour until the Regimental Sergeant-Major appeared:

'Don't none of you think you're going to see your homes and mothers and dads no more 'cause you ain't,' he bellowed. *'We sent out a draft to our First Battalion at Wipers [Ypres] three weeks ago and where are they now? I'll tell yer - they're all bleeding well dead! And that's where you buggers will be in a couple o' months' time - all bleeding well dead!'*

Happily Ridley survived the war, but he was very lucky. He'd twice gone over the top and lost countless contemporaries around him. He'd been struck in the head with a German rifle butt (which although he didn't know it for years had cracked his skull and

caused him to have black-outs from time to time for the rest of his life), he'd been bayonetted in the groin and hand and had once awoken from unconsciousness to find that he was being sewn up in a sheet, having been presumed dead.

Imagine his horror, having survived those ordeals, at having a tall young woman wearing fox fur come up to him when he was convalescing in Torquay in 1917, and hand him a white feather, symbolically suggesting that he should have been fighting in France and that clearly he was a coward. Lance-Corporal Ridley quietly took the feather and said nothing.

Someone who had rather more pleasant memories of his time at Crownhill barracks was David Ben-Gurion, a Polish Jew who, while living in Israel, enlisted in London in what became known as the Jewish Legion, a Battalion of Royal Fusiliers, towards the end of the war.

In the summer of 1918 he wrote to his wife; *'The camp we are staying in is not far from the beautiful port of Plymouth … called Egg Buckland … I was intoxicated by the charming scene … green mountains and valleys covered with silk, fertile fields … The Sabbath is observed here, and on that day we are let off all training, apart from marching to the synagogue together with all the officers, headed by the colonel'* (D. Ben-Gurion, *Letters to Paula* 1971).

After the war, Ben-Gurion was active in the middle east trade unions and later spearheaded the struggle to set up the State of Israel, which came to fruition in May 1948 with Ben-Gurion its first Prime Minister.

Top: *Lance-Corporal Arnold Ridley.*
Bottom: *Private David Ben-Gurion.*

Britain's first fully fledged female Member of Parliament on the campaign trail in Plymouth.

VOTES FOR WOMEN

The First World War, as the Great War came to be known from the late 1940s onwards, undoubtedly changed the world, or at least the Western World.

The class system, while still underpinning British life, witnessed a profound shift away from the upstairs/downstairs culture. Although there was a return to some sort of 'normal' day-to-day life, more and more women entered the workplace, not just because they'd had a taste of the independence conferred by being a wage earner, but also because such a huge of number of young men had been permanently removed from the workplace, cut short in the prime of their lives.

Arising almost inevitably out of this change of circumstances was a realisation that women were not the second-class citizens that society had largely condemned them to be prior to 1914. Clearly this notion had been what had initially created and inflamed the Suffragette Movement.

In 1903 Emmeline Pankhurst who had earlier founded the Women's Franchise League advocating suffrage – votes – for both married and unmarried women, set up the Women's Social and Political Union. At that time no women were entitled to vote.

Pankhurst, supported by a number of other women, including her three grown-up daughters, Christabel, Sylvia and Adela, became increasing vociferous and physical in their campaign to draw attention to the issue and were regularly arrested, however with the advent of war the WSPU, now run by Christabel, advocated abandoning militant activism and support of the government's stand against 'the German Peril'.

Now the WSPU beseeched women to help in any way they could by taking on men's work and at the same time to encourage young men to fight for their King and Country.

As the pressure generally for women to work increased, and as an ever-growing army of women responded to that call, so Britain was able to maintain and increase production of munitions to a level that ultimately helped the Allies in their endeavours to outgun the Central Powers. Women also played a large part in keeping transport systems going and food production at a sustainable level. There could be no denying that without that involvement the war may well have been lost.

Christabel Pankhurst was also a fervent supporter of the Order of the White Feather, and her supporters were among those happy to hand out the symbol of cowardice to any young man in civilian dress – an activity that became somewhat less well-received as the war progressed, but nevertheless was not without impact.

It was hardly surprising, therefore, that despite huge opposition in both Houses of Parliament before the war, when Millicent Fawcett (who was the leader of the less militant National Union of Women's Suffrage Societies) pressed for votes for women at the Speaker's Conference in 1916, she set the wheels moving for the Representation of the People Act in that came into force in 1918.

Initially the campaign had been for the voting age to be lowered to 18, for men and for women, however there were fears that with so many young men lost in the war that would hand an effective majority to women. And so all men over 21 were given the vote as were women over 30 (provided that they were a member or married to a member of the Local Government Register, a property owner, or a graduate voting in a University constituency).

A number of women stood at the election that came after the passing of the Act, including Cristabel Pankhurst, who contested the Smethick Constituency as a member of the Women's Party, working with David Lloyd George's Conservative Coalition. On a turnout of over 18,000 she lost by just 775 votes to the only other candidate, John Davison. Meanwhile, at the same election, a 52-year-old Anglo-Irish woman, married to a Polish Count, the Countess de Markiewicz became the first women to be elected to Parliament. However, as a Sinn Fein candidate contesting a seat in Dublin (and in Holloway Prison at the time), she refused to take the Oath of Allegiance and did not take her seat.

And so the nation waited for its first female Member of Parliament.

November 1919, exactly one year after Armistice and the end of the Great War, Plymouth was gripped by one of the most exciting elections it had ever known.

It was a by-election occasioned by the recent elevation of the sitting MP, Waldorf Astor, to the House of Lords (following the death of his father Lord William Waldorf Astor), on 18 October 1919.

Three candidates contested the vacancy: Isaac Foot, Liberal, who had already served Plymouth as a councillor, and William Gay, Labour, and Nancy Astor, Conservative, but standing on the Lloyd George's Coalition platform and sporting red, white and blue rosettes and ribbons of the coalition.

Isaac's son, Michael, who would later represent Devonport as a Member of Parliament, and lead the Labour Party, wrote:

'I remember going around in a carriage with my sister Sally. I remember going up a street where there was a Labour poster in every window saying "Vote for Gay" and a sign up saying "All Gay for Sutton". The song we children sang was:

> *Who's that knocking at the door?*
> *Who's that knocking at the door?*
> *If it's Astor and his wife, we'll stab 'em with a knife*
> *And they won't be Tories any more.*

'This,' recalled Michael, 'was the first song I was encouraged to sing by my father, who was always a furious opponent of the Tories, and by my mother, who was an even stronger one. But Lady Astor won that election, not only because of her husband and ancestry, but because she was as good an electioneer as some of us will ever see. She had her own way of using the platform and no holds were barred in the way she dealt with hecklers.'

Coming from a fabulously wealthy background the question of the Astor money was an issue raised by hecklers and Nancy's typical reply was: 'I probably have far more than I ought to have, but if some of my Socialist opponents had what I have they would not be here asking for your votes.'

Moreover, 'she was,' according to Michael Foot himself, 'the truest expositor of the women's case and from the start she proved herself a wonderful new speaker on behalf of the people of Plymouth.'

'Vote for Lady Astor and Your Babies Will Weigh More,' was one of the more unusual campaign (*Nancy Astor and Her Friends*), 'it was perfectly true.'

Top: *Lady Astor electioneering.*
Bottom: *Election crowds in town, looking towards Bedford Street*

'Nancy was for pure milk, better working conditions, shorter hours for women and children – in fact all things that did make slum children larger and healthier. 'I want for your children, what I want for my children,' she told her audiences, 'I do not believe in sexes or classes'.'

Despite what was perceived to be the obvious disadvantage of being a woman – indeed a Unionist candidate put himself forward to challenge her on the issue of sex but withdrew before the election - Nancy triumphed.

Isaac Foot's campaign doubtless suffered on account of the fact that he had, as a solicitor, represented a number of Conscientious Objectors during the Great War, however he polled more than the Liberal candidate had in the 1918 Election. William Gay had also contested that one and he too increased his vote, but the turnout was up generally and Nancy Astor won with a majority of over 5,000.

Her cause was greatly helped by her powers of oratory, her compassion, and the fact that the Astors, as newspaper magnates, not only knew the power of a great soundbite, but of a strong image and in November 1919 dozens of excellent and evocative photographs were taken of Nancy on the campaign trail.

And so it was that Nancy Astor became the first woman to take her seat in Parliament.

Above: The declaration outside the Guildhall: left to right; Lord Astor, William Gay, Lady Astor, Colonel Guest, the Town Clerk, CP Brown, Isaac Foot and Lovell Dunstan.
Right: Nancy Astor addresses the crowd from the balcony of the Conservative Club in Princess Square, with Lord Astor and their son, Bill (who would later become an MP) alongside her.

Plymouth & Devonport Mayors/MPs and Stonehouse Chairmen 1900–1914 and post Amalgamation

Devonport Mayors

1900–02	Harman Graves
1901–02	Edgar Leest
1902–03	James Tozer
1903–05	Edward Blackall
1905–07	William Moon
1907–08	Richard Smerdon
1908–09	John Goldsmith
1909–11	William Littleton
1911–12	Myer Freedman
1912–14	Edward Blackall

Stonehouse Chairmen

1900–01	Frank Maitland
1901–02	Samuel Panter
1902–04	William Corbett
1904–06	Isaac Pearce
1906–08	Viscount Valletort
1908–12	Isaac Pearce
1912–13	William Blight
1913–14	William Corbett

Plymouth Mayors

1901–02	Joseph Bellamy
1902–04	Henry Hurrell
1904–05	Richard Winnicott
1905–06	John Yeo
1906–07	J Frederick Winnicott
1907–08	Sir Charles Radford
1908–09	Arthur Spender
1909–10	John Yeo
1910–11	Thomas Wills
1911–12	Henry Hurrell
1912–13	James Godding
1913–16	Thomas Baker

(Amalgamation)

1916–17	John Goldsmith
1917–19	Joseph Brown
1919–20	Lovell Dunstan

Plymouth & Devonport MPs

1900 (Plymouth)	Henry Duke, Ivor Guest
1902 (Devonport)	John Lockie (vice Edward Morton deceased)
1904 (Devonport)	John Benn (vice Lockie resigned)
1906 (Plymouth)	Thomas Dobson; Charles Mallet
1906 (Devonport)	Hudson Kearley; Sir John Benn
1910 (Jan) (Plymouth)	Charles Mallet, Aneurin Williams
1910 (Dec) (Plymouth)	Waldorf Astor; Arthur Shirley Benn
1910 (Jan & Dec) (Devonport)	Sir John Jackson; Sir Clement Kinloch-Cooke

(Amalgamation)

1918 (Drake)	Sir Arthur Shirley Benn
1918 (Sutton)	Waldorf Astor
1919 (Sutton)	Viscountess Astor

The seat of power for the Amalgamated Three Towns – Plymouth Guildhall and Municipal Buildings.

ACKNOWLEDGEMENTS

Having always wanted to produce a book on the first 20 years of the Twentieth Century, the Centenary of the start of the Great War, seemed like an obvious hook to hang it on.

The role of the Three Towns in the Great War has not been well represented by Plymouth historians in the last hundred years, even those who lived through it chose not to make much of it, which is a shame as they could have left us with an interesting perspective.

However I am extremely grateful to Anne and Mike Corry who have spent countless hours going through the local newspapers that were produced between 1914 and 1918 and have managed to distil a flavour of the way the world was reported and perceived back then. The stories and the information that they collated in the course of producing a major exhibition for the City Museum in 2014 have been invaluable.

For images and information I am also enormously indebted to Plymouth City Art Gallery and Museum, Plymouth & West Devon Record Office, and Plymouth Library Services and specifically Nigel Overton, who I had the pleasure of working with on the curation of Plymouth City Council Arts & Heritage WW1 Centenary Exhibition.

The Plymouth Barbican Trust's excellent South West Image Bank has also been extremely supportive as has the marvellous, independently, and voluntarily, run Totnes Image Bank – thank you Colette Hobbs and Barry Weekes respectively.

Derek Tait, another man who loves this city and who has also produced many fine books about different aspects of Plymouth history, has been very generous in allowing me to use many of the images he has collected from this period.

Gerald Walsey, who has already published an excellent account of Devon in the Great War and the definitive guide to Mount Batten as a flying-boat base, was similarly generous.

Dianne Lawer and her husband Harley, have also been extremely kind in allowing me to use images from Di's marvellous collection of picture postcards depicting the lighter side of the Great War, and to have access to the excellent articles that Di has written.

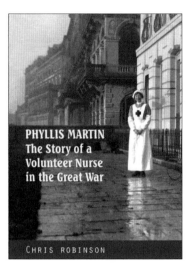

PHYLLIS MARTIN
The Story of a
Volunteer Nurse
in the Great War

CHRIS ROBINSON

I am extremely grateful to John Newbery and his aunt Margaret for access to Phyllis Martin's photograph albums and autograph books, a fantastic resource that helped create a separate project in its own right.

Mavis Hunt, whose aunt was also a Great War nurse, and who married a medical orderly whom she met at Salisbury Road, also made excellent material available.

Graham and Pat Brooks have been similarly helpful with regard to images and information. Graham has a fabulous collection of Scouting ephemera covering the whole history of the Movement, but his early material is particularly fascinating.

Alice Astor has also been extremely kind in allowing me go through some of her grandmother's photographic albums which include many wonderful images of Nancy Astor's historic 1919 election campaign.

I'd also like to thank Lord St Germans for allowing us to quote from the letter from the former head gardener, of Port Eliot, Frank Clayton, who was killed in France in 1916.

Peter Waterhouse, who for years has been collecting naval heritage material and other Plymouth and Devonport related photographs has long been a very useful source of images, thank you, Peter, and thanks too to Todd Wolfenden for the submarine chaser material.

Many more of the images that appear in this book have been supplied by readers of my weekly column in the *Herald*.

Another significant source of images has been that well-loved, erstwhile must-have, local yearbook *Doidge's Annual*, a valuable source of information and photographs that was enjoying perhaps the greatest success of its 80 or so year run at this time (it ceased publication in 1954).

Old books, tourist guides, brochures, and souvenir programmes have also proved useful, as have the inevitable collections of old picture postcards. The first twenty years of the twentieth century were a peak time for these popular, envelope-free missives.

Identifying dates is always a difficult task, but at least being able to decipher a postmark tells us that the postcard could be earlier than a certain date, but not later.

By compiling a collection of several hundred images of a twenty-year period it is hoped that a flavour of the fashions and the times will come across especially with regard to clothing, hairstyles, and transport. There were very few motor cars on the roads, horses – and carts – were still an integral part of everyday life and the electric tram was the state-of-the-art way of getting from A to B. The fact that the lines in the Three Towns were electrified from 1901 is also a key element in helping to identify approximate dates, that, and the fact that there were no motorised omnibuses in the Three Towns prior to 1920.

From a practical and personal perspective, I'd also like to express very grateful thanks to my long-suffering publisher and wife, Clare, my mother-in-law Patricia, New Street operations manager, Rob Warren, former Latimer Trend man Bill Bugler and City Museum and Heritage Curator, Nigel Overton, all of whom have read this looking for typos, inaccuracies and inconsistencies.

Thanks too to Doreen Mole whose organisation of my data base has helped in putting this together.

The internet, and, inevitably, wikipedia have also thrown up innumerable nuggets that have helped bring colour and detail to many of these pages.

Meanwhile, the A-Z list below is to thank those individuals who have sent me photographs from this era over the last twenty years or so – photographs that have helped made this book what it is – I only hope I haven't left anyone out!

So thank you: Ron Andrews, Denise Bailey, Ron Bamsey, Victor Barton, Guy Belshaw, Robin Blythe-Lord, John and Sylvia Boulden, Tom Bowden, Cathy Brown, Barbara Burr, Tim Charlesworth, Arthur

Stewart William Fox Robinson:
My grandfather, pictured post-war with his Great War medals.
Like so many of his generation he put his age up so that he could serve his King and Country.
Born on 17 May 1902 he joined up early in 1918 barely 16-years-old.
After the Armistice he opted to stay in the Royal Marines and just over twenty years later he found himself at war again. Happily he survived that ordeal as well, and came out of the Service shortly after the conclusion of the Second World War after 27 years of service, mostly at sea, but generally based in the Royal Marine Barracks, Stonehouse. It was while there that he met and married my grandmother.

Clamp, Bob Cook, Peter R Damerell, Andy Endacott, Marilyn Endacott, Wendy Evans, Guy Fleming, Arthur Folland, Michael Foot, Crispin Gill, Duncan Godefroy, Dena Goves, Tom Greaves, Tamsin Griffiths, Paul Grosch, Ken Hawke, Ron Hellyer, Alison Highet, Ralph Hoare, Sandra Hunkin, Philip Hunt, Paul Inch, Daryl Jago, Alan Jeffery, David Jennings, Doreen Johnson, Peter Jones, David King, Alan Kittridge, William Henry Lawrence, Mrs CA Legassick, SHC Martin, Brian Moseley, Jimmy Moses, Sid Oliver, Ann Pallant, Joe Pengelly, Derry Purvis, Sam Rendall, Des Robinson, Margaret Robinson, Keith Scrivens, Annie and Mary Smale, Stephen Smith, Gloria Sommer, Ken Soul, Jim Stapleton, Alan Tibbitts, Beatrice Thompson and David Tozer.

While every care has been taken to try and identify individual copyright holders the publishers would be happy to hear from anyone who has information concerning the copyright of any uncredited images.

Chris Robinson *October 2014*

BIBLIOGRAPHY

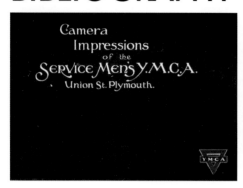
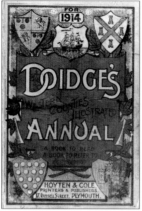

The Aeroplane – The Aeroplane and General Publishing Co., Vol XVI No.22 (June 1919)

Another Great Parade on the Hoe – **RV Walling**, Western Independent (27.9.1964)

Baseport Devonport Warships: Part II, 1877 to 1925 – **Sydney Goodman**, P.D.S Printers Ltd (1983)

Britain in Old Photographs: Around Plymouth – **Tom Bowden**, Alan Sutton Publishing Ltd (1995)

British Almanac and Cyclopedia 1913

British Seaside Piers – **Chris Mawson and Richard Riding**, Ian Allan Publishing (2008)

A Century of Plymouth: Events, People and Places over the last 100 years – **Guy Fleming**, Sutton Publishing Ltd (2000)

China on the Western Front: Britain's Chinese Workforce in the First World War – **Michael Summerskill** (1982)

Devon at the Cinema: An Illustrated History of Cinema Going – **Gordon Chapman**, Devon Books (2000)

Devon in the 1930s: The Way We Were – **Gerald Wasley**, Halsgrove (1998)

Devons in the Great War – **Godfrey Wycisk**, Western Morning News (9.10.1972)

Devonport Dockyard Railway – **Paul Burkhalter**, Twelveheads Press (1996)

Plymouth Yesterday Today – **Vic Saundercock** (1989)

Devons in the Great War 1914-1918 – **Gerald Wasley**, Halsgrove (2013)

thediaryjunction.blogspot.co.uk

Doidge's Western Counties Illustrated Annual – (1900 -1920 inclusive)

Electricity in Plymouth: Its Origins and Development – **Edward W Luscombe**, The Devonshire Association (1999)

The Fighters of the Old Cosmo – A History of Plymouth Boxing 1907-24 – **Clive Tregarthen Mumford** (1975)

Fighting on the Home Front – **Kate Adie**, Hodder & Stoughton (2013)

The First World War – **Robin Prior and Trevor Wilson**, Cassell & Co. (2000)

4th Southern General Hospital Gazette – (1914-18)

From Rattles to Radio, A History of Plymouth City Police Force, **Ernest Dickaty**, typescript (1977)

From South Devon to the South Pole – **Paul Davies**, Kingsbridge Books (2011)

"Get Your Skates On": A History of Plymouth's Roller Skating Rinks 1874 - 1989 – **Diana Lawer**, Three Towns Publishing (2007)

Hard Labour – **Jenny Clegg**, article.

The Historic Defences of Plymouth – **Andrew Pye & Freddie Woodward**, Cornwall County Council (1996)

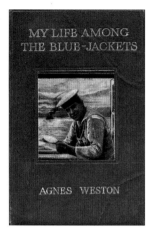
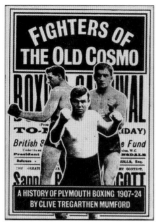

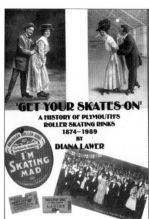

A History of Plymouth: And Her Neighbours – **CW Bracken**, Underhill (Plymouth) Ltd (1931)

The History of the Great War, based on Official Documents – **C Ernest Fayle**, John Murray (1924)

The History of the Great War – edited by **Newman Flower,** Waverley Book Co., (1918)

Images of Plymouth – **Tom Bowden**, Sutton Publishing (2006)

Images of England: Plymouth – **Derek Tait**, Tempus Publishing Ltd (2003)

Introduction To Plymouth and Neighbourhood – Plymouth Corporation of Tramways & Transport Department Offices, Bowering Press (1926)

Isaac Foot: A Westcountry Boy – Apostle of England – **Michael Foot and Alison Highet**, Politico's Publishing Ltd (2006)

Kelly's Devonshire Directory – (1919)

Lest Devon Forgets – **Todd Gray**, The Mint Press (2010)

The Making of the University of Plymouth – **Alston Kennerley**, University of Plymouth (2000)

Memories of the 5th Devons – FCAE article Western Independent (14.2.1954)

Mount Batten: The Flying boats of Plymouth – **Gerald Wasley**, Halsgrove (2006)

My Life Among the Bluejackets – **Agnes Weston**, James Nisbet & Co. (1909)

Nancy Astor and Her Friends – **Elizabeth Langhorne**, Littlehampton Book Services (1974)

Naval Heritage in The West: Part I, II & III – **Andy Endacott** (1986, 1987, 1988)

Notes on the History of the British West Indies Regiment – **Lt. Col C Wood-Hill** DSO (1927)

100 Years of the Co-operative in Plymouth – **Chirs Robinson**, Pen & Ink Publishing (2009)

The People of Devon in the First World War – **David Parker**, The History Press (2013)

Phyllis Martin - The Story of a Volunteer Nurse in the Great War – **Chris Robinson**, Pen & Ink (2014)

Playbill: A History of Theatre in the Westcountry – **Harvey Crane**, Macdonald and Evans Ltd (1980)

Plymouth: A New History – **Crispin Gill**, Devon Books (1993)

Plymouth: A Pictorial History – **Guy Fleming**, Phillimore & Co Ltd (1995)

Plymouth: As Time Draws On Vols 1 & 2 – **Chris Robinson**, Pen & Ink Publishing (1985, 1988)

Plymouth Bygones: Sixty Years of Memories and Pictures – **Guy Fleming**, Devon Books (1991)

Plymouth College, The First Hundred Years – **Chris Robinson**, Pen & Ink Publishing (2005)

Plymouth in the Twenties and Thirties - **Chris Robinson**, Pen & Ink Publishing (2008)

Plymouth in War & Peace – **Guy Fleming**, Bossiney Books (1987)

Plymouth: Maritime City in Transition – **Brian Chalkley, David Dunkerley, Peter Gripaios**, David & Charles (1991)

Plymouth: More Pictures from the Past – **Guy Fleming**, The Devonshire Press Ltd (1996)

Plymouth: Ocean Liner, Port of Call – **Alan Kittridge**, Twelveheads Press (1993)

Plymouth: Pictures from the Past – **Guy Fleming**, The Devonshire Press Ltd (1995)

Plymouth River: A History of the Laira and Cattewater – **Crispin Gill**, Devon Books (1997)

Plymouth 100 Years of Street Travel – **R.C. Sambourne**, Glasney Press (circa 1970)

Plymouth's Electrical Revolution – **Edward Luscombe and Chris Buck**, South Western Electricity Historical Society (2014)

Plymouth's Historic Barbican – **Chris Robinson**, Pen & Ink Publishing (2007)

Plympton's Past in Pictures – **John Boulden** MBE (2007)

The Post Office Directory of Plymouth, Devonport, Stonehouse & District 1908, 1910-11 – Swiss & Co

Regiments of Foot – **Godfrey Wycisk**, Western Morning News (15.11.1971)

Scouting in Plymouth 1908 - 1982 – **Graham E. Brooks and Arthur L. Clamp**, P.D.S. Printers Ltd (1982)

The Second Book of Plymouth - **W. Best Harris**, Oakfield Press (circa 1960)

Showmen of the Past: Hancocks of the West – **Kevin Scrivens & Stephen Smith**, New Era Publications (2006)

A Sporting Century 1863 - 1963 – **Anne Pallant**, Anne Pallant (1997)

Steam Around Plymouth – **Bernard Mills**, Tempus Publishing Ltd (2003)

The Story of Plymouth – **R.A.J Walling**, London Westaway Books (1950)

Strike First They Shall Not Pass Unseen – **Dennis C Teague** – Baron Jay (1982)

Sutton Harbour – **Crispin Gill**, Devon Books (1997)

Three Towns Street Guide: Giving Nearest Main Thoroughfares, Stations and Halts – Clarke, Doble & Co Ltd (1912)

The Trams of Plymouth: A 73-Year Story – **Martin Langley and Edwina Small**, Ex Libris Press (1990)

Urban District Council of East Stonehouse Yearbook 1912-1913 – Valletort Press Stonehouse

Up The Creek, the Royal Naval Hospital, Stonehouse – **Graham Evans**, GV Evans (1994)

Victorian Plymouth: As Time Draws On – **Chris Robinson**, Pen & Ink Publishing (1991)

The War Illustrated, weekly pictorial – Amalgamated Press (1914)

The Western Morning News – Harmsworth, (August 1914)

T. Whitelegg and Sons: Cavalcade of Shows – **Guy Belshaw**, New Era publications (2005)

Wolfesrtans, the First 200 Years – **Chris Robinson**, Pen & Ink (2012)

The World Crisis – **Winston S. Churchill** (1923–27). Volume 1, London: Thornton Butterworth, Ltd.